G000274930

Introduction

introduction

Sacrebleu! There's a revolution happening. The internet is taking over. Smart watches track our every move, TVs, fridges and even lightbulbs are fully connected, and Google and Facebook are worth more than the GDP of most countries. This is the age of the digital revolution folks, and the online generation are here to stay.

It's all old news to the French, of course. They've been celebrating revolutions since the 1790s, when the monarchy was overthrown, a few heads were lost and a new order was created. France is a country that embraces change, and now, as we hurtle through the new millennium, the land of snow-capped mountains, sandy beaches, rivers, forest and lakes, is undergoing a further, unstoppable transformation, this time in the field of camping.

In our first edition of *Cool Camping: France* the number of campsites that had branched out from traditional tent and campervan pitches to something more exclusive, special and luxurious, could be counted on a single hand. Today, among this third edition, you'll find a refreshed collection that represents the new age of camping – an age where luxuries needn't be forgotten and 'glamping' is the buzzword. The result is a more eclectic mix than ever, from pine cone-peppered pitches of old, high in the Alps, to yurts, safari lodges and even tree houses scattered all the way across the country to the Atlantic coast.

Staking their claim as leading revolutionaries in the luxury age are some of our newest glamping finds. The Midsummer Retreat (page 252) in the sunny south-west accommodates just four people, yet furnishes them not only with an enormous Mongolian-style yurt but also a fully-equipped outdoor kitchen space and dining room, while strikingly modern Glisten Camping (page 280) in the Pyrénées boasts white glamping domes that look almost space-age in their wooded setting. So new are the furnished bell tents of Belair Le Camping (page 140), meanwhile, that they have only just opened for their first full season, while another brand new discovery has the most appropriate title of the lot – Le Monteil Revolution (page 168) – revolutionary in name as well as by nature.

Even some of the oldest *Cool Camping* sites from our earlier editions now offer an additional 'pre-pitched' option, whether it's a tipi in the trees or a Romany *roulette* on the riverside. Yet just as the proliferation of digital music has seen the sale of vinyl records soar to an all time high, the glamping trend has its own rebellious counter culture. Amid the châteaux-dotted centre of France there are extra additions to this book that, though new, have a far more timeless quality. Rustic on-the-farm camping is back *en vogue*. Be it river swimming at La Chatonnière (page 146), dining in the old barn at La Vie en Vert (page 268) or admiring the ivy clad courtyard at Camping Goudal (page 232), this third edition of *Cool Camping: France* still showcases the traditional tent-friendly sites that are the bread and butter of what we do.

The main thing that all these campsites – old and new, luxury or otherwise – have in common is that they are all the *crème de la crème* of the country's offering. And all have been personally reviewed by a member of the *Cool Camping* team. Every recommended campsite is accompanied by important practical information – prices, directions,

local attractions and the nearest restaurants – while photos allow you to look forward to the southern sun even if it's raining here on UK soil.

These are, without exception, some of the best places to enjoy a digital detox, to cut yourself off from a busy, online, connected world and enjoy the great outdoors as a rejuvenating force. Yet, thanks to the digital revolution, you can easily book a stay at almost all of these campsites online, starting at *coolcamping.com*. It's a paradox of the modern age, that technology should enable us to escape technology.

Simple holiday planning and a camping experience that's more refreshing than ever before… It's a transformation that brings the best of both worlds, right?

Vive le révolution, we say. *Vive camping!*

James Warner Smith, Editor

campsite locator

ENGLISH CHANNEL

Dunkerque
Calais
Boulogne
BELGIUM
Lille
Valenciennes
LUXEMBOURG
Dieppe
Amiens
Charleville-Mézières
GERMANY
Cherbourg
St Quentin
Le Havre
03 **02** **01**
17
Reims
Metz
Caen
Rouen
Nancy
04
St-Malo
PARIS
Strasbourg
St-Brieuc
07
06
05
Chalons-sur-Marne
08
15
Versailles
Brest
09
Allençon
14
16
18
20
Quimper
10
Rennes
Chartres
Mulhouse
11
13
Orléans
19
Belfort
Vannes
Le Mans
21
22
Lorient
Angers
28
26
25
Dijon
Besançon
St-Nazaire
12
Tours
27
Chalon-sur-Saône
Nantes
Cholet
Bourges
23
SWITZERLAND
29
Poitiers
Châteauroux
Nevers
24
65
60
La Rochelle
30
Niort
57
61
66
67 **68**
Rochefort
56
59
64
69
Angoulême
55
53
58
Limoges
Annecy
31
54
52
50
Clermont-Ferrand
Lyon
51
32
48
49
63
Chambéry
47
46
45
Le Puy
62
Grenoble
37
Brive-la-Gaillarde
Valence
71
70
38
ATLANTIC OCEAN
Bordeaux
41 **44**
79
78
72
ITALY
39
40
43
80
77
73
33
35
36
42
Cahors
81
76
Rodez
34
Agen
90 **89**
Millau
98
87
Avignon
74
Mont-de-Marsan
97
88
Nîmes
Bayonne
99
Pau
Toulouse
Cannes
Nice
100
96
93 **91**
82
Montpellier
Marseille
92
Carcassonne
Béziers
Toulon
75 St-Tropez
Tarbes
94 **95**
83
Narbonne
Foix
86
85
Perpignan
ANDORRA
84

SPAIN

MEDITERRANEAN SEA

Find and book your perfect camping holiday

To instantly check availability for hundreds of camping and glamping sites and book at the best price, visit

www.coolcamping.com

Camping Domaine des Mathevies (p.128)

campsites at a glance

camping le château de martragny

52 Hameau Saint-Léger, 14740 Martragny, Calvados 00 33 2 31 80 21 40 www.château-martragny.com

Consider Norman history and you can't help but think of that famous depiction of the Norman Conquest, the Bayeux Tapestry. For centuries, the intricate masterpiece hung in Bayeux's cathedral relatively un-remarked on until someone noticed it was actually pretty good. Around this time another set of master-craftsmen were at work building the elegant Château de Martragny, one of Normandy's loveliest manor houses, which sits today among over seven acres of herbaceous camping meadows. The château has seen its fair share of drama over the ensuing years – it was, for example, used as a field-hospital during World War II – but its latter years as a family home and farmhouse have paid dividends for the campervan and canvas contingent who dwell here every summer. With flat, well-drained spaces, mature juicy apple trees and a well-stocked fishing pond, it's ready made for camping.

The house, now lived in by the De Buretel de Chassey family, is approached down a long, perfectly straight driveway lined on either side by mature trees. It's a wonderful entrance and has the effect of making you feel oddly privileged to be here, as though you've been granted special permission to camp on someone's large, manicured and well-tended estate. Which of course you have! The majority of the pitches are in the paddocks around the house, while a few can also be found alongside the drive. The former have the newest facilities, housed in a conservatory-like building

with spacious showers, toilets and washbasins – all of which are kept immaculately clean. The old stables and outbuildings are now home to a small onsite shop and bar, while the château's swimming pool and tennis courts are there for campers to use. The pitches along the driveway make do with slightly older facilities, along with a bit more exposure to the to-ing and fro-ing of passing cars, but they still offer the acres of space that make this site a winner; indeed when the rest of the grounds get busy these can be the quieter choice.

The pleasures of relaxing in the château gardens are always a treat, and there is a playground to provide a little extra interest for kids. There's a perfectly square ornamental pond at the very front of the château, stocked with hungry carp for eager anglers, or you can take the short drive back to the coast for some extreme cliff-top fishing. It is a 20-minute drive to the beaches, often via nearby Bayeux where it's worth nosing into the grand cathedral – and the tapestry which is now in the museum next door. Caen is a similarly speedy journey in the other direction, making the campsite a wonderfully central point for your holiday, with the beaches to the north, the Marais du Cotentin National Park to the west and a busy city to the east. It's also pretty conveniently located for the ferry too, making this an easy one-hop stop for a sneaky Gallic getaway!

COOL FACTOR A château near Bayeux with its own rich
tapestry of pristine grassy pitches and ornamental gardens.
WHO'S IN Tents, campervans, caravans, dogs, groups (by
request) – yes.
ON SITE 156 pitches and 4 safari tents (plus guest rooms
in the château are also available). Three sanitary blocks with
toilets, showers, washing machines and dryers. Safari tents
feature a kitchenette and 2 bedrooms (with 1 double bed
and 3 singles). Small shop selling essentials and fresh bread,
a bar serving evening meals, tourist info in reception and a
blackboard with info on local markets and events. Swimming
pool in the château gardens, tennis courts, badminton,
football field, ping-pong tables, children's playground, and
ocassional homemade fun – crafts with the children, drawing
competitions, château tours and boat building on the fishpond.
OFF SITE Normandy's famously sandy beaches, enshrined in
history since World War II, are a short drive away, and there
are excellent museums and memorials all along the coast.
The cemeteries (British in Bayeux, American in Colleville-sur-
Mer, German in La Cambe) allow visitors to appreciate the
magnitude of the D-Day offensive. In Bayeux, you should also
visit the museum of the famous tapestry (0033 231 512 550)
as well as the city's beautiful cathedral (0033 231 920 185),
with its thrice-weekly light show during July and August.
FOOD & DRINK An onsite shop sells local organic cider, jam
and calvados; 5km away in Ducy St Marguerite, Les Vergers
de Ducy (0033 231 802 865) is a good farm shop that also
lays on guided visits of its orchards and cellars. Buy fresh fish
in Courseulles-sur-Mer, 12km from the campsite, and in Port-
en-Bessin, 20km, with its beautiful little harbour. The former is
also home to Hotel de Paris (0033 231 374 507), an excellent
seafood restaurant.
GETTING THERE Once you leave the N13, Martragny is well
signposted. As you draw closer, you will see tourist signs for
Château de Martragny. Follow these to the campsite.
OPEN Mid May–late August.
THE DAMAGE Pitch, electricity and 2 people €31.40–€41.50,
children (under 13) €3.10–€4. Safari tents €500–€570 a week.

le château de monfréville

Le Château de Monfréville, Monfréville 14230, Calvados 00 33 2 31 21 35 42 www.châteaumonfreville.com

A thousand years ago, the cling-clang of armour and haughty laughter of the French aristocracy reverberated from the walls of this picturesque château, whose grey stones and round tower were as attractive and romantic a sight then as they are today. Since its commission by William the Conqueror, Château Monfréville has housed all sorts, from the family of Walt Disney to invading German soldiers during World War II, but today this scenic abode is an altogether more bucolic affair, hosting a thoughtfully-run campsite on a quintessentially French estate that offers the perfect family getaway. The quaint rusticity of the place is apparent the second you arrive, when you're whisked off from the château's leafy apple orchard by vintage tractor to the vehicle-free pitches in the grounds. It's a spacious site, limited to just 25 tents so campers are guaranteed to never feel crowded. There is ample room for children to play, open spaces where Bert the donkey can graze, and a natural swimming pond that is perfect for an authentic camping dip!

The greenery of the château's gardens are unmarred by sanitary blocks. Instead campers head into the cellars of the castle where a set of well-kept washing facilities are complemented by power sockets, fridge freezers and a washing machine. And, if a quick blast under the hot showers isn't enough for you, back outside a steamy hot tub is sure to help you unwind. Those who wish such luxury to continue can forego the tent to stay in one of the site's two small well-equipped gypsy caravans, furnished with an eye for detail and with room for up to four in a double bed and bunk beds; there's also ample storage space, two gas hobs, tables, chairs and every kitchen utensil you could possibly need; all you'll need to bring is your toothbrush.

Overlooking the stunning Contentin and Bessin nature park, the Château de Monfréville is the perfect place from which to grab a bike from the free-to-borrow stock onsite and head into the trees, discovering migrating storks, hooting owls and the gregarious bullfrogs who offer a dawn chorus each morning. A longer cycle ride takes you to the coast (a 15-minute journey by car), where you can visit the historic sandy beaches of D-Day and the fascinating museums that go with them, while Bayeux and its famous tapestry is also close at hand.

At its heart, however, it is not so much the pleasant countryside and rich history of Normandy that make Château Monfréville so special, as the owners Zoe and Paul, whose all-round warmth and attentiveness is very welcome indeed. Their smallholding of animals and the tiny onsite honesty shop reflect the easy-going, rural atmosphere of the site. Children can socialise with fellow campers, parents can relax beneath the shady trees, and everyone tends to leave vowing to return the following year.

COOL FACTOR A family-friendly and very personable château campsite with lots of space for each pitch.

WHO'S IN Tents, glampers, large groups (on request), families – yes. Caravans, motorhomes, campervans, dogs – no.

ON SITE 25 grassy pitches and 2 gypsy caravans, with showers, loos and a washing-up area in the cellars of the château that would give some people's homes a run for their money. There are 2 showers, 2 loos and hand basins in the ladies and the same in the gents. Campers can also use the washing machine in the château on either a self-service or laundry basis. There is a fabulous natural swimming pond (kept clean by the plants that surround it) a bubbling hot tub, a ping-pong table, table football and loads of ball games such as badminton and boules, while there is also a selection of bikes free for everyone to use. There are no cars allowed on the campsite and no dogs because of the chickens and ducks – a classic vintage tractor transports everyone to and from their pitches.

OFF SITE Le Château de Monfréville is a small château by French standards but more than makes up for it with its extensive grounds and a prime position overlooking the Regional Nature Park of Cotentin and Bessin. It is also conveniently located for Utah and Omaha beaches (20 minutes drive away), where the Utah Beach Museum (0033 233 719 236), Omaha Beach Memorial Museum (0033 231 219 744) and the Bayeux War Cemetery are perhaps the most poignant of D-Day and World War II sights in a region that is full of such things. The charming medieval city of Bayeux is home to the famous 11th-century tapestry and a lavish cathedral, and Mont St Michel (0033 233 601 430) is just an hour's drive away – as is Giverny, home of Monet's renowned Gardens (0033 232 512 821).

FOOD & DRINK A basic honesty shop stocks essentials such as marshmallows, logs, charcoal, the château's own eggs and homemade jams. The bread fairy delivers pastries every morning to your tent and Thursday evening is 'moules frites night', when campers gather in the barn for a night of feasting. Once a week they also fire up their enormous wood-fired pizza oven (made from one of the château's old boilers). Sunday's are whole roast chickens and chips! Normandy, known as the bread basket of France, has a superb larder of cheese, cider and seafood and markets every day of the week. Nearby Isigny (4km) boasts a cheese factory (0033 231 513 333) and a (separate) caramel factory (0033 231 516 650), both of which you can visit. The fishing village of Grandcamp Maisey also has good places to eat: try A La Maree (0033 231 214 100), La Tinquettte (0033 231 226 490) or La Belle Marinière (0033 231 226 123) – all excellent.

GETTING THERE From Calais, Caen or Ouistraham head to Bayeux. and then take the turn-off to La Cambe (D113). At the stop sign turn left, then, at the roundabout, take the 3rd turning to Monfréville. Drive over 4 small bridges and after the last one take the 2nd turning on the right. The campsite is about half-a-mile down on the right-hand side. Ignore the Monfréville exit sign as it is a bit further on, and don't take the left turn to the church. From Cherbourg follow the signs towards Caen and St Lo (N13); take the turn-off to Isigny-sur-Mer (D5) after Carentan. At the stop/give way sign, turn right and then immediately left to Monfréville (5km). Follow the signs to Monfréville (not the Mairie) and you will find the château at the top of the hill on the left.

PUBLIC TRANSPORT The nearest train station is Lison, about 11km away, connected by direct train to and from Paris (2hrs). There are no bus facilities in the area so a car or a bike is essential to get around.

OPEN May half-term–mid September.

THE DAMAGE Tent and 2 people from €30.50; tent and 3 people from €36.75; tent and 4 people from €43.75. Extra persons from €7.20 per night. Tents over 5m cost an extra €7.20 per night. Gypsy caravan from €200 for 2 nights.

camping bel sito

Camping Bel Sito, L'église 50270 Baubigny, Manche 00 33 2 33 04 32 74 www.camping-normandie-belsito.com

Like a long line of solidified lava, a thin, red tarmac track runs from Baubigny through the dunes. At the height of summer, the midday sun brings it up to lava-like temperatures, and barefooted children walking back inland hop along its surface as if dancing across hot coals. The curious effect is of a pathway worn down only along its edges, where beach-goers traipse along in the cooler sands on either side. At one end of the path lies the beach; at the other, through a sandscape of rolling marram grass and craters studded with wind-shattered shells, is Camping Bel Sito, a refreshingly understated spot that is the ultimate antidote to the holiday parks scattered across the rest of Normandy. Indeed the very notion of a holiday park seems alien here: elsewhere swimming pools, evening 'animations' and daytime kids clubs are the very staple of camping existence, whereas here affable owner Edith shuns these gaudy go-to recipes for apparent campsite success.

"We respect your peace", she says, welcoming you into the spacious camping area that's home to up to 85 pitches; "we do not propose any noisy entertainments". There is a small playground, a ping-pong table and Wi-Fi up by the main reception building, but otherwise the aptly-named Bel Sito has a thoroughly undeveloped feel. Not unloved, though – the facilities, while basic, are immaculate, and decent showers with free hot water seem almost a novelty compared to the 50-cents-a-minute fumbling of other sites.

The main joy of this site, however, is its overall atmosphere. The convenience of a beach just 900m away would be a treat no matter what the campsite was like, but to find such a relaxed, old-school set-up is truly a privilege in such a location. Edith describes her philosophy as "a return to the traditional values of simplicity and conviviality", and it's to these specifications the campsite firmly adheres. Guests socialise in the late lingering light of summer evenings and children play hide-and-seek among the dunes that spread out from the campsite's edge; the sea is visible to every pitch owing to the tiered layout of the site: when sunset falls it looks stunning, no matter where you are.

Given the proximity of the dunes, the pitches are in some places more sandy than grassy, but head to the bottom of the site, where there is a small lake, and the ground is generally a little firmer. It is here, too, come the evening, that the true stillness of the place can be appreciated. In the distance Sark Island and Jersey can just be seen, while in the foreground that warm, lava-like ribbon of tarmac disappears towards the beach. It's a simple yet perfect scene, reflective, in a way, of the campsite itself: Nothing too fancy, and nothing unnecessary. Isn't that all you really need?

COOL FACTOR Peace, simplicity and panoramic views over the Baubigny dunes to the sea beyond.

WHO'S IN Tents, campervans, caravans, dogs (on a lead) – yes. Groups – no.

ON SITE 85 pitches, all with electricity. 13 showers, 10 toilets, a washing-up area, 2 washing machines and 1 dryer. A playground and 2 table tennis tables. Wi-Fi is available in a specific area of the campsite at an extra charge.

OFF SITE The Cotentin Peninsula is lined with excellent beaches, the nearest of which is just a 5–10 minute stroll from the campsite through the Baubigny dunes. It's huge, running north to south for several miles, so you're never short of space. Back inland, the vast Regional Park of Cotentin and Bessin is great for cyclists – and there's a particularly good route following the path of the River Douve. It's a 10-minute drive south to Barneville-Carteret from where you can get a ferry out to Guernsey (01481 723552) – an excellent day-trip and well worth doing if you're in the area for long enough (remember you need your passport to visit).

FOOD & DRINK There are bread and croissants sold on site during July and August, while year-round a small selection of essential groceries is available in the reception building. There's a big billboard suggesting local restaurants and cafés in the local area or ask Edith in person for specific suggestions. In terms of specialities, the region is renowned for its shellfish – notably oysters from Saint-Vaast-la-Hougue and Pirou – as well as cider and calvados, made from locally grown apples and pears.

GETTING THERE It's 34km from Cherbourg to Baubigny. From Cherbourg you take the D650 and 6kms after Les Pieux, turn right to Baubigny. From here follow the brown signs to the campsite.

OPEN Mid April–mid September.

THE DAMAGE A pitch and 2 people from €15.50–€24.40.

camping lez-eaux

Castel Château de Lez-Eaux, 240 avenue de Lez-Eaux, 50380 Saint-Pair-sur-Mer, Manche 00 33 2 33 51 66 09
www.lez-eaux.com

The long, tree-lined avenue that leads you into Camping Lez-Eaux is like a shaded runway landing you at your perfect holiday destination. At its end you taxi into a maze of camping pitches dotted, like a busy terminal, with folk from all across Europe: Belgians in board shorts, Dutch in wide-brimmed sunhats and French holidaymakers folding out their deckchairs. To say it's a hidden corner of France would be like calling *Babybel* a traditional French cheese; but for all its broad European appeal, Camping Lez-Eaux is still an exceptional place to stay: the grounds are spacious, the facilities excellent and your children will have befriended their continental companions before you've even unpacked the car.

Based around a 15th century château, Lez-Eaux – translating as 'close to the sea' – is a family-run site that's now into its fifth generation. Over the years, the camping area has steadily grown and altered shape, gradually spreading beyond the charming stone building with its outlying fishing lake. Despite a string of chalets and static caravan accommodation, the site still sticks to its traditional camping roots: tents cover the vast majority of the grassy pitches, each with ample space and an electricity hook-up if you wish to use it, and a number of classic vintage campervans pepper one or two of the sunnier spots. The atmosphere is laid-back and family-friendly, and the variety of activities they lay on during the peak summer period can

give weary parents a pleasing time-out if the kids are still running wild.

The real quirk of this campsite, however, is not in its essentials – which include fresh croissants every morning and a very well-kept outdoor swimming pool – but in some newer additions, which few other sites can match. Six metres up, in a pair of old oaks on the edge of the site, two strikingly cool tree tents are the envy of every canvas camper. Inside, the tree trunk forms a centre column around which everything is orientated, with a plush double bed and a single for kids. Each tent is reached by a spiral, wooden staircase, while a rope pulley system allows you to hoist your breakfast basket up and down every morning – a playful if not the most practical way to start the day!

Elsewhere, sports pitches, paddling pools and tennis courts provide welcome distractions, although for most the morning is one of readying and picnic-making for a day on the beach. It takes just four minutes in the car to reach the nearest beach, while a route designed for cyclists will lead you to the same spot in little over half an hour (ask at reception for a map and information). From here you can skirt the coast south along shoreline roads, taking in historic settlements and endless beaches, or skip north a couple of kilometres to the seaside resort of Granville, a historic, walled town that is home to a range of shops, cafés and restaurants.

COOL FACTOR A family-friendly spot, with loads of activities onsite and 2 quirky treehouse options.

WHO'S IN Everyone! Tents, campervans, caravans, families, couples, dogs (on a lead) – yes.

ON SITE 121 camping pitches (all include electrical hook-ups), 59 chalets and 2 treehouses. There are 3 toilet blocks, 1 heated and open all year, while the others are open subject to demand. Coin-operated washing machines and tumble-dryers. Onsite activities include an indoor swimming pool, paddling pool and 3 slides, an outdoor pool, bouncy castles, football and volleyball pitches, a tennis court (€5 per hr), a kids' playground, a kids' clubs (July & Aug), a fishing lake and an onsite local market (July & Aug). Cycle hire also available.

OFF SITE At reception you can buy tickets for trips to nearby Jersey and Chausey islands – if you can, get one of the first boats across, as the islands each deserve a good day-trip. Closer to home, the campsite is just 8km from Granville, whose well-preserved old centre is surrounded by 15th-century ramparts and dominated by the ancient church of Notre-Dame du Cap Lihou – an imposing granite building built by the English during the Hundred Years' War.

FOOD & DRINK There is a licensed bar onsite that also serves takeaway meals in the evening. The small reception shop has a few essentials, plus freshly baked bread and pastries each morning. For more choice, drive the 8km to Granville where a huge selection of restaurants will keep you busy: Picorette (0033 233 599 349) is a popular choice throughout the day, while OXC3 (0033 233 694 682) is the place to go for dinner.

GETTING THERE From the A84 take the exit to Granville where you take the D973 towards Avranches (signposted). Continue over the roundabout on the D973 and after 4km the campsite is on your right.

OPEN April–mid-September.

THE DAMAGE A camping pitch for 2 people, a vehicle and electric starts at €26 a night.

forest escapes

Château de la Baudonnière, Les Chambres 50320 La Haye-Pesnel, Manche 01273 803030 www.forestescapes.com

Gifted with a French château set within beautiful 100-acre grounds, most campsites would simply add a couple of toilets and sit back and welcome the campers in their droves. Not so at Forest Escapes. Instead of just tucking you away in the dappled shade of the woodland, they've decided to raise their game by offering exquisite glamping accommodation along with an 'all-inclusive' option that includes homecooked meals and a wealth of activities. The result is pure French glamping heaven.

Forest Escape's 'woodland village' sits in the heart of the Normandy countryside, just north of Avranches. It's an apt description for a place that gains, over the course of a week's stay, a real community feel. There's a convivial atmosphere, aided by fantastic group meals washed down with lashings of local wine, yet it's also full of tranquil, private spaces to enjoy quiet family time.

The site's treehouses are perhaps the stand-out feature. There are two of these – the playfully named Les Singes (Monkeys) and Les Ecureuils (Squirrels). The latter is the larger of the two, with a three-bedded bunk room and a mezzanine floor with a double bedroom; Les Singes sleeps one less and is all on one level. Both have their own eco-toilet and Indonesian shower room on the ground. In addition to the treehouses, the site has three traditional Mongolian yurts and a woodland cabin, each of which shares facilities in the Ranger's Lodge in the centre of the glamping glade. As well as the toilets and washing facilities, breakfast is served in the lodge (lunch and dinners are served in the château; dinner is

accompanied with wine and cider).

The lodge also serves as a main meeting-place and home of onsite amusements. Nothing is compulsory but it's hard not to get involved! There's a wide range of activities available – canoeing, climbing, archery, orienteering, fencing, raft building, clay pigeon shooting, bike touring, animal petting, bread-making... you name it. Many can be undertaken as a family while others are just for kids, leaving the adults to do something different – like taking the scenic walking tour across the bay to Mont St Michel, arguably France's most famous landmark outside of Paris. With its spectacular medieval architecture and outstanding views, it's approached by crossing a dramatic tidal causeway. Your knowledgable guide will make sure you follow a safe route and point out interesting features along the way (including quicksand!).

COOL FACTOR All-inclusive luxury glamping – and bundles of active fun for families.

WHO'S IN Glampers only. Tents, campervans and caravans – no.

ON SITE Three yurts, 2 treehouses and a woodland cabin. The communal ranger's lodge has showers, toilets, communal areas and a breakfast room. The main château also has dining rooms, communal areas and toilets. The 100-acre estate also includes a mini-farm and they even have their own cider press. There are plenty of supervised children's activities, if parents wish to go off an do their own thing, and a full programme of outdoors activities with qualified instructors, including climbing, canoeing, bread-making and fencing to name but a few; they also run tours like the spectacular walk across the bay to Mont St Michel.

OFF SITE A quaint little town 15 minutes' from the site, Villedieu-Les-Poêles is home to the interesting Bell Foundry (0033 233 610 056) copper workshop and pewter museum. It also hosts a great morning market every Tuesday. The nearest beaches are at Carolles, Juilloville and Dragey, and you can walk the scenic stretch between Carolles and Jullouville. One of the best zoos in France (0033 233 613 074) is only 8km from the site at Champrepus: it has a diverse range of wild and farm animals, along with a botanical garden and a delightful café.

FOOD & DRINK Woodland villagers have their breakfast provided at the Ranger's Lodge and lunch and dinner is taken in the château complex. It's all included in the price (plus tea, coffee and squash provided throughout the day), which includes a civilised amount of wine and the site's own cider – served with dinner and into the evening.

GETTING THERE Full transfer to and from nearby airports and ferry ports can be included in bookings.

OPEN Open for just 6 weeks in summer (basically all of the UK summer school holidays).

THE DAMAGE Prices are all inclusive and per week (Sat–Sat). Treehouses £520 per adult, £490 for children (6–16); yurts £470 for adults, children from £155; woodland cabin £495 per adult, children from £155. Children under 2 free.

le bois coudrais

35270 Cuguen, Ill-et-Vilaine 00 33 2 99 73 27 45 www.leboiscoudrais.com

"Turn left at the crossroads and look out for the drapeau Britannique on your left," grinned a helpful couple. There's a French flag flying outside the site, too, but it's mostly British and Dutch campers who appreciate the friendly, family-run, traditional camping at Le Bois Coudrais, a small and very peaceful campsite situated around 25km inland from St-Malo in the north of Brittany. At night the peace and quiet is only disturbed by leaves rustling in the poplars, but the myriad birds deliver a dawn chorus, so if the other kind of twittering disturbs you, then best drive by.

The reward for getting up early is the sweet smell of fresh croissants delivered before 8am, and perhaps a chance to visit the site's own goats, chickens and ducks. Children so enjoy petting and feeding them that the animals need to be put on a diet come summer's end. Campers may feel the need to self-impose one too. In high season the owners bake cakes and make burgers, chips and salads, so you can eat outside the bijou café-bar next to the swimming pool or have them freshly delivered right to your pitch.

And once the delights of the site are exhausted there is plenty to do in the surrounding area, with Mont St-Michel 20 minutes by car in one direction and the fairytale feudal castle at Fougères, with towers and turrets in all the right places, around half an hour in the other. There's also St-Malo and Dinard, the Brittany capital of Rennes, tree-top walking at nearby Villecartier, and any number of glorious country walks.

COOL FACTOR Traditional camping in north Brittany.

WHO'S IN Tents, campervans, caravans, dogs (on leads) – yes. Large groups – by arrangement.

ON SITE Large pitches spread over 3 areas, and just 25 pitches overall. The Top section has electric hook-ups and is nearest to the washing facilities – ideal for caravans or vans. The middle area is better for tent camping, with shady trees and a field with plenty of space for ball games in the evenings. There's a bright wash-block with free hot showers and good laundry and washing-up facilities. Kids' play and animal-petting areas. Heated swimming pool. Free Wi-Fi. There's also 4 gîtes and pre-erected tents for hire. No campfires, BBQs okay.

OFF SITE The local visitor centre has a café, shop, play area and is the start-point for walks, strolls and offroad cycling.

FOOD & DRINK There's a small café-bar at the campsite. Le Bois Coudrais is possibly the only site that will deliver the food right to your tent pitch. Though only when time allows, so not if all 25 pitches are ordering something at once! Elsewhere, The Auberge de la Cour Verte in Dol-de-Bretagne (0033 299 484 141) is a welcoming mid-range restaurant. Or treat yourself to the best seafood at Côté Mer, 4 rue Ernest Lamort, with menus from €27 (0033 299 896 608).

GETTING THERE From Combourg follow the signs to Mont St-Michel on the D796 and then Cuguen on the D83. The site is signposted on the left about 2km after Cuguen. From Pontorson take the D90 to Trans-la-Forêt, then the D83 towards Cuguen. The site is signposted on the right before the village.

OPEN Mid May–mid September.

THE DAMAGE Camping, car, 2 adults costs €20 a night; extra adults €4. Children (up to age 14) €3. Electricity (10 amp) €4. Tax de sejour €0.20 per person per night.

camping milin kerhé

Rue du Moulin 22200 Pabu, Cotes d'Armor 00 33 2 96 44 05 79 www.milin-kerhe.com

The Brittany coastline has no shortage of cool camping destinations, but Camping Milin Kerhé stands out from the pack. For a start, not many campsites can boast such an idyllic setting. Pristine terraced fields hugged lovingly by enchanting woodland and a majestic, meandering, salmon-rich river, Camping Milin Kerhé is the very picture of tranquility; and the general laid-back air of the place is mirrored in the camping options on offer. Want to pitch your tent? No problem. Fancy rocking up in a VW relic-on-wheels? Go ahead. Too lazy for all those pegs and guy-ropes? Rent one of their spacious and quirky hanging tents slung up in the woodland! Moreover, there's more than enough onsite fun to please everyone, from kayaking and nature trails to volleyball and boules.

It's all a bit too easy to take for granted once you've been here for more than a few moments. The setting simply lends itself to the site's inimitable laid-back, relaxed and wonderfully natural style – simply thinking of a rowdy holiday park would be a criminal offence here. Instead, the beautiful River Trieux slides calmly past, sparkling in the French sunlight and catching your eye as you try to peacefully work through the new book you've been reading. It couldn't be further than the swarming Europarks that have popped up in recent years – and that's just the way we like it.

The Trieux shouldn't hold back tiny campers either. For those worried about the river, there is a fence separating the pitches from the water and most of the time it's families that form the bulk of the customers here. The resulting atmosphere is wonderfully social, with little ones quick to

breach any language barriers with a lively game of volleyball or a bit of hide-and-seek amongst the trees. The all-round bonhomie of the place is largely down to your amazingly welcoming hosts Jonathan and Margareth Low. Their hospitality knows no bounds and their midweek evening BBQs are the stuff of legends! Breathe it in folks, breathe it in...

COOL FACTOR Tranquil, idyllic waterside camping in the heart of Brittany.

WHO'S IN Tents, campervans, motorhomes, dogs – yes.

ON SITE The 2.6 hectares site is spread out over 3 terraces. It encompasses 55 pitches for tents and a separate emplacement for caravans and campervans. A spacious and airy sanitary block contains 6 showers, 8 toilets, washing machines and separate gents and ladies wash blocks. There are also electric hook-ups. There's plenty of wildlife on site to spot, including kingfishers, owls, deer, koypu, otters and a huge bat colony. Guided bat and nature walks are held in high season, and kids will love playing with the dwarf goats and ducks. Campers have free use of the canoes, kayaks and rowing boats. There is a volleyball pitch, boules pitch, table tennis, a children's play area, a swimming hole in the river above the weir and a cliff with 3 climbing routes. At the reception you'll find information and permits for river fishing for salmon/trout/coarse species in the river. There is also a suspended tree tent up that can be rented (see the website for more details).

OFF SITE Beyond the neighbouring mountain biking trails and hiking routes, the historic Breton towns of Guingamp, Pontrieux and Treguier are worthwhile attractions. The beautiful island of Brehat is also worth a day trip, not least for its charming harbour and lighthouse. Other beauty spots worth visiting include La Roche Jagu, a wonderfully preserved medieval fortress high above the river.

FOOD & DRINK There's a small shop in reception selling beautiful Breton produce, fresh bread delivery each morning and a food truck, serving pizza, fish and chips and Galettes and crêpes on alternative nights. There's also a lovely bar-restaurant a 10-minute walk away. The nearest supermarket is 5 minutes by car. During the high season, the Low family put on a delicious weekly evening BBQ.

GETTING THERE By car the site is an hour from the Roscoff ferry port and and hour and a half from Saint Malo. By car, take the N12 to Guingamp and from the centre follow signs for Pabu (3km). Once in Pabu, continue along rue de la Poterie for 800m and turn left at restaurant into Rue du Moulin. The campsite is at the end of the road.

PUBLIC TRANSPORT Trains run from the ports of both Roscoff and Saint Malo to Guingamp. There is a bus from Guingamp station to Pabu (No. 2) but there are only a few services per day.

OPEN Mid May–late September.

THE DAMAGE Pitches €5.50–€6, plus adults €4.50–€6, children €2.50–€3), dogs €2 (low season only), electricity €3. Pitches with firepits are an additional €1 per night. There's also a hanging tent for €30–€40 (and price per person) per night.

le ferme de croas men

Croas Men 29610, Plouigneau, Finistere 00 33 2 98 79 11 50 www.ferme-de-croasmen.com

In a part of northern Brittany bestowed with place names like Plouezoc'h Trudujo, and Beg ar C'hra you'll find more prosaically named, La Ferme de Croas Men, nestled in the rolling countryside. The flowery roadside signs that lead you there were all painted by Monsieur Cotty, who started the campsite 20 years ago and also created the many *objets trouvés* sculptures around the site. Not that he considers himself purely an artist. This is also a working dairy farm shared by four generations of the Cotty family and an ark-full of animals. With a herd of 45 cows, there are also donkeys, goats, sheep, ducks, rabbits, chickens and Max the pig to feed. For children, this menagerie is a real hoot.

La Ferme de Croas Men is much more than a glorified petting farm, though: it also hosts a museum demonstrating just how much farm life has developed over the last century. The antique farm machinery is displayed next to Ty Coz, the original family cottage, which is decorated just as it might have in 1900, complete with a beaten-earth floor, a massive table and benches, four-poster bed, vintage dresser and grandfather clock, which stands opposite photos of the great grandparents.

The Cottys, among whom Raphael speaks excellent English, allow their smaller visitors to watch the milking, feed the animals and witness the farm in action throughout the day, asking only that adults are present to ensure safety and that animals are allowed to rest between 11am and 4pm. There are tractor rides in July and August and plenty to see in the countryside around, with beautiful sunken-road walks starting from the farm itself.

The historic port of Morlaix is just 10 minutes' drive away, while the closest beaches and coves on Brittany's heather-covered northern coast – the wonderfully named Armorican Corniche – are about 5 minutes further. Morlaix is famous for its colossal viaduct, the remarkable 16th-century house of Queen Anne of Brittany, and for repelling an English attack in 1522. The English sailed up the estuary and found the town undefended and in true medieval style proceeded to invade. However they made the mistake of lingering in the wine cellars until the locals returned to drive the inebriated intruders away, subsequently adding *'S'ils te mordent, mords-les!'* ('If they bite you, bite them!') to the town's coat of arms.

Fortunately, there are no worries about overstaying your welcome any more, with spacious pitches, cabins, or tents waiting for you. You can even raid the cellars too, with some fantastic local wines on offer from the Morlaix market. Consider it your own personal nod to history. Holidays are supposed to have a cultural element, after all.

COOL FACTOR Proper camping on the farm with a few added comforts.

WHO'S IN Tents, campervans, caravans, dogs (on leads), large groups, young groups by arrangement – yes.

ON SITE 50 large pitches, all with electricity, and 2 wash-blocks. There are also 2 wooden roulottes (gypsy caravans), chalets, cabins and wood-and-canvas tents to hire. The most central wash-block is the better of the two, with efficient warm showers, laundry sinks, disabled access, a parent-and-baby room, washing machine and chemical disposal point. Next door is a reception with walking routes and tourist information, toys, books and board games for the kids. Campfires permitted.

OFF SITE There's a local market somewhere every day of the week, one of which is in Morlaix, so fans of 'produits régioneux' can get a daily fix if they fancy, and discover lovely Breton towns and villages in the process. There are loads of beaches and coves to explore, with the sandy shore, surf and sailing schools at Locquirec recommended. But if the weather's awful you might prefer the big indoor pool with slide and hot tub at Plouigneau.

FOOD & DRINK You can eat at the campsite, where milk, eggs, butter, yogurt, preserves, honey, cider and apple juice are either homemade or locally produced and can be bought at reception. The Crêperie L'Hermine (0033 298 881 091) on the quiet rue Ange de Guernisac, in the heart of Morlaix, makes a traditional Breton pit-stop after the Saturday morning market. Alternatively, go for a lunchtime treat of fresh seafood on the terrace of the Brasserie de la Plage (0033 298 793 070) overlooking the beach and harbour at Locquirec.

GETTING THERE Take the Plouigneau exit off the N12, but don't go into Plouigneau; head for Lanmeur on the D64. Drive for just 150m and you should see the first of the pale-blue signs directing you to the farm, 6km away.

OPEN April–October (all year for renting).

THE DAMAGE Camping with a vehicle plus tent or caravan and 2 adults €14.44; extra people over 7 years €3.50, small children €2–€2.80. Electricity (6 amp) €3.50.

camping la pointe

La Pointe, 29150 Saint Coulitz, Finistere 00 33 2 98 86 51 53 www.lapointesuperbecamping.com

La Pointe lies just outside the picturesque town of Châteaulin, close to a tree-lined bend of the canalised River Aulne. The site is British-owned – Marcus and Julie took over from another English couple in 2008 – but it attracts a loyal following of French *campeurs*, along with British and Dutch regulars, who appreciate the warm, considerate welcome, spacious pitches and good facilities.

Set in a conifer-lined valley at the foot of a deciduous forest, the site was recently incorporated within the borders of the Parc Naturel Régional d'Armorique. A tinkling stream runs down one side, and the pitches, separated by hedges and flowers, sit on terraces rising up the wooded hillside. Experienced campers themselves, the owners know what their customers want – there's a spacious play area for the kids and a chill-out room; outdoor furniture for lounging and a handy fridge-freezer. If you fancy having a BBQ, they are available for hire, and there's a daily *boulangerie* delivery as well as fresh eggs and vegetables from the garden. Along with the woodland, the canal path is ideal for a walking, running, cycling or fishing (the canal is a grade-II salmon stream), but adventure junkies won't need to travel far either.

To get a bird's eye view of the Breton countryside, take a trip to the summit of Ménez-Hom, the highest peak in the Black Mountains. At just over 1000 feet (330m) it's no Everest, and you can actually drive almost to the top, but it offers a panorama of Western Brittany and the Crozon Peninsula like no other. The paragliders who use the peak get an even loftier view looking north towards Brest, south to Quimper, and west, where the coastline curves around the sweep of the Baie de Douarnenez with its extravagantly long, level stretches of sand. Near Douarnenez, Pentrez beach is conveniently connected to the site by bus in July and August and was home to the sand-yachting world championships recently. You can hire a sand-yacht of your own if you can handle the adrenaline thrill, while surfers who want to catch the Atlantic swell can head for Pen Hir Point. Those of more sedate tastes will find pleasure here, too – Marcus and Julie are keen bird-watchers, and they recommend the rugged cliffs around Pointe du Raz and local marshland sites near Le Faou to fellow twitchers.

Another essential excursion is to the remarkable medieval town of Locronan, a perfectly preserved, cobbled and car-free haven which became famous in the 14th century for making sailcloth. The sand-coloured granite houses and 15th-century church have made it a favourite location for film-makers, and it's so reminiscent of Hardy's Wessex that Roman Polanski's version of *Tess of the d'Urbervilles* was filmed there. The town feels quite touristy in the afternoon, so it's probably best to go on a Thursday evening, when there's an atmospheric 'starlit' market during high season.

In short, there's plenty to do around La Pointe and you won't want to leave. The visitors' book is full of comments like 'I only meant to stay one night and I'm still here a week later'. Which says it all, really.

COOL FACTOR A very warm welcome and cool, shady pitches in the forest, even in high season.

WHO'S IN Tents, campervans, caravans, and well-behaved dogs, large groups by arrangement – yes.

ON SITE 60 camping pitches all with electric hook-ups, and 1 fully-equipped canvas tent lodge. Campfires are allowed (but not in the forest) – please ask first. The wash-block is large enough to accommodate a much bigger site, with plenty of sparkling-clean sinks and showers, plus laundry wash-rooms. Next door there is an information room and book exchange; there's free Wi-Fi, too. The communal room isn't fancy, but it has a table tennis table and space enough to relax on a rainy day when you can't get out. The fully-equipped tent lodge has room for up to 4 glampers and is situated on one of the terraces overlooking the site. Campers with their own canoes can launch just outside the campsite and bikes are available to hire. There's a motorhome service point.

OFF SITE Châteaulin, a stroll along the river from the site, is a lovely, floral riverside town, with a good weekly market and supermarkets, restaurants, tennis and a heated indoor swimming pool. There is a centre there that hires out kayaks, canoes and pedalos for use on the calm waters of the River Aulne, which forms part of the 315km of the Brest–Nantes canal. Beaches, water sports, and sand-yachting are 16km away. Quimper, the medieval capital of Finistère, is a 20-minute drive away. Brest is about 40 minutes, and is home to the Océanopolis aquarium (0033 298 344 040),

which isn't cheap but is great for a family day out. There's also an excellent open-air boat museum, Le Port-Musée, in Douarnanez (0033 298 926 520).

FOOD & DRINK *Boulangerie* deliveries mean you can guarantee your pain au chocolat for breakfast, and fresh eggs and fresh vegetables are available, too. On Thursdays in high season it's crêpe night onsite, but otherwise there are special places to enjoy Breton crêpes close by. The Crêperie St Côme (0033 298 265 586), on an old farm at St-Côme, near Pentrez beach, has no less than 580 different crêpes to choose from. Marcus and Julie also recommend Crêperie de l'Enclos in Pleyben (0033 298 263 868), where they may add truffles, foie gras, peach and other exotic gastronomic flavours. In Châteaulin, Le Miniscule (0033 298 862 866) is an easy-going, friendly pizza and seafood bar/restaurant, where moules-frites costs around €10.

GETTING THERE It's about an hour's drive from Roscoff, but if you're coming from Rennes take the N12 and then change to the N164, signposted Quimper. Once you get to Châteaulin, drive down to the river in the centre, cross the bridge, and follow the signs to Quimper on the D770. After 1km, turn left (signposted St-Coulitz), and the campsite is 100m further down on your right.

OPEN Mid March–mid October.

THE DAMAGE Camping, car and 2 adults €15.50–€18 (€12-€13 on bikes). Extra adults €4., children €2.50. Electricity €4 (prices vary depending on season).

ACCUEIL

camping du letty

32 rue du Canvez, 29950 Bénodet, Finistere 00 33 2 98 57 04 69 www.campingduletty.com

Beach holidays have one small problem. After you've splashed about in the shallows and lounged about on the beach for a few hours, getting sandy, salty and suntanned, you really don't feel like changing out of your swimwear and stepping into a car that's also been gently roasting for a few hours. The answer is to stay as close to the sea as possible, and Camping du Letty is the perfect solution, enabling you to stroll to the showers before ambling back to your pitch refreshed and ready for action. Or inaction if you prefer – Camping du Letty is an excellent place to do nothing. However, as in many of the other larger coastal sites, there's also plenty happening on site if that's what you're after – with bars, a disco, restaurants and entertainment, and a swimming pool and aquapark, complete with slides and a retractable roof.

Yet campers can have a lovely, peaceful holiday here if they wish. A short distance along the corniche from the shops and restaurants of the summer resort of Bénodet, the site is run by two generations of the Le Guyader family. Marc and his parents have their work cut out – the site is spread over 25 acres and has around about 550 pitches – but their enthusiasm and commitment are plain to see, and what's more the site has been established for decades, so the shade-giving trees are mature and the abundant hedges give each bit of the site a real sense of seclusion. In fact it's surprisingly easy to forget that you're in the midst of the biggest tentopolis along this stretch of coast.

The campsite abuts Plage du Groasguan, a strip of golden sand along a slinky lagoon at the mouth of the River Odet. Across the placid water the Dunes Dominiales de Mousterlin stretch away, into a sandy horizon that blocks out the sea's swell. The result is a choice between a backwater that's ideal for paddling while parents can comfortably lie back on the shore, or a real beach and bigger waves just a short hike away from the site, where the beach is overlooked by a lighthouse that winks flirtatiously at every passing vessel after dark.

As you stroll along the shore, past the colourful art-deco changing rooms, and then further along Plage du Trez and around Pointe du Coq, you'll be getting closer to the old port of Bénodet, where you can buy seafood so fresh that it may still be flapping about – perfect to fry up back at the campsite in a butter and white wine sauce. Indeed freshly-caught fish is just another reason to enjoy being right beside the seaside.

COOL FACTOR An exquisite sandy beach on your tent-step.

WHO'S IN Tents, campervans, caravans, and dogs (on leads), large groups and young groups by arrangement – yes. But everybody must keep quiet after 10pm.

ON SITE 542 pitches, most with electric hook-ups, and a mass of services to match, including 6 wash-blocks scattered around the site – one of which even has a shower for dogs. There's also a well-equipped *salle du musculation* (gym), a swimming pool, a kids' club, a library, free Wi-Fi, a well-stocked *épicerie* (minimarket), squash and tennis courts, volleyball and archery areas, sauna and massage rooms, and even a hairdressing salon. Takeaway food, from pizzas to main meals, is available every lunchtime and evening. There's canoe and kayak hire and water sports on the beach. Motorhome service point. No campfires, but BBQs okay.

OFF SITE There are plenty of great cycle or canoe rides around the nature reserve and waterways adjacent to the site. Bénodet has more beaches, the grande promenade along the corniche, ferry trips across the River Odet to Ste Marine or upriver to the impressive medieval centre and double-steepled cathedral of Quimper, ancient capital of La Cornouaille (Cornwall). In the other, easterly direction, the fishing port and resort of Concarneau, complete with its

remarkable rampart-enclosed fortress island, Ville Close, lies on the coast, with the artist-favoured Pont-Aven around 35km further on.

FOOD & DRINK The Monday-morning market in Bénodet (or the Wednesday one in Ste-Marine), may tempt you off site for food; and there's a Champion supermarket in Bénodet too. There are plenty of bars and restaurants along Bénodet's seafront, but back in the town itself Le Café Foutu (0033 298 570 038) is a particularly good pick, with a large wine selection and a seafood buffet for aorund €30.

GETTING THERE From Quimper, take the D34 and follow the signs to Bénodet. At the Rond Point de Penfoul, bear left on to D44 (avenue de Fouesnant) and follow the road for 1.5km until Rond Point de Ty Pin. Turn right on to route du Letty, then fourth right on to rue de Canvez and second left down impasse de Creisanguer.

PUBLIC TRANSPORT Take a train from Paris to Quimper, catch a ferry to Bénodet, then take a taxi to the site.

OPEN Mid June–early September.

THE DAMAGE Pitch and 2 people €24–€48.50 (including electricity); the best beach pitches €36–€69.50 (including electricity and private water point); children (3–6yrs) €4–€7; dogs €2–€5; tourist tax for over 18s €0.66.

COOL FACTOR Peaceful, lakeside camping in the grounds of a classic 19th-century Breton château.

WHO'S IN Tents, campervans, caravans, dogs – yes.

ON SITE 170 pitches, most with electricity (10 or 6 amp). Lakeside spots available. Wash-block with immaculate toilets and showers. Washing machines, dryers and even a dishwasher available. Wi-Fi €3 per day. Open-air swimming pool. Small onsite shop stocking basics.

OFF SITE The Parc Regional de la Grande Briere boasts the Loire Valley's most diverse wetland bird population. Explore France's second largest marshland on a leisurely cruise in one of the iconic punts or *chalands*. If it's beaches you're after, La Baule-Escoublac is famous for its pristine 12km-long sands which attract the French uppercrust every summer. Besides its casinos and luxury villas, La Baule also hosts one of the world's most prestigious show-jumping events, the Grand Prix de la Ville de La Baule. The port of Saint-Nazaire is also close by – the scene of arguably the most daring allied raid of WWII, when British commandos ram-raided and destroyed the dry dock there. Some of Brittany's most historic towns and cities are also worth a visit including Nantes – home of the Château des Ducs de Bretagne (0033 251 17 49 48) – and Vannes, with its ancient city walls and timber-beamed houses.

FOOD & DRINK There are plenty of excellent restaurants in the area. Le Clos de Mélanie (0033 240 880 839) is one of the closest and serves a pleasing menu of French classics. For something more sophisticated, Le 11 (0033 240 422 328) offers a vibrant set menu and they also have an artisan shop attached. Deffay's onsite eatery is a decent and convenient shout, though it only opens in high season 7pm-10pm. But the pizzas are deservedly popular.

GETTING THERE From the N165 join the D33 at junction 13. Then follow the tourist signs for Camping du Deffay.

OPEN May–September.

THE DAMAGE From €14.80 – €26.60 for a non-electric pitch and 2 people. Dogs are free.

huttopia lac de sillé

Sillé Plage, 72140 Sillé Le Guillaume, Sarthe 00 33 2 43 20 16 12 www.huttopia.com

Huttopia Lac de Sillé isn't a small campsite, with over 150 pitches in total. Yet you could be forgiven for thinking it's almost half that size – not least because it is completely dwarfed by its surroundings, with over 3,500 hectares of pristine forest and a huge lake (the imaginatively named 'Grand Etang' or 'Big Lake') in the shape of a teardrop glistening in the sun. Pitches vary wildly across the site. At its furthest point, where the trees are thickest, there's a real woodland feel, while closer to reception the space is more open, with motorhomes and caravans in among the larger family tents. There's an array of glamping accommodation options too, in particular safari tent-style lodges in various sizes and wooden cabins equipped with everything you could possibly need.

The campsite is, however, best-known for its activities, with a whole range possible around the lake, including mountain biking, watersports, swimming, climbing, zip-lines, archery, fishing and more. The campsite itself has multiple facilities, including ping-pong tables, volleyball courts and bikes available to hire. There's an indoor area with board games and books in case it rains and Wi-Fi should you need it. The focus is definitely on families, but if kids and noise all become a bit too much there's a pleasant 2km walk through the woods to nearby Sillé-le-Guillaume. It's a tiny town with a sleepy feel but all the French essentials – cute cafés, excellent delicatessens and even an old château. It's a quiet contrast to the buzzing little hive that is Huttopia Lac de Sillé.

COOL FACTOR Great facilities in a beautiful woodland and lakeside location.

WHO'S IN Tents, campervans, motorhomes, caravans, families, groups, couples, pets... everyone!

ON SITE 129 camping pitches and 37 glamping units (wood and canvas tents, chalets and roulottes). Heated swimming pool, free Wi-Fi around the snack wagon area and reception, a playground, boules, table tennis, table football, volleyball court, tennis, and bikes available for hire. A shop sells essentials and there's tourist information in reception.

OFF SITE The campsite is right by the Sillé Beach activity park – bring bikes or rent them on site to follow the various marked trails. It's 2km to Sillé Le Guillaume (0033 2 43 20 10 32), where you should pop your head into the Collegiate Church of Our Lady of Assumption and the Château of Sillé. The town of Le Mans (0033 2 43 28 17 22) – 30km away – is also worth a visit, with a walled historical quarter that can be explored easily on foot.

FOOD & DRINK The snack wagon offers simple food that you can eat on the terrace overlooking the pool – open the May bank holiday weekends and throughout July and August. There's a small grocery store in the reception area and bread and croissants are available to order in advance. For something elsewhere, walk (or drive) to Sillé Le Guillaume where there are plenty of options.

GETTING THERE Follow the D304 to Sille-Le-Guillaume and turn north onto the D5. Continue through the town and turn right onto the D105. After 200m, turn left, signposted 'Plage Hippodrome'; the campsite is on your right.

OPEN Late April–late September.

THE DAMAGE A pitch and 2 people from €14.50 per night. Additional adults €3.70–€5.60; children under 2 free, children 2–7 years free in low season, €3.80 in high season. Pets €2.30–€4.50. Glamping starts at €46 per night.

forest view

L'Espérance, Dorceau, 61110 Rémalard en Perche, Orne 00 33 2 33 83 78 55 www.forestviewfrance.co.uk

Peter and Sarah Wilson took over Forest View in October 2012, transforming the wilderness they found into a comfortable, easy-going site that lies by a quiet crossroads between the edge of the Forêt de Saussay and a landscape of gently rolling farmland. While the forest is huge and forms a significant part of the Parc Naturel Régional du Perche, the site itself could easily be called Lake View, because it's the reflections in the fishing lake that most people love to gaze at.

The lake is stocked with rudd, roach, pike and tench, but there's a firm policy on angling, and even if you land a giant carp it must go back into the water. Most people come here to ride horses or bikes, to paint, watch birds or walk in the woods of tamarisk and hawthorn. You can easily arrive and leave your car keys in your pocket, taking off on foot to explore everything that's on offer.

The irony is that for all its beauty this region is often bypassed in the rush to get further south. Yet it's a land of forests, ancient abbeys, and garden-fronted manors. The longer you stay the less you'll want to leave. The area is famous for its lace, its powerful Percheron horses, and for unspoilt thousand-year-old villages such as Chapelle-Montligeon, where an early-20th-century, Gothic Revival cathedral, Notre-Dame de Montligeon, rises somewhat bizarrely above the fields. It's also known for its wonderful cider and hospitality, both of which can be sampled back at the site during one of Forest View's unique 'Plat du Jour' evenings, when campers relax around long tables at the site's farmhouse restaurant, sharing tales of the day's adventures.

COOL FACTOR Cool views, warm hospitality, hot meals and cold ice creams. Plus a whole lot of history.

WHO'S IN Tents, campervans, caravans, and dogs (on leads), large groups by arrangement – yes.

ON SITE 25 pitches, 19 with electric hook-ups, and 3 Chambre d'Hote rooms. Separate ladies and gents wash-blocks, each with 3 showers and 3 toilets, plus 2 washing-up sinks, a washing machine and basins. Great fishing available. Wi-Fi is free. Campfires are prohibited but raised BBQs are welcome. Bike hire is available. You can order freshly baked bread and pastries from the office for the next day.

OFF SITE Spectacular hikes and rides from the site into the adjacent Forêt de Saussy – maps available. Bretoncelles and Rémalard have markets on Mondays and Thursdays respectively, with larger ones in Nogent le Rotrou and Mortagne au Perche on Saturdays. The sensational stained glass and soaring spires of Chartres Cathedral are just 44km away.

FOOD & DRINK Owner Sarah serves homecooked meals in the campsite's 300-year-old restaurant and bar 3 times a week (Tues, Thurs, Sat) – they offer a 2-course *Plat du Jour* menu, encompassing everything from Sarah's acclaimed Pork and Cider Lyonnaise to her celebrated Toulouse Sausage Cassoulet. Book at least one day in advance. The bar is open every evening in season 7pm–10pm.

GETTING THERE Make your way to either Bretoncelles or Rémalard and the site is on the D38 between the two villages. See www.forestviewfrance.co.uk for full directions and maps.

OPEN Mid April–mid October.

THE DAMAGE Pitch prices start at €12.30 per night.

camping senonches

Etang de Badouleau, 28250 Senonches, Eure-et-Loir 00 33 2 37 37 81 40 www.huttopia.com

Nature comes to the fore at Camping Senoches, which is part of the Huttopia group and situated within France's second-largest state-managed woodland, just an hour and a half from the capital. Paris may be within suprisingly easy reach, yet there's plenty to keep you out of the city, with a great deal of nature-related activity nearby, including an appealling swimming lake.

Somewhat off-puttingly the campsite describes itself as a 'camping village' but the car-free tent pitches are still spacious, well spread out among the trees and each come with their own picnic table area. The descritpion alludes, instead, to the spectrum of glamping options on offer. There are more luxury wood and canvas lodges available to rent here than there are regular tent pitches, and they speckle the area like a small settlement. Inside, each are smartly finished with ample room for families, while outside, other campsite luxuries include a swimming pool and a restaurant (breakfast is included in the price). Plans are even afoot to add a spa and wellness area, with a subtle wooden finish to match the surroundings.

Along with the amenities, the surroundings are the real draw of the site, with horseriding, mountain biking and hiking on hand, along with fishing in the Étang de Badouleau, which is adjacent to the site. The campsite restaurant sticks its great terrace arms right over the water, so that you can sit and watch others try to land their catch too. Once you're done there, make a trip into the town of Senoches and visit the castle – or head for the renowned cathedral city of Chartres, which is just half an hour away.

COOL FACTOR Well thought out woodland glamping and camping for families within easy reach of Paris.

WHO'S IN Tents, campervans, caravans, cars, families, couples – yes. Cars left at the gate.

ON SITE Large, private pitches for tents, each with its own picnic table, and a large number of glamping options – wooden cabins and wood-and-canvas lodges mainly. Several shower- and wash-rooms are dotted around. Good baby-changing facilities. Swimming lake, with a bar/restaurant stretching over it on stilts. Upstairs has a good stock of board games. There is a vast array of children's activities daily, concerning nature and art, and adult activities in the evening. Indoor swimming pool and wellness spa planned. Site shop sells essentials and some local produce.

OFF SITE Reception has plenty of information. The town of Senonches is charming and appears to have dropped from the sky into the centre of the forest. There is an 11th-century castle and plenty of interesting architecture. The Parc Régional du Perche is 450 acres of natural and cultural heritage, with fortified manor houses, farmsteads and villages that you can explore on foot or by bike. Chartres is 40km away, with its medieval old town and cathedral.

FOOD & DRINK A bar and restaurant overlook the lake with outdoor seating, serving grills, pizza and fresh breads and pastries at breakfast. Both Chartres and Senonches have great restaurants to discover.

GETTING THERE From Paris take the N12 to Dreux, then the D928 towards Digny; then head towards Senonches following the Huttopia signs. From Chartres take the D24 towards Senonches and follow the Huttopia signs.

OPEN April–November.

THE DAMAGE 2 people, tent, car €18–€25. Glamping prices vary depending on date, size of group and accommodation. See website for details.

huttopia rambouillet

Huttopia Rambouillet, Route du Château d'Eau, 78120 Rambouillet, Yvelines 00 33 1 30 41 07 34 www.huttopia.com

If you've ever camped in the national parks of North America, you'll have a pretty good idea of what the best forest camping should be like – and that's what Huttopia is all about: providing natural, untouched and simple campsites with all the essential facilities you need for a family holiday. Despite being less than an hour from central Paris, Huttopia Rambouillet ticks all those boxes perfectly. For starters, it's dominated by nature, with not a manicured lawn, pruned hedge or indeed a marked-out pitch in sight. Instead, campers arrive and loop their way around, carefully picking the best spot they can find, hopefully one where the roots aren't going to be poking through the bottom of the tent and digging into your back. Trees still rule the roost here – it's up to you to work around them.

The camping pitches themselves come in various types. 'Forest Spots' are the smallest, tucked in among the trees and suitable only for tents, while 'Nature Spots' are more open, less wild and suitable also for campervans and caravans, while 'Normal Spots' offer pitches of the more regular campsite kind – grassy, open and with electrical hook-ups. Plus there is a stash of eco-friendly glamping accommodation – cabins basically built from French Douglas fir that gives their fully-furnished interiors a wonderfully earthy aroma.

As for activities and facilities, the choice and quality is bigger than you might imagine – and perhaps somewhat at odds with a supposedly 'wild' site – but the swimming pool is an eco-friendly affair supplied entirely by natural water (it has two basins: one for swimming and the other full of filtrating plants and minerals): the water is crystal clear and there's not a single chemical added.

As for everything else, there's a reception backed by friendly staff, taking orders for the next morning's bread delivery, a small grocery area selling essentials and a lounge with board games and books to borrow in case it rains. They reflect the impeccable quality of all the facilities on site, regularly cleaned and well looked after. So even while you're camping North American-style beneath the trees, you know the essentials are well taken care of and always within easy reach.

COOL FACTOR Nature and trees, complete with all their lumps and bumps, together with exceptional family facilities.

WHO'S IN Glampers, campers, families, couples, tents, campervans, motorhomes, caravans – yes.

ON SITE 116 tent pitches, ranging in size and accessibility, and with plenty suitable for motorhomes too. Wood and canvas glamping cabins are also available. Excellent shower and toilet blocks, cleaned 3 times a day, including spacious family bathrooms, baby-changing and disabled facilities. There is a natural swimming and paddling pool with a pleasant poolside area, a café-restaurant (open daily July/August plus weekends out of peak season), a bar (open until 11pm) and a reception area with a small shop and plenty of tourist information. There are also swings, a playground, table tennis, volleyball and boules, plus an indoor lounge area with board and card games, books to borrow and a TV. There is no Wi-Fi on site but a computer with internet is available. No campfires.

OFF SITE Go fishing in the Etang d'Or lake, just next to the campsite. For this, you need a fishing permit which you can buy at the campsite reception. There aren't any fishing rods for hire though, so be sure to bring one with you. Bikes can be hired and there's a large map showing some of the best local routes. Alternatively, head into town – the former royal city of Rambouillet – where the Château de Rambouillet (0033 134 830 025) features a magnificent garden and the Chaumière aux Coquillages ('Shell Cottage') – home to one of the most beautiful shell and mother-of-pearl decors in Europe.

FOOD & DRINK The campsite's café-restaurant opens for breakfast or you can order fresh bread and pastries the evening before. They also do lunch and dinner, generally from around €10, including made-to-order pizzas (made with organic flour and tomatoes) cooked in a wood-fired oven. BBQs are available for anyone to use in the communal areas dotted around the site.

GETTING THERE From Paris take the A13 and then the A12, then the N10. Go through Trappes, then Rambouillet and then take the Les Eveuses exit. From here the campsite is clearly signposted.

PUBLIC TRANSPORT The nearest train station is in Rambouillet, 3km away.

OPEN Easter–end of October.

THE DAMAGE A pitch for 2 people and a tent, campervan or caravan starts at €18.50 per night in low season. Additional adults €6–€8.50; children under 2 years old free; children between 2–7 years are free in low season and €5.40 in high season. Pets €2.60–€4.20. Glamping accommodation begins at €63 per night and ranges right the way up to the largest *cabanes* (for up to 6 people) which peak at €154 per night in high season.

camping etangs du moulin

02320 Suzy, l'Aisne 00 33 3 23 80 92 86 www.etangsdumoulin.fr

All kids love playing 'cowboys 'n' injuns'. Some grown-ups do too, for that matter. So, if you're the type to get giddy at the theme from *Bonanza*, then saddle up partner and mosey on down to Picardy's darn-tootin'est camping experience. Camping Etangs du Moulin is a slice of The Old West in the rural French north. Run by affable host Agnès ('her's the sheriff round these parts' – ok, we'll stop now!) along with husband Sebastien, this is the ultimate getaway for your tiny Tontos, not to mention all bigger Buffalo Bills. Just outside the blink-and-you'll-miss-it hamlet of Suzy, the Etangs du Moulin's variety of western-themed accommodation is sure to bring out the John Wayne in any intrepid pioneers. There are 30 level grass pitches for tents, caravans and modest-sized motorhomes, but those seeking the authentic experience should opt for one of the hand-built pioneer waggons. Kids will love these charming chucks, sited near a swimming lake, which can sleep a family of up to five; they're named John, Lucky, Clint, Calamity and Charles and come fitted with a double bed, a triple bunk, kitchen, shower and toilet. Best of all, they're equidistant from both the playground and saloon so mum and dad can enjoy a few scoops at the rum-hole while the littl'uns get in character.

But it isn't all about the kids. For those looking to really push the pony out, La Village Boheme features a trio of handsome roulottes, secreted away from the rest of the site. These gorgeous gypsy caravans are pretty much self-contained and you can even indulge in a spot of pampering with chilled champagne waiting on arrival, meals brought to your door and a full-body massage (just... erm... like real cowboys).

Elsewhere, there's a tipi reservation that features five Native American-style canvas abodes, each sleeping two couples and complete with wood-burning stoves, BBQ and outdoor seating – plus the 'Cheyenne refuge reserve' provides an atmospheric communal area for cooking and dining.

For those who like their camping with a large dose of comfort, there are also six wooden cabanes that enjoy excellent views from their

enviably-elevated position atop stilts. They range from a two-person love shack to the family-sized Fisherman's Hut waterside cabin, which has a spacious veranda for spotting the trout leaping from the lake. The newest cabanes are the Cabane de D'Jo, with views over the lake from the king-sized bed and a wooden bath, and the Cabane du Grizzli, with a round bed overlooking the lake, and a hydro-jet shower. Both are set amongst trees by the water's edge, so you can kick off your boots and enjoy a spot of fishing from the veranda as you take in the tranquility of the setting.

As the name suggests, there are an abundance of carp-filled lakes, and rods can be hired onsite. For those not so keen on angling, there's a heated outdoor swimming pool and a varied choice of activities on offer, including pony-trekking. And while you can't exactly rustle cattle, there's a proliferation of tiny, fluffy wild rabbits to herd. Finally, while France and gastronomy go together like Butch and Sundance, the culinary delights on offer at Etangs du Moulin are of a distinctly more American flavour. The onsite Tex'n restaurant is something of a local institution, with vacationing vaqueros joined by the natives for a carnivore-friendly menu of pub grub favourites and *pintxos* to accompany the selection of quenching bières d'Abbaye. Campers can also order from a selection of BBQ packs to slap on their own personal grill – bison steak anyone?

COOL FACTOR Playful cowboy camping that's paticularly ideal for families.

WHO'S IN Tents, glampers, caravans, dogs, motorhomes – yes.

ON SITE 30 different size pitches for tents and caravans, 4 roulottes, 5 tipis, 6 wooden lodges (including 2 on the lakeside) and 5 pioneer waggons in a separate area. Facilities include toilets and free hot solar-powered showers, and electrical hook-ups (5amp). Children's playground and other activites, including volleyball, ping-pong and pedal go-karting. Massage treatments on offer. Heated swimming pool and 6 carp-filled fishing lakes – rod hire is €8. Pony-trekking is €8 for adults and €6 for kids. Wi-Fi included.

OFF SITE The site lies on the western outskirts of the 22,000 acre St Gobain Forest, a vast woodland that boasts some lovely walks. Take a stroll to the ghostly ruins of the abbey of Saint-Nicolas-aux-Bois or the mysterious Grotto Roches de l'Ermitage. The Château de Coucy (0033 323 527 128) in Aisne is one of the country's most impressive, while the department's capital Laon boasts some of France's finest medieval architecture. Take the town's funicular to enjoy some expansive views. Historians of the Great War should also seek out Chemin des Dames, and make a visit to the harrowing subterranean trench museum, Caverne du Dragon. Visit also the fascinating Familistère de Guise (0033 323 613 536) created by the region's most famous son, the 19th-century polymath Jean-Baptiste André Godin.

FOOD & DRINK A variety of BBQ packs are available to order onsite. Breakfast hampers and sophisticated evening meals can also be arranged. The Tex'n restaurant serves decent pub grub and pintxos to snack on. The saloon boasts a selection of Belgian beers and cocktails – try 'The Scalp' if you dare! Suzy doesn't have much in the way of shops, but Anizy-le-Château (just 10 minutes' drive away) has a supermarket, butcher and baker. Laon hosts a market every Thursday: be sure to pick up a wedge of *mariolles*, Picardy's famous cow's-milk cheese.

GETTING THERE From Calais/Lille, take the A26, then exit 12 and follow the road towards Laon/Saint Gobain. From Paris, take the N22 and exit after 10km towards Soissons/Laon and then towards Anizy-le-Château/Pinon/ Faucoucourt. Continue straight until you reach Suzy.

OPEN All year.

THE DAMAGE Camping pitches from €10 per night. Roulottes from €99 for 2 nights. Cabanes from €152 for 2 nights. Waggons from €110 for 2 nights.

camping de troyes

Camping de Troyes, 7 rue Roger Salengro, 10150 Pont-Ste-Marie, l'Aube 00 33 3 25 81 02 64 www.troyescamping.net

There's something very fitting about the fact that the medieval town of Troyes – the capital of the Champagne region – has a town centre shaped like a champagne cork. It's a lovely centre, too: a huddle of medieval buildings that stand out proudly against the town's more workaday charms. Though formed in the Roman era, most of Troyes' architecture dates from the Middle Ages, when it was an important trading town. Just along the road, in Pont-Sainte-Marie, Camping de Troyes is the town's official campsite. Though a former municipal spot, the owners here have done everything in their power to transform it into something much more alluring than the word 'municipal' suggests. What could be mistaken for a motorhome-filled nightmare is, in fact, a beautiful, green tent haven surrounded by shrubs and trees. And while you can easily feel you have your own private space, the site isn't exactly sprawling, so being at the peaceful end of things doesn't mean a long walk if you get caught short in the middle of the night.

The site is modern, but not overly manicured, and the pitches aren't regimented. Squirrels rustle amongst the old trees, flowers splash colour around the perimeter and a swimming pool injects some playful fun into it all, accompanied by evening campfires arranged when the weather permits. The overall feel is that of a well-organised site, with good facilities plus a heated outdoor swimming pool, games room and restaurant. Those using it as a handy stop-off point on the way to Southern France will leave thoroughly refreshed and ready to get on their way.

Campers hanging around for longer will want to spend some time exploring the delights of Troyes of course, but once you've done that you, can busy yourself with the nearby Parc Naturel Régional de la Forêt d'Orient, just 20 minutes away by car. The forest's natural lakes offer plenty of outdoor activities which are best accessed by using the excellent La Vélovoie Verte ('Green Bicycle Path') – of which detailed maps are available at reception, along with bikes to hire.

COOL FACTOR A handy stop-off point when journeying across France but also a bit of a gem in its own right.

WHO'S IN Tents, campervans, caravans, dogs – yes. Large groups allowed, but owner checks details before confirming.

ON SITE 104 pitches, 26 for tents; 22 hook-ups, 3 in the tent area. Heated outdoor swimming pool, games room, restaurant. 12 free showers, 11 toilets and wash-block. Disabled facilities and baby-changing room. Bike hire, small shop and daily bread-delivery service. Small play area, kids' bikes for hire. Ice-pack freezing. No campfires.

OFF SITE Troyes is one of the Champagne region's most historic cities with wonderful medieval streets converging on the Cathédrale St-Pierre et St-Paul, which has a spectacular series of 180 stained-glass windows. Elsewhere Troyes has a number of decent museums, including a particularly good modern art gallery (0033 325 762 680) and even its own beach at Lac de la Forêt d'Orient.

FOOD & DRINK The onsite restaurant is fairly basic but the Bistro du Pont (0033 325 809 099) is only 300m along the road and serves decent local dishes. For something more exotic, Libanais (0033 325 706 068) serves homemade Lebanese food at reasonable prices.

GETTING THERE From central Troyes, head 4km north to Pont Ste-Marie (signposted), along Avenue Robert Schuman, then follow signs for 'Municipal Camping'. Just after a set of traffic lights you cross a river and there is a big blue sign directing you to the entrance on your right.

PUBLIC TRANSPORT Troyes is easily reached by train or bus from most major French towns. A bus service runs to and from the centre to within 50m of the site.

OPEN April–mid October.

THE DAMAGE 2 people, vehicle, tent €18.90; extra adults (13 years plus) €5.45, children (2–12 years) €3.40. Advanced booking not required.

les grèbes du lac de marcenay

5 rue du Pont Neuf, 21330 Marcenay, Cote d'Or 00 33 3 80 81 61 72 www.campingmarcenaylac.com

Marcenay, in the Châtillonnais area of Burgundy, is one of 23 villages famed for Chardonnay and Pinot Noir wines. At one time the lake here was used by local monks as their source of piscatorial sustenance. Today, however, it attracts a somewhat more diverse collection of people, who come to sunbathe on its sandy banks, row or paddle across the large expanse of water, or just to watch the local wildlife. Fortunately, there's also a lovely campsite nestled right next to it.

Les Grèbes du Lac de Marcenay is everything that a campsite should be, with all the ingredients you need for a properly old-school camping experience: a remote location far away from any road noise; a substantial lake; an incredibly friendly and helpful welcome in the guise of owner Dirk Jansen; and a laissez-faire attitude to where you pitch your tent. That it's off the beaten track won't appeal to people who like to be within walking distance of a choice of bars and restaurants, but this isolation is all part of its appeal.

When Dirk took on the site it was a tired municipal affair in desperate need of some attention. One of the first things he did was remove the barrier at the entrance and throw away the rules telling campers what they could and couldn't do. 'People don't want to see that when they're on holiday', he explains in his dulcet Dutch tones. Since then, he's been quietly turning it into a relaxed lakeside idyll. Dirk has spent years in the campsite business, but you can tell that he still has a passion for it, as well as 101 plans for things he wants to develop when time and funds allow.

The site itself seems to attract a mixture of people: young couples touring France who just want to stay for a few days, and older folk who come back year after year for week-long vacations. There's a regular crowd of musicians too, who appear for impromptu concerts around the campfire or in the main music hall – a hoot when you fancy joining in but also wonderfully shielded by the campsite shrubbery if you want to remain in the peace of your pitch. Away from the traffic, the layout is safe for kids who want to run wild and have fun without causing undue parental anxiety.

The main camping area is a lush, wooded plot with reasonably spacious pitches. Each is set in a clearing, partially surrounded by shrubs or trees, so there is a real sense of privacy. Open fields and vineyards on one side contrast with the lake on the other, which is about 5km all the way round edged by a forest – an ancient natural feature that remains the site's greatest asset. There is something very special about being near the water and, though you can't actually camp on the lakeside itself, it's a mere hop, skip and a jump away across the footbridge.

COOL FACTOR Relaxed, remote lakeside chilling.

WHO'S IN Tents, campervans, caravans, dogs, large groups (owner checks details before confirming) – yes.

ON SITE 90 pitches, all with electric hook-ups, if needed; 13 toilets, 17 showers, plus 2 disabled toilets and showers and a baby-changing room. A small play area is provided for children, with kids' bikes and a free-standing outdoor pool. In the main reception there is a games area with a pool table and free Wi-Fi. The laundry is also in the main reception building and there is a self-catering kitchen along with a wood-fired stove. There is a facility for freezing ice packs. No individual campfires are allowed, but there is a communal fire just to the side of the main site. There is also a windsurf to borrow, a Canadian canoe and some oars and paddles.

OFF SITE There are 3 different walks around the lake, ranging in length from 5km to 10km. Dirk also rents bikes at a reasonable €3.50 for 2 hours and will lend you local maps – the quiet roads around the campsite are not too hilly and ideal for cycling. Or you can try pony-trekking next door for €18 an hour (ask at the campsite reception).

FOOD & DRINK You can pre-order fresh bread and pastries at reception every day and they carry a very small selection of food and drink, including the local sparkling wine, Crémant de Bourgogne. Dirk is also a fan of hosting traditional crêpe evenings every now and then, whipping them up outside reception for just €2 each. For traditional French food served in what feels like someone's front room, complete with dressers and a mounted boar's head, the Auberge de la Baume, in nearby Balot (0033 380 814 015), is well worth a visit.

GETTING THERE The site is on the D965 between Laignes and Châtillon-sur-Seine. Follow the signposts to Lac de Marcenay and 'Camping'.

OPEN May–September. Advanced booking rarely required.

THE DAMAGE 2 adults, tent €15.50; extra adults €5, children (2–11 years) €4.

camping de l'ill à colmar

Camping de l'Ill, 1 allée du Camping, 68180 Colmar, Haut-Rhin 00 33 3 89 41 15 94 www.campingdelill.fr

Every country has its 'Little Venice'. In fact, almost anywhere with a canal seems to be staking a claim, so it's no surprise that the pretty town of Colmar is getting in on the act. However, unlike some places (we're looking at you, Birmingham), its river-woven, timber-house-lined centre is thoroughly deserving of the accolade. If you want a picture-perfect scene, this historic centre is the place to find it. For much of the 19th century the town was in fact part of Germany and has a rather unique culture as a result, with the German language blended into street names and a pleasing mix of French and German cuisine. Not only is it the regional capital for wine but the local beer isn't half bad either.

Camping De L'ill À Colmar is situated in the Horbourg Wihr district on the eastern edge of town, perched on the banks of a river. Despite being less than half an hour's walk from the town centre, the leafy setting gives the campsite a far more rural feel. Pitches are spread among mature trees with the best of the bunch right on the waterside, so be sure to ask for one of these if they're available. Pre-pitched safari tents are on offer, if you want a little luxury or simply don't care for the effort of pitching your own tent, and larger pitches are available if you're arriving as a group.

Facilities abound. There's a small onsite restaurant, a living room with books and board games, free Wi-Fi, a heated swimming pool and a water play area. Yet, while it all keeps family campers (and particularly children) happy, it's the location that remains the winning feature. Colmar itself has a wonderfully compact and walkable centre, while canoeing on the local rivers and adventures in the Ballons des Vosges Nature Park – a vast mountainous region a few miles west – mean that you are never short of options for ways to spend your time.

COOL FACTOR Riverside camping on the outskirts of Colmar, where France and Germany combine.

WHO'S IN Tents, campervans, caravans, pets – yes.

ON SITE 150 camping pitches spread across 12 acres. Heated swimming pool, paddling pool and water play area, a central lodge with internet and free Wi-Fi, a playground, boules pitch, table tennis, table football, volleyball court and indoor board games. 'Camper's cornershop' for any essentials you've forgotten, a library corner and tourist information in reception. Snack-bar (with a sun terrace and special 'meal nights' during peak season) and activities for children during school holidays.

OFF SITE It's a half hour walk into the old centre of Colmar, where the tourist office (0033 389 206 892) is a good place to get your bearings. The main area that is crossed by canals of the River Lauch (which formerly served as the butcher's, tanner's and fishmonger's quarter) is now called 'Little Venice' and is the most picturesque part. There are no fewer than 6 different churches – all but one of which were built in the 13th-century – and a handful of museums. The Unterlinden Museum (0033 389 201 550) is the most renowned of the lot. Elsewhere, head west into the Ballons des Vosges Nature Park (0033 389 779 034) for hiking, biking and general outdoor fun.

FOOD & DRINK The bar-restaurant onsite serves excellent homemade pizzas, along with a host of other snacks and drinks. It's only open over public holidays and through July and August. Outside of those times there are still plenty of great eateries in Horbourg Wihr (a short walk) and Colmar – a slightly longer walk but with more choice.

GETTING THERE From the centre of Colmar follow signs to Horbourg-Wihr. As you leave town you'll cross a dual carriagway and the River Ill. The campsite is immediately on your right after the river.

OPEN All year (except Jan and Feb).

THE DAMAGE A pitch and 2 people from €14 per night. Adults €3.90–€5.10; children under 2 years old free, and children between 2–7 years are free in low season and €3.30 in high season. Pets €2.40–€4.50. Glamping from €42 per night.

camping merry-sur-yonne

5 Impasse des Sables, Merry-sur-Yonne 89660, Yonne 00 33 3 86 34 59 55 www.campingmerrysuryonne.com

A series of limestone cliffs loom 150ft high above the village of Merry-sur-Yonne, hugging a row of houses against the River Yonne. On summer weekends they're dotted with the bodies of rock climbers, suspended from ropes as they clamber around on the impressively irregular face. From the top, the view is stunning: the river sweeps in a wide meander, a thick wodge of trees skirting its edge and, below, inside the river's bend, there's a tent-speckled, family field – Camping Merry-sur-Yonne. Climbing the famous 'Roches du Saussois' is just a small part of the attraction here. Though the cliffs may be a mere five-minute walk from your tent it's easy to get side-tracked by something else along the way – a giant outdoor chess set covers a section of the camping meadow, there's an excellent playground for kids and the pair of onsite tennis courts even come with raised umpire's chairs, so you can authoritatively wag your finger and yell the words "out!" from up on high.

The main field itself is populated by the full variety of camping types. Tents, campervans and caravans are all welcome, with electricity on just over half the pitches, while modern glamping pods and a gîte are also available to hire if you fancy slightly plusher accommodation. Pets are welcome (there's even a dog-washing point) and the English owners speak the full range of French, German, Italian and several other languages. Everyone is made to feel welcome.

When you venture out there's plenty to be found nearby. The Burgundy region is famous for its wine and there are several vineyards in the vicinity that offer tours and tastings – just flick through the ideas and information sheets in reception. Historic Auxerre, a 35-minute drive away, is also an excellent starting-point, with a grand cathedral and Benedictine abbey, now a museum, both standing tall over the waterfront. Magnificent canal boats chug upstream in the direction of the campsite – it's considered one of the most beautiful inland boating areas in all of France – and you can even hire your own for a morning, afternoon or day-long excursion.

COOL FACTOR A scenic riverside setting and a wealth of things to do for active campers.

WHO'S IN Tents, campervans, caravans, groups, dogs – yes.

ON SITE 50 pitches, 30 with electricity. The wash-block has individual cubicles, each with a toilet, shower and sink. Disabled facilities and baby-changing rooms. Laundry with washer, dryer and ironing board. Fully-equipped communal kitchen with fridge, freezer, kettle, toaster, microwave. Playground, tennis courts, ping-pong and a games room with pool, table football and arcade machines. Dog-wash station. Caravan service point. Free Wi-Fi. Bike rental.

OFF SITE Le Roches du Saussois, a Mecca for rock climbers, is a 5-minute stroll from the campsite. Though much of it is very challenging, there are hundreds of routes and something for every level of climber. Chablis, Irancy and many other famous wine villages are less than 20 minutes' drive away, most with vineyards you can tour, while in the village of Merry-sur-Yonne itself the beautiful Canal du Nivernais and the River Yonne can both be explored by boat. You can also fish in the river or visit one of the fishing lakes nearby, while walking, cycling and horse-riding are all on offer nearby.

FOOD & DRINK There is an onsite grocery store with local produce and a bar-café serving snacks and drinks all day and an à-la-carte table service 12–2.30pm and 5–9pm. Takeaway options also include pizzas, fish and chips and ice creams. Elsewhere, Le Hostellerie de la Poste in Clamecy (0033 386 270 155) is highly recommended.

GETTING THERE From the N65 join the D606 and then the D100 (towards 'Clamecy'). After Mailly la Ville, you will see Merry-sur-Yonne on the right. Turn into the village, cross the canal, and follow the road sharply left by the church. Bear left by the war memorial.

PUBLIC TRANSPORT There's a train station in Chatel Censoir (5 mins away), connected to Dijon, Auxerre and Paris. Regular bus services run direct from the village.

OPEN All year.

THE DAMAGE Grass pitch €12 per night (€15 with electricity). Hard-standings with electric €17 per night. Price includes up to 6 people, the car, pets and the tent.

au bois joli

2, Route de Villeprenoy, 89480 Andryes, Yonne 00 33 3 86 81 70 48 www.campingauboisjoli.com

Au Bois Joli means 'pretty wood' and that's a fine indication of what to expect from this site. Perhaps all woodland areas have their charm, yet there is a little extra magic about this site and the trees that arch over it. Approaching Andryes down open and meandering roads, carved through vast farmscapes that blend at the horizon with rich blue skies for much of the summer, it is impossible to resist a smile. The site and its region are definitely worth further investigation. Perhaps it's the wealth of Burgundy sunflowers arching aloft before the summer harvest that makes even the most inanimate entity appear jolly. Or it could be that the inspiring, vast skies endorse an air of drifting creative thought. Whatever the explanation, it's blindingly obvious why Robert and Henriëtte de Vries elected to settle here, amid the cheerfully swaying branches.

Au Bois Joli was created with a sharply observed philosophy in mind: respect for nature, for peace of mind, and for a carefully nurtured atmosphere of good will. The site layout, its location and ambience converge effortlessly towards this end, yet only a daily investment of hard work and passion maintains the delicate balance. The camp is quietly adjusted around the campers all day, with the owner's high expectations making the site a cut above most others; indeed it has been awarded a prestigious 'Clef Verte' for its ecologically sound methods and reverence for nature. In turn, nature seems to be thanking Au Bois Joli, with Robert and Henriëtte proud to record each new winged visitor or blooming flower to appear. If you're lucky and catch either host during a quiet moment, it's absorbing to spend some time learning about the site's unique micro-environment and how they tend it.

Consideration for the environment is also extended to their human guests, especially young children. Camping au Bois Joli is a site that's built for safety: trees that lends themselves to climbing have soft wood chippings below; the ample and imaginative play areas have the same soft precaution; and children even have a wash-block of their own.

Adults can luxuriate in the shade of mature trees or blister in the sun beside the pool, all the while soaking up epic views. For a small deposit, books can be borrowed from the site library or magazines borrowed from the racks outside reception. At the highest point of the site a gate leads to a wild wood, for which access has been negotiated, and within moments it's possible to be quite alone. Alternatively the prepared welcome pack, tailored to the length of your stay, has suggestions for offsite activities that demand varying degrees of exertion.

It is difficult to criticise a campsite whose owners are forever meditating upon greater improvements that seem superfluous, given the high standards already achieved. But if we must be critical: the grass needs combing, the trees are not symmetrical, and the site isn't open all year. I suppose the latter could be construed as the only real shame.

COOL FACTOR Relaxation and tranquillity, in contact with abundant nature.

WHO'S IN Tents, campervans, caravans, nature-lovers, families, children – yes. Loud and busy people, late-night owls – no.

ON SITE 89 pitches, with a wide, open area among trees for pitching tents anywhere. There are also 3 large nature fields where there is 'free camping' (unmarked pitches without electricity), and there's also a fully-equipped safari tent that sleeps 5 people comfortably. Communal campfires are lit twice a week by the owners (weather dependent). There are 19 superb shower booths, ample toilet blocks, disabled access and a dedicated wash-block for children with low access facilities. 3 washing machines (€4.50 including powder) and a tumble dryer. Playground, table tennis tables, volleyball, skittles, mock castle and sandpit. Clean and well-maintained swimming and paddling pool, with a decent poolside area. There's a mini resto – The Tavern – with a terrace, plus a shop selling organic produce, and a daily bakery delivery, library and magazine rack. Free Wi-Fi in certain areas. Freezer available.

OFF SITE One must-see is the astonishing contemporary construction of a medieval fort at Guédelon, which is being built using only 13th-century tools and materials. Work began in 1997 and completion will be in about 2035. Auxerre, Avallon and Clamecy all have markets once a week. The campsite is an official kick-off point for the newly renovated cycle paths beside the canal between Auxerre in the north and Clamecy to the south, a 62km stretch that is one of a total 800km of canal paths being worked on. Vézelay, a world heritage site, is a short drive from the campsite and also well worth exploring.

FOOD & DRINK The Auberge des Sources (0033 386 415 514), beyond Clamecy, has a good reputation, as does the warm and inviting 2 Pieces Cuisine (0033 386 272 507) in Clamecy itself. The latter has a great candle-lit terrace on the junction of 3 pedestrian streets, and the family feel of the place is wonderful.

GETTING THERE From Auxerre, take the N151 (towards Bourges) and in Coulanges-sur-Yonne the D39 to Andryes, 3km away, where you will see the campsite signs.

OPEN April–November (avoid the high-season peaks for the best of the peace and quiet).

THE DAMAGE Pitch and 2 people €17–€31. Children (up to 11 yrs) €3.50–€5. Cotton Lodge Nature Tent from €150 for 2 nights.

la forêt du morvan

58370 Larochemillay, Nièvre 00 33 3 86 30 47 93 www.campinglaforet.nl

There's always something a little magical about camping in forests. They're dark, mysterious places full of unseen dangers, lurking beasts, and the constant fear of getting lost. Even on the sunniest of days a dimly lit forest interior can feel like a very quiet, twilit world, where even the birds seem to keep away. Luckily, perhaps, the site at La Forêt du Morvan isn't quite in the heart of the forest and has cleared plenty of space for its 25 pitches to let the sunshine and birds in. But there's no question that it's the forest that makes Morvan special: almost half a million acres of prime French countryside that was officially made a Parc Régional in 1970, and is now something of a playground for the not-so-rich and not-so-famous. Hills, lakes and forests are the main attractions, best explored using a combination of shoes, pedals and oars (or an outboard, if you're lazy). Just make sure you take a map.

As for the site, there are two main camping areas on the south-facing slopes; one above and one below the main buildings. Most of the pitches have expansive views down across the valley. The others lay along the edge of the forest and have a little more shade. Tents are available to rent, if you haven't brought your own, while one particularly handy feature is the availability, for hire, of private bathrooms, which is a great idea for families. You can keep your clobber in there and you don't have to cart it around every time the kids need a scrub-down. It's not cheap, but well worth it if you're here for a week.

COOL FACTOR Stunning views, newts to catch and the chance to enjoy pure camping freedom.

WHO'S IN Tents, campervans, small caravans (large ones may not get down the drive), dogs – yes.

ON SITE Facilities in the old barns, with hot showers, private bathrooms, weekly campfire, a nice spring-fed lake with a slide, arts and crafts, kids' disco, tractor tour, sports and games in the forest. Free Wi-Fi.

OFF SITE There is lots to do and visit around the campsite (just ask the owners), including nice walks (maps provided), and campers are kept informed daily about regional events. Autun is the nearest town of any significance, and has a Roman amphitheatre and a 12th-century Gothic cathedral.

FOOD & DRINK There is a small campsite shop with basic products and fresh bread is delivered to your tent every day (order the evening before). Twice a week you can join the owners for a regional 3-course meal and, on Sundays, you can make your own pizza at the weekly pizza night. If you want to eat out, head to L'École Buissonière (0033 386 304 721) in Millay or Le clos de la Bussière in Semelay (0033 386 309 166).

GETTING THERE The campsite lies halfway between Nevers and Beaune, north of Luzy, south of Villapourçon. Take the D27 north or south, between Larochemillay and Le Puits. The site is just off the main road, 4km north of Larochemillay.

PUBLIC TRANSPORT There are trains to Luzy. If you contact the owner in advance he can arrange to pick you up from the station.

OPEN April–October.

THE DAMAGE Pitch (including 2 people) and car €10–€24.50 per night, depending on season. Rented tent (sleeps 2–5) €39–€68.50. Private facilities cost €7.75 per night in high season and €5.00 in the low season.

domaine du bourg

Domaine du Bourg, 04 chemin des Terriens, 03230 Gannay-sur-Loire, Allier 00 33 470 43 49 01 www.domainedubourg.com

Domaine names are a tricky business in France. Call your estate something fancy like Domaine de Beauregard and the neighbours think you're pretentious. So this place keeps it pretty simple, and in fact concentrates on doing just what it says on the tin. 'Domaine du Bourg', it says on the gate – 'Small Market Town Estate' – and what's inside is fairly straightforward too. Dutch owners Peter and Trudi de Lange have converted some old farming buildings into a cracking, pretty sizeable home, along with four gîtes, three B&B bedrooms and some dorm rooms for hikers. Beyond the huddle of buildings, meanwhile, is 250 acres of camping space with a trio of canvas safari lodges, a wooden gypsy caravan and a clutch of just 25 grassy pitches (so you can do the maths to work out how much room there is).

The small market town in question is Gannay-sur-Loire, a sleepy little place if truth be told, but the quiet roads and gentle countryside are ideal for exploration by bike. These are available for hire from the site and come equipped with maps showing the local routes. The site is also on the new 'EuroVélo6' cycle route, which stretches across six countries from the Atlantic coast to the Black Sea. The French section starts at St Nazaire and follows the course of the River Loire through Orléans and Nevers, before swinging north through Switzerland, Germany, Austria, and Slovakia and south through Hungary and Serbia, finishing in Romania. So there's no real excuse for coming here and just lounging around.

The Loire also beckons budding water babies down to its glistening depths. There are plenty of lazy watersports available, including kayaks you can hire from the site. The slow, soothing pace of the river is the perfect antidote to all your worries. Drift along in the sun on what is undoubtedly one of the most beautiful rivers in France (and also the country's longest). The Loire is pleasantly free from noise, buildings and commercial traffic. Instead the banks are either alive with chirping wildlife or quaint historic villages – the perfect place to pick up yet another buttery croissant or stop for a picnic as you glide gently along.

COOL FACTOR Smallsville camping with plenty of room to stretch out.

WHO'S IN Tents, campervans, caravans, dogs (as long as you scoop any poop) – yes.

ON SITE 25 car-free pitches (electricity available). There is also a 3-person gypsy wagon, 3 safari lodges (sleeping 4–6), and a *gîte etape* or hiker's cabin (sleeping up to 12). A brand new half-timbered building houses free warm showers toilets, washbasins and dish-washing facilities. Toilet paper is supplied so you can leave your rolls at home. There is also a disabled room and baby facilities. Elsewhere there's a small pool and a covered seating area (where meals are served).

OFF SITE This is a fairly quiet site, so the best thing to do is capitalise on that quietness and hire a bike or kayak. Bikes can be rented from the site at €10 per day and kayaks are available at €14 per half day and €23 per full day, including transport to and from the river. It is one of the most beautiful sections of the Loire, well-known as 'France's last wild river' and an excellent place to explore by whatever means you chose. Along with the EuroVélo6 route you

can follow the 'Loire by Bike', 'Burgundy by Bike' or 'Grand Randonnée nr 3'. Peter and Trudi know them well and are more than happy to give advice on where to go.

FOOD & DRINK There's a small Proxi convenience store, a pâtisserie, a butcher, and Les Vanneau, a little restaurant-café with a terrace, in the village.

GETTING THERE From Nevers take the D13 and D116 to Decize. Head out of town on the D978a and turn left onto the D116 for Ganny-sur-Loire. Once in the village cross the river and you'll see a triangular green sign with a road veering off to the left. Follow that road for 100m and the site is on the right.

PUBLIC TRANSPORT The closest you can get to the site is 12–16km away, at one of several nearby railway stations at Fours, Cercy-la-Tour or Decize.

OPEN April–November (permanent accommodation is open all year-round).

THE DAMAGE Pitches €6–€10. Adults €2.50–€3.50, children (up to 12 yrs) €1.50–€2.50. Dogs free. Gypsy-wagon €150–€425 per week. Safari lodges €400–€875 per week. Hiker's cabin €10 per person per night; gîtes €150–€800 per week.

camping la grande sologne

Rue des Peupliers, 41600 Nouan-le-Fuzelier, Loir-et-Cher   00 33 2 54 88 70 22   www.campingrandesologne.com

Trivia time: how many French rivers are designated UNESCO World Heritage Sites? Just one – the Loire. Snaking its way through some of central France's most gorgeous towns and cities, the unspoiled Loire Valley is at once both wildly tranquil and beautifully untamed. Throughout the ages, the mighty Loire has conveyed warring armies, nourished those who dwell by her banks, and fed the imaginations of myriad painters and poets. The iconic, château-dotted settlements which line the river's unwieldy banks bring the history of France's gilded past vibrantly to life. Within this spellbinding landscape, just south of fabled Orléans, lies the Sologne region – a land of enchanted forests, moorlands and lakes; of timber-beamed cottages and brick farm dwellings, unchanged for hundreds of years. And it is within one such charmingly sleepy town (Nouan-le-Fuzelier) that we find another of the region's hidden treasures – Camping La Grande Sologne.

When your host has previously run not one, but two Cool Camping-approved sites, there's no denying she knows a thing or two about what campers want. After eight years charming guests at both Camping de Troyes in Champagne and Camping Les Grèbes du Lac de Marcenay in Burgundy, Marie stumbled across this underloved little spot in the Loire. Picking up sticks (in every sense), Marie and her team (completed by co-manager Eric and affable Irishman Bill) rolled up

their sleeves and set to work creating the fantastic site we see today.

La Grande Sologne boasts nine hectares of spectacular camping. Out of the 165 pitches, 150 grassy ones are for just about anyone and everyone. Some are shaded, others are in a dappled half-shade, while some have no trees at all, so you're covered for every eventuality. What brings real charm to the place is the campsite's beautiful central lake. Spread over two spectacular hectares, guests are free to fish the abundant carp, black-bass, perch, bleak, roach, rudd, crucian, breme and tench that inhabit the tranquil waters. In 2016, even sturgeons were added to the list.

If you don't have your own gear, you can rent a mobile home or a ready-equipped tent, or, if you really want to scale up the glamping experience, you can stay on the remarkable 'Flotente' cabin, floating on the edge of the lake. There is also a waterside Bivouac tent with the best views of the water (Flotente excluded). You can even see the sun glimmer on the surface from tucked within your bed.

The transformation of this place since Marie's arrival is really something quite special, and there is no doubt you'll be charmed by its natural beauty. A UNESCO World Campsite? Sadly they don't exist yet. No doubt if they did, Camping La Grande Sologne would be somewhere on the shortlist.

COOL FACTOR A waterside wonder with a knowledgeable host who has earned many a Cool Camping plaudit in her time.

WHO'S IN Tents, campervans, caravans, motorhomes, trailer tents, groups, dogs – yes.

ON SITE 165 pitches, with 150 set aside for tents, caravans, campervans and motorhomes. All are spacious and have 10amp electrical hook-ups. There are also 4 pre-erected tents, mobile homes, a 'floating tent' for 2 people to sleep on the water and a Bivoac tent. There are 3 sanitary blocks (disabled and family facilities available) and a fully-equipped laundry. Free Wi-Fi available at site reception and on a third of the pitches. Heated outdoor swimming pool, plus games/activities available (including minigolf, trampoline, billiards, badminton) and a tennis court opposite. A small onsite shop sells all basic provisions, plus ice creams.

OFF SITE Orléans, the capital of France's central region, has some beautiful medieval architecture including the imposing Gothic Cathédrale Sainte-Croix. The city is also synonymous with France's most famous heroine, St Joan of Arc, for it was here that she relieved the besieged city, thus earning the nickname 'The Maid of Orléans'. Be sure to visit the timber-clad Maison de Jeanne d'Arc (0033 238 683 263).

FOOD & DRINK In high season, you can buy freshly baked bread and croissants every morning, while the little snack bar, Calypso, is open from 6pm for simple meals, fresh salads and tasty desserts. There is also a takeaway. Ask Marie for eating out recommendations: L'Etna Pizzeria (0033 254 882 348) is popular with locals and tourists alike. They have a nice terrace and a kid-friendly menu of pizzas and other Italian favourites. No visit to Sologne could be complete with a thimble or two of it's most famous export, Chambord, a sweet raspberry liqueur from the Château de Chambord (0033 254 504 000) which has been made the same way for 300 years.

GETTING THERE From the north, take the A10 towards Bordeaux. At Orléans, take the A71 for Bourges/Clermont Ferrand amd take exit 3 for Lamotte Beuvron, then the RD2020 towards Nouan Le Fuzelier for 7km. Cross the town centre and turn left at the public garden and train station. From the south, take the A71 towards Paris and take exit 4 for Salbris, then the RD2020 towards Nouan Le Fuzelier/Orléans for 15km. Shortly after entering Nouan, turn right just after the petrol station.

OPEN April–October.

THE DAMAGE Tent and 2 people €16.20– €21.30 (tourist tax included). €2 euros reduction per night for campers staying more than 2 nights out of season.

ferme pedagogique de prunay

Ferme de Prunay, 41150 Seillac, Loir-et-Cher 00 33 2 54 70 02 01 www.prunay.fr

Gazing at the turrets and gleaming towers of Azay-le-Rideau, Villandry or Valençay, which are so picture-book pretty they look more like Disneyland Paris than the France of yesteryear, it's easy to forget that not all of the châteaux decorating the Loire Valley exemplify state-of-the-art Renaissance luxury. Chinon, by contrast, is a fortress, all practical purpose and no frippery, while Amboise and Blois were also built purely with defence in mind.

Ferme de Prunay looks perfectly peaceful among this Loire landscape but the farm originally formed the core of a Gallo-Roman fortified village. The ancient moat that curls around two sides was built to keep marauders out and today provides a gentle afternoon's fishing practice. Similarly, when the owner, Michel Fouchault, dug out the swimming pool, he unearthed many graves and bones – something that hopefully won't bother campers as they dive in!

Traditions run deep here, but it's perfectly safe and calm now: the farm has been in the Fouchault family for six generations, with 494 acres of crops beyond the floral borders of the site. The feeling of spaciousness the land provides extends to the enormous pitches, some of which are big enough to accommodate a car, a caravan and a few badminton courts for good measure. There's never any danger of feeling hemmed in between caravans and motor homes, and there's a real variety to the pitches, too, some of which are fringed with

hedges and trees while others enjoy more open space and expansive views next to the fields. Many of the pitches have their own plum or apple trees, which campers are welcome to plunder, or you can select a pitch overlooking a huge bank of wild flowers (planted to attract butterflies and bees) and the open fields. Those who choose the views should know that their freedom comes with a price tag, as they're further away from the wash-block. But it's worth it – the blooming horizon is a wonderful sight to wake up to.

The Ferme de Prunay also operates as a *ferme pédagogique*, or teaching farm, with school visits off season. Those opportunities continue throughout the summer, so children and their parents can learn how corn is ground and how to bake bread, for instance, or go on guided walks, which pass by the local goat farm or vineyard. Opportunities to buy the wine, cheese and honey are included of course.

It's all a part of the generally easy-going atmosphere of the Ferme de Prunay. The bikes around the site are free to use, as is the fridge, cooker and indeed all of the facilities, while impromptu tractor rides are always a hit with kids. Hitch a lift in the right direction and you can pet the farm animals too – pigs, rabbits, chickens, donkeys, goats, turkeys and a horse are all eager to lick your hands, peck your fingers or squawk loudly in your direction.

COOL FACTOR Camping on the farm – a short ride away from great rivers and grand castles.

WHO'S IN Tents, campervans, caravans, and dogs (on leads) all welcome.

ON SITE Large pitches suitable for tents, campervans and caravans. Cabins and gypsy caravans also available. The wash-block has the option of family shower rooms and disabled access. The well-organised site has welcome letters and information in English, French, Dutch and German. The café-bar is open from 8am (for bread and croissant deliveries) until 9pm and also sells ice creams, basic bar food and pizzas. There are tractor-train rides around the site (in high season), animal petting and kids' play areas, table tennis, volleyball court and basketball areas at the front of the site, which is where (supervised) campfires take place. There's also a new heated swimming pool and an indoor room with games for toddlers.

OFF SITE There are discount vouchers available on site to get into many tourist locations in the Loir-et-Cher département, including the wonderful château at Blois (0033 254 903 332) 16km away, where Joan of Arc was blessed in 1429 before she left with her army to drive the English from Orléans. Also in Blois there's the Maison de la Magie (0033 254 903 333), a spectacular House of Magic museum situated opposite the castle. The beautiful town of Amboise is well worth the 20-minute drive along the Loire, both for its château and Le Clos Lucé (0033 247 570 073), the house where Leonardo da Vinci lived his final 3 years – now a museum displaying models of his amazing drawings. It's possible to hire canoes to use on the Loire itself, or the rivers Loir and Cher, which feed into it.

FOOD & DRINK The farm is a member of the regional tourist organisation 'Bienvenue à la ferme' and can recommend many local suppliers, including La Cabinette for goats cheese in Onzain, 8km away, where there's also the best range of shops locally. Organic Touraine wine is produced at the Domaine Château-Gaillard in Mesland, about 3km from the site, and there's a great market in Amboise on Friday and Sunday mornings. There are many restaurants to choose from in Blois, and just about anywhere near the castle is good. L'Orangerie du Château de Blois (0033 254 780 536) stands out as a special gastronomic treat, in a beautiful building with stunning interiors and a lovely terrace opposite the castle – menus start from around €35.

GETTING THERE From the A10 take the Blois exit, then follow signposts for Angers and Château-Renault until Molineuf, then for Chambon-sur-Cisse and then Seillac on the D131, where you'll pick up the roadside signs to Ferme de Prunay.

OPEN Late March–early November.

THE DAMAGE 2 adults, plus pitch, plus electricity €20–€33. Extra adults €8–€10.80, under-5s €4–€4.80.

le moulin fort

37150 Francueil, Indre-et-Loire 00 33 2 47 23 86 22 www.lemoulinfort.com

Walk through the woods along the south bank of the River Cher from the campsite at Le Moulin Fort at dawn, and if the weather's good there's every chance you'll start hearing voices from the sky. The gods calling to you at last? Well, you never know. But more likely it's the occupants of a couple of Montgolfière balloons drifting overhead towards the château at Chenonceaux. Keep walking through the trees for five minutes and you'll see why. Built across the river is one of the Loire valley's finest sights. When it catches the morning rays, the sandstone of Chenonceau glows gold and is perfectly reflected in the almost still waters of the river. It probably looks even better from the basket of a balloon, but if you don't have a head for heights you can always catch the *bateau-mouche* that operates from the riverbank opposite the charmingly appointed site of Le Moulin Fort.

Occupying a strip of riverbank along the River Cher, the site lies just a little upriver from the château and a stone's throw from a weir. It's overlooked by willows, fringed by waist-high grass and is a perfect picture of sleepy French tranquillity – the kind of place that makes you realise that weeping willows and lazy water somehow go together like baguette and cheese, onions and berets, Gainsbourg and Birkin. Le Moulin Fort has the kind of lackadaisical air that will have you sitting staring into space whilst time ticks by almost as slowly as the waters of the river. Before you know it, the sun will be going down, the waters darkening, and you'll wonder where on earth the day went.

But before you idle away your life on the riverbank, remember that this is the Loire Valley and there's a lot to see. Chenonceaux is a picture-postcard kind of place with ivy-clad hostelries and narrow streets of honey-coloured buildings, vaguely reminiscent of the Cotswolds. The château itself is open daily – the price of admission is worth it just for the gardens and the views alone. Catherine de Medici laid out some of the parks and added one of the galleries around the time when Mary Queen of Scots was a visitor.

The nearby town of Amboise has another of the most picturesque châteaux of the Loire, sitting high on its ramparts on the south bank of the river. The town is also famous for being the last residence of one of the world's great artists, Leonardo da Vinci. Da Vinci spent his final years at Le Clos Lucé in Amboise on a pension of 1000 écus soleils (that's quite a lot, apparently), all courtesy of François I who was a fan of Leonardo's work. He wasn't a man of enough taste to spot his most famous painting, though, and it's rumoured that the Mona Lisa, never much of a hit during the artist's lifetime, used to sit in a corner of his studio here, leaning against the wall. Perhaps that's why she looks so rueful – though sometimes you wonder if she wouldn't rather swap her current place behind bullet-proof glass at the Louvre in Paris for the quieter surroundings of Leonardo's house at Amboise. Or even a spot overlooking the willow trees at Le Moulin Fort.

COOL FACTOR Idyllic site on the willowy banks of a quiet tributary of the Loire.

WHO'S IN Tents, campervans, caravans, well-behaved dogs – yes. Large, noisy groups are not encouraged as it's all about peace and quiet by 11pm.

ON SITE Two good clean sanitary blocks with separate ladies and gents facilities. There is a busy bar/restaurant in the mill house (often so busy you'll need to book) that serves decent food and beer. There's also a swimming pool, a kid's pool and a small play area. Campers can fish for carp, perch, bream, trout and catfish in the river – permits are available at reception. Wi-Fi is available in the bar and on the main terraces (€1 per day).

OFF SITE There are bikes for hire at the campsite to enjoy the quiet back roads of the Cher. Treat yourself to a hot-air balloon flight over the château (about €200 per person, including children – who must be of a certain age/height to see over the edge of the basket). The dawn flights afford unrivalled views of the Loire valley and Château de Chenonceau (0033 247 239 007) in the middle of the river.

FOOD & DRINK Classic French cuisine can be enjoyed across the river on the terrace of La Roseraie (0033 247 239 009), where they serve a 3-course 'bistrot' menu at lunchtimes for just €16.50. Also in the village, the Cave des Dômes (0033 247 239 007) sells the wine that's bottled at the château.

GETTING THERE Follow the D976 east from Tours on the south bank of the Cher, bypassing Bléré. There's a main junction between the villages of Francueil and Chenonceaux. Turn left there, heading for Chenonceaux, and the campsite is on the banks of the river, just before the bridge on your right.

PUBLIC TRANSPORT The site lies 1km from Chenonceaux train station which is connected directly to Tours, from where there's a shuttle service to and from Tours Airport and also the TGV station at St Pierre de Corps.

OPEN May–September.

THE DAMAGE Pitch, plus 2 adults €15–€25. Additional adults €3.50–€5.50, children (4–12) €3–€4.50. Electricity €4.

le chant d'oiseau

49390 Mouliherne, Maine-et-Loire 00 33 2 41 67 09 78 www.loire-gites.com

The open grassland and forests surrounding Le Chant d'Oiseau make an ideal habitat for the barn owls and tawny owls that live in the loft above one of the site's three gîtes. All sorts of other birds, from herons and hen harriers to buzzards and hoopoes, love it around here too, which is surely how the house got its moniker. The name appears on a map from 1750, but the building itself could be centuries older – the date 1626 was incised into the stone walls of the hayloft by workers tallying up bales.

The property is now owned by Stu and Syb Bradley, who moved their family here from Doncaster in 2005, bringing with them an easy-going conviviality from South Yorkshire that blends in perfectly with the Loire region's reputation for 'la doucer de vivre' – essentially enjoying life at the same leisurely pace at which France's longest river flows through the valley (Flaubert called it 'the most sensual river in France'). They're relaxed about campers arriving late, and offer to come and find those searching for the site after dark, even making them a nice cup of tea on arrival – just the kind of welcome visitors cherish after a long drive from a channel port. An earlier arrival means you can relax with a glass of Samur wine in the newly rebuilt 'barn', a beautifully constructed homage to traditional building techniques, completed in the spring of 2014 and which serves as an al fresco Wi-Fi area, communal eating space and quiet retreat.

The barn is also home to the wood-fired oven that Stu recently installed, where superb pizzas are cooked once a week. On Mondays and Fridays during the summer they also serve a four-course homecooked French meal using fresh locally-sourced ingredients, and they heat up the pizza oven again on Sundays in high season to bake the troglodyte (and Angevin) favourite, *fouée* – small parcels of bread dough into which savoury or sweet fillings can be added: goats' cheese, *rillettes* (pork pâté), *confiture*, Nutella... delicious!

These events are all optional, but they can make camping here so much more appealing. New for the 2016 season was the communal BBQ and firepit area. You can forage the lanes for wood and kindling and return to make a fire and toast a marshmallow with family and new found friends. Cycling is also a prominent feature of the area with safe country roads and lanes to explore. Stu is happy to lead keen two-wheeled fans out on local (and not-so local) excursions when time permits. Otherwise he has plenty of maps and advice on where to go and what to see, available from the office.

Ironically, it was really surfing that led the Bradleys into camping. After decades tenting in Cornwall and France they wanted their own site but when plans to set up on the Cornish coast proved too expensive, they decided to move abroad instead. At Le Chant Oiseau their aim was to incorporate all the best features from their favourite campsites; they are passionate about the house and region, and a knowledgeable source of recommendations on places to visit nearby. Surfing or no surfing, we think they've done a pretty unbeatable job.

COOL FACTOR Birdsong and conviviality in the heart of the Loire countryside.

WHO'S IN Tents, campervans, caravans, large groups (by arrangement) – yes. Pets – no.

ON SITE 10 pitches all with electricity. 2 showers, 2 toilets and 3 basins, all with wheelchair access. A communal BBQ and a firepit (bring marshmallows), plus a gas cooker, oven, fridges, kettle, microwave and food-preparation area in the Kampers' Kitchen. Freshly made pizzas are cooked once a week and 4-course meals are available 2 nights a week in peak season. Wi-Fi, table tennis, outdoor games, a pool table, a small swimming pool, kids' play area, bikes and book exchange are all available. Three gîtes also available to rent.

OFF SITE Medieval Mouliherne and its twisted-spired church is 5km away, and there are peaceful walks and bike-rides through the woods and fields. The elegant city of Saumur, with its fortress-château, multi-arched bridges and houses built in local tufa limestone, is a 25-minute drive. Stu (and the Michelin Guide) rate the Musée des Blindes tank museum (0033 241 530 699). The town also has a great market on Saturdays and is renowned for its sparkling white wines.

FOOD & DRINK Cooked food is available on site twice-weekly on Mondays and Fridays, as well as pizzas (Wednesday) and *fouée* (Sundays in high season). Milk, fresh eggs, ice creams, draught and bottled beers as well as wine by the carafe is also for sale. Daily bread and croissant deliveries (amazing *croissants aux amandes*), booked the night before. Le Grand Bleu (0033 241 674 183) is a lovely family-friendly seafood restaurant on rue du Marché in old Saumur.

GETTING THERE It's easiest to get to the nearby village of Mouliherne and follow the signs to Le Chant d'Oiseau from there. Otherwise, it's off the D58 between Vernantes and Mouliherne. Count 5km from Vernantes or Mouliherne and then look for a crossroads with campsite signs.

OPEN March–November.

THE DAMAGE Pitch and 2 people €15–€25 (including electricity). Extra people over 5 years €5.

flower camping la bretonnière

85150 Saint-Julien-des-Landes, La Vendée 00 33 2 51 46 62 44 www.la-bretonniere.com

Seduced by the tourist hype, many of us flock to Paris or the Riviera for our fix of fine dining and delectable foreign weather. The more discerning French meanwhile head straight for the west coast. Sandy, pine-covered beaches front a varied coastline of Roman cities, slumbering *villes* and a scattering of small islands. Follow the sunflower-flanked roads a few miles inland and you'll find Camping La Bretonnière, the perfect base for exploring the region. Situated around a pleasant fishing lake, the green fields of La Bretonnière play host to over 150 pitches along with a small number of holiday huts and safari tents. With such variety, campers can decide on exactly what size space they want, from smaller 'nature' spots all the way up to roomy 'privilège' pitches, ideal for caravans and motorhomes. Trees and tall hedgerows provide plenty of shade from the summer sun, although when it comes to cooling off most people know exactly where to head.

Overlooking the natural waters of the lake, a recently built swimming area is the perfect remedy for those used to more British weather. Two covered swimming pools and a wading pool are accompanied by a play area where fountains squirt water in all directions. The space is a delight for kids, and, surrounded by decking with a small wooden bar, it's not a bad spot for parents to lounge about either. Sitting in the balmy summer sun you can enjoy a drink or two while the little ones clown around in their own watery world. The poolside fun is complimented by a hedge-lined field on the other side of the campsite where there are tennis and volleyball courts, a football pitch, pétanque court and a children's play area.

As much as these onsite activities will soak up your day, Flower Camping La Bretonnière is also an excellent base for hopping in the car and heading elsewhere. Most people are attracted to the beaches sweeping north to the incredible island of Noirmoutier. Cut off by the sea at high tide, this charming offshore paradise is reconnected when the water recedes, revealing the famous Passage du Gois, an old paved causeway that can still be crossed by car if you get your timing right. In the opposite direction the town of La Roche-sur-Yon, a few miles inland, has changed its reputation since it was described as "the dullest town in France" by an English guidebook in the early 1800s, and is now populated with a good stock of excellent bars and restaurants.

This delightful position that provides access to both the coastline and the quieter inland attractions makes Flower Camping La Bretonnière a good place to start exploring Western France. Something that can only start, however, when you persuade yourself to leave the poolside sun lounger and put down that bottle of local vino!

COOL FACTOR Spacious pitches and glamping options on a massive site with loads to do – you'll never need to leave!

WHO'S IN Tents, campervans, caravans, dogs – yes.

ON SITE 165 pitches, most with electric hook-ups. Wooden chalets and safari tents also available for hire. Two indoor swimming pools (1 heated), a padding pool for the children and a fish pond. There is also a football pitch, tennis court, beach volleyball area, playground and indoor TV room. Five well-equipped sanitary blocks have toilets, showers, basins and electric points, along with baby-changing facilities and disabled facilities. Free Wi-Fi is available.

OFF SITE It is just over a 10-minute drive from the campsite to the sea, where the coast offers plenty of good beaches. The land ends at Noirmoutier (0033 251 398 071), an island of sandy inlets, pine forests and salt marshes that is 50 minutes away by car but well worth the drive. More locally, an activity centre with high-wire and ropes course is just 2kms away, surrounded by quieter roads that are good for cycling. During mid-August there is a fireworks display on Lake-du-Jaunay, 3kms away, while every other Thursday during July and August sees an 'ancient traditions fair' take to the streets in Challans (0033 251 931 975).

FOOD & DRINK The site has a bar, bakery and grocery stocking all the basics. For something extra special, head to Domaine de Brandois (0033 251 062 424) in neighbouring La Mothe-Achard, an elegant château restaurant serving traditional French cuisine.

GETTING THERE Follow the A87 around La Roche su-Yon onto the D160. Turn right onto the D12 (signposted St Georges), then take the next major left onto the D760. Follow this to La Mothe-Achard where you join the D12. Follow this for 6km to Saint-Julien-des-Landes. The campsite is 2km after the village on the right.

OPEN April–October.

THE DAMAGE Pitch and 2 people from €12.90–€33. Pets €2–€5. Extra people €3.50–€6, under-3s free. Extra vehicle €3–€5.

camping le verger

27 Jean pierre Pigot, Bellecroix, 17139 Dompierresur-Mer, Charente-Maritime   00 33 5 46 34 91 00
uk.campingleverger17.com

The climate, the history, the café culture, it's no surprise camping is so popular in France. But it's become so commonplace that all too many campsites lack that unique Cool Camping feel. Happily some still manage to buck this trend, and Camping le Verger is a great example – the perfect small-time site that everybody is searching for, exuding the warm, friendly atmosphere of a business run on a wonderfully personal level.

"It's less a campsite and more our garden", the owners Catherine and Sylvain tell us, though to be more precise it is part garden, part orchard. Beneath the fruit trees, grassy spaces provide ample room for camping, yet despite it all they curb the numbers at just 25 places to avoid overcrowding. Pitches are not designated in any specific way and on arrival you're given a cute wooden sign to stick in the ground, claiming your numbered spot. After that simply kick back in the shade or, if you've picked the right time of year, pick fruit from the trees to eat.

Cycling seems to be the big thing round these parts. The neighbouring canal has an adjacent bike path that leads from here all the way into the quaint old port of La Rochelle (8 kms away), an easy and enjoyable ride that you can finish off nicely with a cold drink overlooking the Atlantic in one of La Rochelle's many harbourside bars and cafés. You can also easily cycle to the nearby Ile de Ré – a quaint sandy island that has some of the best beaches in Western France and is itself criss-crossed by cycle paths. Plus cycling there means you avoid the €16 fee for the toll bridge. A savvy little trick.

It's these tips and more that mark Sylvain and Catherine out as well-practiced hosts. Their time living here means they know the area like the back of their sun-tanned hands, and the size of the site means they have time to afford you a personal service, chatting you through the local hotspots and dropping a phone call to the village restaurant if you want to make a reservation. It's all part and parcel of allowing you to camp in their garden – in itself a wonderfully friendly gesture that perhaps sums the couple up.

COOL FACTOR A tiny orchard campsite. No forbidden fruit here, but still a beautiful little Eden.

WHO'S IN Tents, caravans, campervans, motorhomes, cyclists and pets (by arrangement) – yes. Large groups – no.

ON SITE 25 pitches (no designated spaces; pitch where you want). Four showers, 4 toilets, disabled facilities, washing-up sinks, chemical waste disposal. Free Wi-Fi. Access to a freezer for free ice-pack freezing. Bikes for hire (half day €9, full day €12, with further price reductions for multiple days). Fruit picking from the trees is allowed in the right season. Electric hook-ups available.

OFF SITE The nearby port of La Rochelle, 8kms west, is an excellent place to visit, with a historic harbour and old centre and of course a host of great places to eat. A cycle path leads from the campsite to the town; it takes half an hour, but is a rewarding route that begins 500m from the campsite and ends right at the port. Ile de Ré (20 minutes by car) has some of the best beaches in the region and can be reached via a €16 toll bridge, or you can park by the toll booths on the mainland for free and walk/cycle across the 3km bridge. Or you can cycle the whole way!

FOOD & DRINK A small onsite shop serves fresh bread and croissants in the morning, wines, beers and tasty local products. La Rochelle is the obvious choice when eating out but it is also worth visiting the daily market in the town centre, particularly good on Wednesdays and Saturdays.

GETTING THERE Leave the N11 at 'Dompierre sur Mer' and follow the signs to 'Belle-Croix'. After you cross the canal and enter the village there's a roundabout. Turn right towards La Rochelle and just before the sign 'end of Belle-Croix' turn left.

PUBLIC TRANSPORT The campsite is on line 39, by the 'Belle-Croix Fontoreux' bus stop. Buses run every 30 minutes from La Rochelle.

OPEN June–September.

THE DAMAGE A car and a small tent €5, a car and a medium size tent €7 and a motorhome €8. Adults €5, children (under 12) €3, pets €1.50 and electric €5. Minimum 3-night stay.

camping de l'océan

62 Allée de la négade L'amélie, 33780 Soulac-sur-Mer, Gironde 00 33 5 56 09 76 10
www.camping.ocean.pagesperso-orange.fr

Soulac–sur–Mer, claims the tourist office, is 'close to everything except boredom'. They're not wrong. This seaside resort on the Bay of Biscay is dense with activities to suit all ages, all within easy walking or cycling distance of each other. Starting at La Pointe de Grave, 141km of cycling tracks run south down the Médoc coast to Les Landes, taking in wild beaches, stunning lakes, château vineyards and scented pine forests. Long, sandy stretches front Soulac's compact town, where bijou boutiques and eateries suit all tastes. The resort has been protected from urbanisation, the streets look cute in their neo–classical splendour, and the locals appear to be a friendly bunch.

The campsite is located on the northern tip of the Médoc, where the Gironde Estuary meets the Atlantic Ocean on the Côte d'Argent (Silver Coast). The drive from Bordeaux takes close to two hours, or you can journey south across the estuary from Royan. As for Soulac, locals claim it was the country's first beach resort and they celebrate their heritage every June at a lively carnival. The rest of the time it is a calm, quaint resort, home to Camping de l'Océan, undeniably the nicest campsite on the Soulac block, safely situated 300m back from Plage de l'Amélie. Their set–up is exemplary. A snack bar, reception and wash–rooms are designed to blend in with the surroundings, while pitches are generous and well spaced out. Everything you need is on site, but if it's not, just grab a bike and get pedalling until you find it. Soulac won't leave you wanting.

COOL FACTOR Stress-free haven for beach-lovers, surfers, families, solo travellers and everyone in between.

WHO'S IN Tents, campervans, caravans, dogs – yes. Large groups, young groups – no.

ON SITE 300 pitches. 10 communal hook-ups, 3 washing areas (Le Soleil, La Mer, La Forêt), 30 strong, hot showers and 40 toilets, including disabled. Shop and snack bar open daily in July and August. Washing machines, tumble- dryers (€5/€3). Wi-Fi €1.50 per hour (cheaper in town). 10 communal BBQs. Tennis is free in June and September, otherwise €6 per hour. TV and games room, table tennis. No campfires.

OFF SITE Cycling trails offer an exciting way to explore. Horseriding, skate-boarding, and sky-diving are all easily accessible from Soulac. The Romanesque Notre-Dame-de-la-Fin-des-Terres Basilica is a UNESCO World Heritage Site. The Courdouan lighthouse, the oldest in Europe, can be found at Le Verdon-sur-Mer. If the Atlantic surf is too wild there are sandy lake beaches at Hourtin lakes, a 45-minute drive away.

FOOD & DRINK Unusually named, Le KU-G du Pop (0033 556 418 244), serves fresh fish dishes and modern cuisine. Bear in mind that most bars and restaurants in Soulac take cash only.

GETTING THERE Head northwest out of Bordeaux on the D1 towards Castelnau-de-Médoc, then take the D1215 towards Soulac-sur-Mer. Turn left on the allée Montaigne towards L'Amélie-sur-Mer and look for a left turn on the D101. The campsite is signposted down the track.

PUBLIC TRANSPORT Regular trains in summer from Bordeaux to Soulac. Prebook a taxi (0033 5 56 09 79 57).

OPEN June–mid September.

THE DAMAGE Pitch with 2 adults €29.50, children 2–10 years €3.50, under 2 years free. Hook-ups €5. Dogs €2.60.

camping chez gendron

1 Chez Jandron, 33820 Saint Palais, La Gironde 00 33 5 57 32 96 47 www.chezgendron.com

'CHEZ GENDRON' read the large black letters, stamped along the oak barrels at the entrance to the site. It's clear you're in the wine region. In fact, though nestled snuggly among the vineyards of Gironde, one of the oldest regions for red wine in the world, not all of the grapes around here are destined for those dark and fruity bottles of Merlot. Turn left at the campsite entrance and you're straight across the border into Charente Maritime, a region just as famous for its cognac and with just as many green corduroy-like vineyards as Gironde.

Unsuprisingly, the views from Camping Chez Gendron, looking directly across the Gironde valley to the distant river, 5km away, are stunning. To make the most of the spectacle it's best to go for a wander, as the camping area itself is dotted and shaded by shrubs, trees and mature vegetation that can sometimes block the view. It makes for a pleasantly green place to pitch your tent, though, and the campsite has a relaxed, natural feel, with only two hard standings in favour of more grassy camping spaces.

The facilities are precisely what you would hope for: clean, well-maintained and providing everything you need, but without the artificial clamour of a large commercial campsite. There's a swimming pool and an adjacent, shallower paddling pool, both overlooked by the campsite's bar, which has a pleasant terrace for enjoying a glass of wine. Kids can enjoy games like volleyball or table tennis and, when they're finally worn out, they can find a quiet spot by the tent to snooze in the shade.

The tourist information folk love to tell you about the city of Bordeaux, bustlingly urban Royan and the beaches of the west coast – all, admittedly well worth a visit and within a reasonable driving distance. But really the modest local surroundings of the campsite have their own quiet charm, largely absent of people but full of wildlife and easily explored by bike. Vineyards, sunflower fields and pockets of woodland furnish the immediate vicinity, levelling out into flat marshy riverbanks along the Gironde estuary. It takes around an hour and a half to pedal to Blaye, home to a huge and fascinating military citadelle, open every day with free admission to the main area. It's a great spot for a picnic too.

The overall feel of the campsite, then, is much like the local wine it so proudly alludes to with its grand, oak-barreled welcome signature: natural, smooth and well-rounded, with beautiful bouquet and a very pleasant finish!

COOL FACTOR Wines on your right, cognac on your left and a patchwork of sunflowers, forests and rivers in between.

WHO'S IN Tents, campervans, caravans, dogs – yes.

ON SITE 46 grass pitches, all with electricity, and 2 hard-standings with a water tap each; 2 static caravans, 2 wooden lodges and a gîte available to rent. Sanitary block with 6 showers, 1 family shower, 1 room with baby facilities, a washing and a drying machine. Swimming, football, volleyball, a climbing frame and trampoline, table tennis, billiards, darts, horseriding and mountain biking in the woods behind the site. Free Wi-Fi available.

OFF SITE The campsite lies on the border of Gironde, famous for its Bordeaux wines, and Charente Maritime, which is equally well-known for its cognac, so tasting a local tipples is a must. Chez Gendron organises visits to the local wine châteaux, just ask at reception. Elsewhere, it's just under 30 minute's drive to Blaye with the magnificent Citadelle-de-Blaye (0033 557 421 209), a historic military stronghold made up of barracks, amouries, powder magazines and officers' quarters. Cyclists will enjoy the local paths with good routes upriver along the Dordogne, back along the Gironde estuary or between the vineyards. Mountain bikers will find no less than 40km of off-road trails just behind the campsite.

FOOD & DRINK Fresh bread is delivered from the bakery each morning. A small onsite restaurant serves fresh, mainly organic, food and cold drinks. If you want to explore the local area, try the village of Saint Ciers-sur-Gironde, only 2km from the campsite, which has a large supermarket and a weekly market, along with one or two decent restaurants.

GETTING THERE From the north on the A10 take exit 37 to Mirambeau, then turn right and follow the D137 south in the direction of Bordeaux, turn right on the D151 (direction St Ciers sur Gironde) and follow the camping signs.

PUBLIC TRANSPORT The nearest bus stop is 500m away from the entrance. Buses run from Bordeaux to Blaye and then from Blaye to Saint Palais.

OPEN March–October.

THE DAMAGE Pitch per night €8.18–€11.70; people €4.30, children (up to 4yrs) €1.65, dogs €1.05.

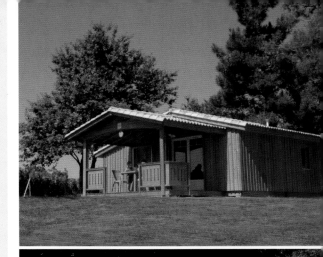

panorama du pyla

Route de Biscarrosse, Pyla sur Mer, Bassin d'Arcachon, Gironde 00 33 5 56 22 10 44 www.camping-panorama.com

Arcachon – what a surprise! This glitzy west coast resort is home to a natural, powerful and somewhat elegant tourist attraction. It might only be a sand dune, but what a sand dune it is. The King Kong of all sand dunes in fact, busting all other imitations out of the water.

Traffic is bumper-to-bumper during summer months on the single autoroute to La Teste-de-Buch, which leads to the suburbs of Arcachon's 'Winter Town' maze of magnificent Victorian villas. These ornate wooden-balustrade holiday homes belong to wealthy Bordelais and feel surprisingly tropical against the wooded hillside. You can share their coastal idyll for a while by pitching up at Camping Panorama du Pyla. This fantasically well-equipped site boasts a fancy restaurant, ice cream parlour and crêperie and two swimming pools – all of which creates a boisterous atmosphere in high season, to say the least. The ergonomics of the place work, however, with amenities grouped near the entrance to the site so that the noisier activities precede the quiet calm among the coniferous trees. Terraced slopes allow personal space at numerous pitches, but for greater seclusion aim for a spot by the side of the dune. These pitches are still near the beach – the sea glistens through the trees – but you're further away from any of the pedestrian paths. Temperatures average 22°C (72°F) in summer, although sea breezes make the midday heat bearable. If climbing the dune feels like walking on hot coals, use the steps etched into the slope at the start of every summer. After the sun has set and you've washed the sand off, steam oysters over a bed of pine needles (it's what the locals do) and dream about the wonderful surprises that lie in store tomorrow.

Tourists aren't the only visitors flocking to the one-mile-wide bay. The Banc d'Arguin nature reserve, a UNESCO World Heritage Site, is a nesting site for thousands of birds attracted to the shallow coastal waters and protected mudflats of Île aux Oiseaux. But both birds and tourists are outnumbered by the oysters that thrive along the Cap Ferret Peninsula, where colourful cabanes sit on stilts storing the daily catches gathered in sprawling fishing nets. Cap Ferret is an upmarket but laid-back shoppers' paradise serviced by regular, 20-minute ferries that zip back and forth from Le Pyla. But if shopping's off the menu, make sure oysters are on. Pick a restaurant with views across the bay and feast on shellfish that is plated over ice within minutes of being caught. Afterwards, you can walk off lunch by climbing the 258 steps of the Pointe du Cap lighthouse. The view at the top is of a landscape that hasn't been destroyed by waterfront hotel or property developments.

Next to the campsite the view is just as impressive. The largest sand dune in Europe was an 18th-century 'accident' that the wind slowly blew in over time. It measures 3km in length, and is 500m wide and 107m high. From the campsite below, matchstick silhouettes can be seen trekking towards the summit, the reward for their 30-minute climb being a sublime pinky-blue sunset that engulfs the Bay of Arcachon, from the campsite across the waters to Cap Ferret.

COOL FACTOR A unique destination. Silvery-blue sea in front of you, Europe's biggest sand dune on your right, and oysters for breakfast (possibly).

WHO'S IN Tents, campervans, caravans, dogs – yes. Large groups, young groups – no.

ON SITE 450 pitches, including 50 for tents by the sea (less shaded and sheltered from the elements, but with great sunset and sunrise views). All pitches have electric hook-ups. 70 clean, modern shower rooms and 60 WCs. 2 rooms for disabled (although wheelchairs will have difficulty in the sand). Two outdoor pools, La Panorama restaurant, small shop, bar, beauty centre, bouncy castle, sauna and Jacuzzi (free to guests), tennis court, bike hire, mini-golf, minimarket, washing machine (€6 including washing powder), drier (€4), Wi-Fi access throughout (chargeable). Baby cots for hire. No campfires.

OFF SITE Ferries run between Arcachon and Cap Ferret and make trips across the bay. The famous Médoc cycle trail starts at Cap Ferret and runs up the Médoc Bleu coastline along 141km of flat trails to the northern tip of the Gironde Estuary at Pointe de Grave. The trail passes the Lacanau lakes, Montalivet-les-Bains and Soulac-sur-Mer (see Camping de l'Océan, p.96), passing magnificent ocean beaches and pine forests. Paragliding tandem flights with or without an instructor (if qualified) courtesy of Air'v parapente (0033 665 478 676). Personally guided wine and food tours of the Médoc region in Bordeaux –

full-day, tailor-made outings that include collection from your campsite, a vineyard ramble, tastings and a 3-course lunch, from €185 per person. Or visit at the end of June via Bordeaux, where every 2 years a wine festival with a mile-long 'wine road' of outdoor bars, wine stands, and food booths is staged.

FOOD & DRINK Commercial oyster-farming started in 1859 so, naturally, seafood is popular here. Pinasse Café in Cap Ferret has waterside views and an excellent ambience (0033 556 037 787). Many oyster huts (cabanes) offer tasting (dégustation) sessions. At the site, the crêperie and ice cream café is situated in the middle of the site, making it hard to resist late-afternoon refreshment.

GETTING THERE From Bordeaux follow the A63/A660 towards Arcachon. Exit at La Teste-de-Buch (signposted Dune de Pyla) and follow the signs.

PUBLIC TRANSPORT Fast TGV trains run from Paris to Bordeaux, and stopping trains from Bordeaux to Arcachon, from where buses run past the site 6 times a day. Or book a transfer from Bordeaux airport with the site – from €130 for 4–8 people.

OPEN Early April–end of September.

THE DAMAGE Two adults €18–€50; additional people €7–€9, children under 3 years free, otherwise €7 per night. Bike hire €12 per day. Tennis free in low season, otherwise €9 per hour. Cots and high-chairs free except in high season when they cost €2 per day. Bungalows €39–€185 per night.

camping du toy

1284 Route Des Carroues, 40990 Herm, Landes 00 33 5 58 91 55 16 www.camping-du-toy.com

Covertly hidden in the heart of the Landes Forest and close to the natural lakes of Aquitaine, Camping du Toy is a long-established campsite that has been attracting keen campers for decades. The welcoming and knowledgeable owner Vincent has been at the helm here for more than 30 years, so it's fair to say that he knows a thing or two about running a successful site. With just 35 pitches, Vincent's privileged campers have a choice of pitching up in either the sun or the shade. A charming French farm building houses the site's immaculate showers, sinks, and toilets, while onsite oddities aplenty are dotted around to catch your eye – original mosaics, sculptures and tree-carvings, all lovingly created by Vincent's fair hands!

A major pull of this part of France is the amount of interesting places to visit. Known for its neo-classical architecture, Bordeaux's wide avenues, world-class museums and a distinctly un-touristy atmosphere, make Aquitaine's capital so much more than just a convenient stop between Paris and Spain. To the west, meanwhile, seaside escapes beckon with several excellent beaches less than half an hour away.

Back at Camping du Toy, guests gather around the large communal kitchen and get to grips with some of the region's famously fine cuisine, including goose liver, duck breast and asparagus. Such meals are the perfect way to end the day, while children burn off steam in the well-equipped play area, the long grass or the thick hedgerows – the rich onsite natural environment that is just another reason for this campsite's well-earned longevity.

COOL FACTOR Quaint family camping in a tree-speckled natural landscape around a 100-year-old farm house.

WHO'S IN Tents, caravans, mobile homes and dogs – yes. Large groups should call ahead first.

ON SITE 35 pitches, all with electricity and a water point nearby. 6 showers, 5 toilets and 2 washing machines (€3.50; detergent included). Wi-Fi available. There is a children's playground with a log fort, slide, carousel, zip wire, swings and a trampoline. There is also table tennis, boccia, football, volleyball, badminton and tennis. Vincent will kindly lend campers equipment for games. Communal BBQ area.

OFF SITE Just north of Vieux Boucau, the beautiful beach at Messanges is only about 25 minutes' drive away from the campsite. Its undulating white sand dunes and crashing Atlantic waves attract scores of families and surfers. The pretty village of Soustons is one of the true jewels in the Landes' crown, and the famous Lac Soustons, surrounded by ancient pine forests, is perfect for sailing, kayaking, windsurfing and swimming.

FOOD & DRINK The onsite BBQ is accessible to all campers. There is also a communal kitchen with a gas stove and oven as well as 3 fridge-freezers which can be used for a small fee. Herm, 1.5km away, has a restaurant, bar and small supermarket. There is a larger supermarket at Castets (4km away) while Magesq has a couple of fine-food supermarkets. Nearby Dax also hosts a traditional farmers' market every Saturday.

GETTING THERE Taking the N10 from Bordeaux to Biarritz, exit at Castets. You will reach a roundabout. Take the first exit 'Z.I. Cazalieu' and follow the road until you see the signs directing you to the campsite.

OPEN March–October.

THE DAMAGE Pitch and 2 people (including electricity) €15–€18.50, children (under 11 yrs) €2–€2.50. Dogs €2–€2.50.

simply canvas

Bonac, 47120 St-Jean-de-Duras, Lot-et-Garonne 00 33 6 81 76 85 94 www.simplycanvas.eu

Sandra and Santi, the owners of Simply Canvas, couldn't be accused of being orthodox. They met in a Vietnamese monastery – she was a nun, he was a monk. After leaving the monastery, destiny brought them to the Dordogne, whereupon they were married. The end? Not quite. They then set up a campsite that sought to encapsulate peace and equilibrium. As such, a Zen-like calm pervades every inch of Simply Canvas. Chickens potter past fat Buddha statues in the allotment; kittens bounce across the lawn as hammocks swing gently in the breeze – tune in, turn on, doze off. A lazy wander through the lavender leads to the graphite-black, kidney-shaped swimming pool – built like that to soak up and retain the heat of the sun (why run a manmade heater when you can harness nature's own?).

The accommodation is equally relaxing, with six safari tents furnished in traveller's paraphernalia – ornate globes, wicker furniture, peacock feathers. Each tent faces its own direction to maximise privacy. The site operates an honesty bar, so it's up to you to declare how many glasses of chilled rosé you've been tucking into while watching the extraordinary pink sunsets. There's a high-beamed, candy-lit barn that is a playroom for kids on rainy days, a venue for yoga classes and also the kitchen and dining room. Because there are only six tents the atmosphere is intimate; you'll soon get to know your fellow guests, either sitting al fresco or meeting on the way to your personalised shower (your name is chalked on the door).

Amongst all this is the garden itself – Sandra and Santi's pride and joy. Their permaculture ethos ensures that everything is grown organically and sustainably, with each plant strategically placed in order to help the growth of those around it. The idea is to simulate the patterns of natural eco-systems and create a fruitful garden that simply maintains itself. It's just another way that the site continues its cycle of natural harmony. Simply canvas? It's simply wonderful.

COOL FACTOR Zen-like calm filters through every inch of this garden-cum-campsite.

WHO'S IN Glampers and dogs (on leads) – yes. Campervans, caravans, tents, etc – no.

ON SITE Six well-equipped safari tents (3 cottages also available). Everything you need is on site: a sun-heated swimming pool, table tennis table, lounge-lizard hammocks, volleyball, kids' swings, soccer field, communal fire and BBQ; private, personalised shower and toilet. There are 6 safari tents (and 3 cottages); all include breakfast and linen. There is even tent Wi-Fi (although the speeds are at a slower, countryside pace).

OFF SITE The great thing about glamping in France is that there's no need to rush – with a climate like this you can easily just loll around the swimming pool all day. If you do want to take off for a while, though, head for Bergerac for a *dégustation* of its famous red wine. With scores of roadside vintners en route, it would be rude not to). Nearly every day there is a farmers' market in one of the surrounding bastide (medieval) villages, and St Emilion and Bordeaux are within reach for a (half) day outing. To see the lush valleys from a different angle treat yourself to an afternoon's hot-air ballooning (0033 553 890 223).

FOOD & DRINK Breakfast on site is an informal affair; Sandra makes smoothies, cooks eggs, or returns from the village laden with fresh baguettes, pains au chocolat and croissants. You can eat outside the barn at the long table, which gives on to great views of the fields. Sandra and Santi are also known for their delicious dinners: a few times a week they whip up a fabulous Mediterranean buffet with veggies from the garden, salads, local meat and cheese. In neighbouring Eymet, Le Pub Gambetta (0033 553 233 341) on the central town square is welcoming and authentic.

GETTING THERE From Bordeaux, follow the signs for Périgueux, joining the A89 shortly before Libourne. Exit at junction 12 and take the, D708 to Margueron, then take the left turn in the village towards Miramont-de-Guyenne. After about 5km, turn left when you see the sign for Briquet/Bonac or look for the road sign 'Simply Canvas and Permaculture'. Follow this 220m, and you have arrived.

OPEN April–early October.

THE DAMAGE Low season (April, May, June, September) €85 per night for 2 people, €20 per extra person including breakfast and private bathroom. Minimum stay 2 nights. High season (July & August) €850 for a family safari tent for a week (4 persons) including breakfast and private bathroom.

la parenthèse – camping les ormes

47210 St Étienne de Villeréal, Lot-et-Garonne 00 33 5 53 36 60 26 www.laparenthesecampinglesormes.com

Out of Africa meets Ibiza chic in this leviathan of taste and scale. It's hard to imagine a more stylish campsite, but don't be fooled by the über-cool bar complete with shiny chrome taps and de rigueur grey tables – Les Ormes is actually as rough and ready as you want it to be. Apart from the high-luxe tents, there are 100 great tent pitches for traditional camping in shady meadow areas. Of course, you can indulge in a bit of fantasy glamping if you wish, and the site's 25 safari tents are just the ticket, each individually finished, hidden in mature groves, and perfectly set apart in order to nurture your film star fantasies. Each tent has its very own verandah, twinkling candelabra, and lavish interior that seems to jump right out of the pages of a *Tatler* shoot, with a chaise longue, scatter cushions, fresh flowers, retro furnishings and cool self-catering facilities, all finished off with a dash of élan. There's even a raised outdoor platform with a tent atop should your kids want to escape, but which is close enough should the bogeyman come calling.

By the restaurant, on a gentle elevation, there are hammocks strung between the trees so that you can maximise the splendid views of the sunsets, which incandesce in the low-slung hills. The crowd is mid-thirties to forties, the atmosphere decidedly laid-back – perhaps something to do with the chillsome tunes wafting by, or the smell of deliciously grilled food from the gastro bar. As for facilities, there's a great deal to keep you busy and ensure you never need to leave the site. After a faux African sunrise and delicious cappuccino and breakfast in the whiter-than-heaven café, head off to the tennis court or to the pond for a spell of fishing; or maybe it's volleyball, or a wander over to the petting zoo... Now they're just showing off! And we didn't even get to the black granite swimming pool with silver bus that doubles as a snack bar.

Coolness aside, kids are in their element here, perhaps because the site is so huge; but it's secure too, so their parents are able to really relax, safe in the knowledge that if one of them tries to escape, the chances are a hundred per cent they'll be spotted by one of the many staff who drive around in beat-up, ancient Renaults. Apart from the kids' pool there are swings and climbing frames, and if they really want to go feral there's the mature elm woods – from which the place takes its name – to run wild in. There's even a kids' restaurant, where they can eat with their new buddies, undisturbed by their embarrassing parents.

Yes, if Carlsberg did campsites it would probably look something like this. Run by a pair of families who came together and took over the site in 2016, aspiring to creating a camping environment where visitors can truly take a break, La Parenthèse – Camping Les Ormes is finished to perfection. But like everything that's finished well, they make it all look so easy. Which, of course, is exactly the point.

COOL FACTOR A campsite that redefines comfort with its laid-back ambience, efficient facilities and general panache.

WHO'S IN Tents, campervans, dogs (on leads), glampers – yes. Caravans and large motorhomes – no.

ON SITE 100 pitches; choose from forest or field, your own tent or glamping. Two large toilet and shower blocks, laundry, tennis court, swimming pool and stylish pool bar as well as a kiddies' pool. Sandy lakeside beach, a petting zoo and an authentic restaurant in an old barn. There's also a kids' café and a Ben & Jerry's fridge bursting with your favourite Phish Food and Chocolate Fudge Brownie flavours.

OFF SITE At the border of Dordogne, you can easily visit the Périgord and the beautiful old town of Bergerac, whose old town undulates through a series of sun-dappled courtyards to the river and makes for a lovely morning visit. Closer to home, there are a number of fortified medieval villages (bastides), including Villeréal, Monflanquin and Monpazier, all vibrantly French with arcaded squares and weekend markets selling everything from foie gras to local cheeses. There's also an 18-hole golf course right next to the campsite.

FOOD & DRINK Etincelles (0033 553 740 879) in nearby Ste-Sabine-Born village has a Michelin star and is celebrated for its authentic French cooking. To be honest, though, the campsite restaurant has a terrific menu.

GETTING THERE Take the A10 towards Bordeaux and just before Orléans take A71 in the direction Paris/Blois. After around 80km – just before Vierzon – turn onto A20 to Toulouse/Limoges. Near Brive-la-Gaillarde, pick up the A89 to Bordeaux and exit at junction 15 to Bergerac, then follow the N21 and D121 through Bordas and Castillonnès to Villeréal. From here the campsite is clearly signposted. Follow these to the entrance.

OPEN Late April–late September.

THE DAMAGE A pitch and 2 people with electricity from €18. Glamping accommodation from €500 per week. Visit their website for more information.

camping lestaubière

Pont Saint-Mamet, 24140 Douville, Dordogne 00 33 5 53 82 98 15 camping-lestaubiere.fr

You may come to the Dordogne full of good intentions – the caves you wanted to visit, the vineyard tours you had planned, the museums you fancied nosing around in – but once you reach the thinly spread little village of Lestaubière, most plans begin to unravel. Camping here is like stepping into a time vortex, in which somehow, no matter how hard you try, the outing you had organised is lost to a day of swimming, sunning or simply hanging around the campsite. Not that this is a bad thing. Finding a campsite as relaxed and sociable as this is exactly what most families are after. Just make sure you book a stay long enough to take it all in. There's plenty here to do!

With 100 pitches centred around a swimming lake, the campsite itself is probably larger than the rest of the village put together – though this is testament more to the size of the village than the site. In fact, the site has a deceptively intimate feel, with the camping divided into two separate fields and the terrain broken up by trees and shrubs. When you enter, you can turn right, heading off to one camping area, or left, leading you around to the second, along with the central reception building where there's an indoor games room and library for rainy days. Rainy days are rare though (that's why you came to sunny France, remember?) so it's not the library that will be soaking up your time but the inviting swimming pool, circled by a deckchaired terrace and overlooked by a small café-bar where you can enjoy a drink as you supervise the children. For something a little wilder, the oval-shaped swimming lake is the real treat. Long reeds cover much of the edge, while

a short stretch of sandy beach is the perfect entry point to swim out to a wooden platform that's ideal for jumping in. There's also a beach volleyball court, a boules court and an excellent playground for children. By the time you've done all that and dried off it's easy to see how the day has disappeared.

If you do manage to make it further than the campsite gates, the rewards are well worth it. Empty country roads seem designed for summer cycling, while a 25-minute drive south to Bergerac presents you with one of the most idyllic towns in the region, plus the opportunity to hop in a canoe and paddle down the river. There's life beyond the campsite vortex after all!

COOL FACTOR A fun, relaxed and sociable spot with plenty to soak up your time.

WHO'S IN Everyone! Tents, campervans, caravans, pets – yes.

ON SITE 100 camping pitches, almost all with electricity. 3 sanitary blocks equipped with modern toilet and shower facilities, baby baths, dishwashing, disabled access, washing machines and dryers. 2 chemical disposal points. Wi-Fi, a library with books and magazines and a games room with billiards, table football and board games. Beach volleyball, table tennis, 2 boules courts, a swimming pool and separate toddler's pool, plus a swimming lake with beach area and wooden diving platform. Fishing is permitted.

OFF SITE There's a tennis court 500m from the campsite and it's 25-minute drive south to historic Bergerac on the banks of the River Dordogne. The old town centre has a variety of boutique shops in half-timbered buildings. Visit the 12th-century Maison de Vins de Bergerac (0033 553 635 755), where there's an exhibition showing the history of Bergerac wines and its 13 appellations. At the top of the main square – Place Pelissiere – the lovely Saint Jacques Church is also worth popping into. Bergerac is also a great place to hire canoes to paddle the river (0033 553 229 588). You can rent them here and get picked up further downstream.

FOOD & DRINK There is a campsite bar with terrace which does snack-type food, hot and cold drinks, beer and wine. They also serve a variety of full menus during the week and pizzas can be ordered daily. Fresh bread can also be ordered every day, and it's 15-minute walk into the village where there is a small shop and bakery.

GETTING THERE From Bergerac head for Perigueux on the N21 and take the N6021 towards Pont St. Mamet; pass through the village and the campsite is on the right. From Perigueux, head towards Bergerac on the N21, take the N6021 towards Pont St. Mamet North, and the campsite is on the left before you reach the village.

OPEN Mid April–end of September.

THE DAMAGE Camping pitch €6.75–€12.75; adults (older than 7yrs) €5.25–€8, children (younger than 7yrs) €3.25–€5. Electricity €4.50–€5.50. Pets €1.50–€3.50.

camping la brugère

24510 Saint-Felix-de-Villadeix, Dordogne 00 33 0 5 53 61 13 02 www.labrugere.info

La Brugère, in the heart of the Dordogne region, is a farm. Or so the owners René and Lieke like to tell us. They gesture to the sheep in the neighbouring field, gnawing the grass back to its brown, sun-dried stems, and to the cattle in a meadow in the bottom of the valley. It's a working farm, with real life crops, and tractors and ducks and things. Yet despite its early days as a mere side-note to the agricultural proceedings, it's the campsite that has become the real centerpiece of La Brugère. And who would have betted otherwise? After all, what kind of farm has a kidney bean shaped lake that's just asking to be swam in? Or perfectly placed trees that are just asking to be pitched under? And, for that matter, sheds with old haylofts that are just aching to be transformed?

Yes, La Brugère has a proper rustic feel and this is precisely what makes it so special. But the reality is, no matter how much they insist La Brugère is a farm, it's the camping that's to die for.

Spread in a meadowy space, gently sloping towards the lake at the very bottom, and dotted throughout with young trees, the site has around 25 grass pitches. At the entrance, by the yard buildings, a chalky white track leads you in but otherwise the short grass – maintained by those friendly sheep – is left for campers to enjoy. To avoid scorching, campfires are also not allowed, but in the peak season René and Lieke light a communal campfire outside the main farm shed, as well as hosting their renowned weekly BBQs – a great communal gathering where campers can socialize and bring their own meat and food

to cook. The same shed has been delightfully converted to be used as a small onsite shop and bar throughout the season. Along with coffee, ice cream, alcoholic and soft drinks, they also serve a few tasty family dishes. Pizzas, made in their wood-fired pizza oven, and spit-roasted chickens are a staple, while the occasional *plat du jour* will see paella, fish curry or a *confit de canard* appearing for a change.

It's an attitude to cooking that's perfectly suited to the sort of site this is. Casual and spontaneous, yet delighting every camper who's willing to give it a try. What more could you ask for?

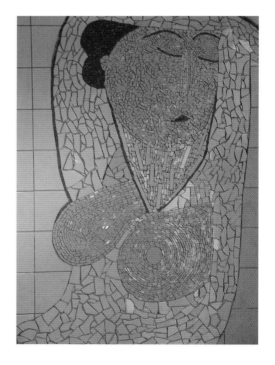

COOL FACTOR Casual camping, rustic charm and a natural lake for swimming.

WHO'S IN Tents, campervans, caravans, dogs, groups – yes.

ON SITE 25 grass pitches with the option of electricity. 3 showers, 5 toilets, washing-up area, a washing and drying machine for use and a freezer (free). There is a small lake you can swim (or fish) in, volleyball, table tennis, space for ball games, a sandpit for little ones and a swing. The converted cow shed has a small shop and bar, with a log fire lit inside on particularly cold days. Free Wi-Fi. No campfires, but BBQs allowed. The farm also hosts cattle, sheep, ducks, 2 cats and a dog.

OFF SITE There is a large forest 500m away with excellent marked trails and maps at the entrance – you can also ask René and Lieke for some paper copies. The routes are multi-terrain so mountain biking is popular, though those who want to stick to the roads won't have many problems – the quiet country lanes are ideal for family cycling. For culture, shops, cafés and restaurants, the nearest spot is Bergerac (see p.113).

FOOD & DRINK An old cow shed has been transformed into a multi-functional space where the owners run a bar during peak season. In the morning they serve coffees and offer a bread service; you order in the evening and they collect from a bakery in Bergerac each morning. During the day and evening the bar is open for ice creams, coffee, tea, wine, beer and soft drinks. They also serve pizza from a wood-fired pizza oven, spit-roasted chicken and chips (after 7pm). The site also hosts a grand BBQ feast every week – bring your own meat, fish or veg. Otherwise, there is a restaurant in the village and the nearest supermarket is 12km away.

GETTING THERE From Perigeux: take the D8 and follow it through Vergt. About 1km out of Vergt, follow the D21 towards Bergerac; after about 7km, there's a petrol station on the right. Take the 2nd road on your left (opposite La Brande restaurant). From here follow the signs.

OPEN April–mid September.

THE DAMAGE Tent or caravan/camper pitch with car, 2 adults and electricity €14.50–€15.50 per night.

la grande veyière

24480 Molières, Dordogne 00 33 5 53 63 25 84 www.lagrandeveyiere.com

Surely, few areas sum up the appeal of France better than the charming Périgord. The River Dordogne carves this fabled region in two, its banks lined with picturesque villages, high bridges and dozens of illustrious castles – the scene of centuries of combat and conquests. Today the clanking of sword and armour has given way to that of tent poles and fold-up chairs, in what is one of France's most popular camping destinations. Chief amongst the region's most popular sites, La Grand Veyière is arguably the Dordogne's best family-friendly campsite, a secluded, bucolic bolthole that makes for an ideal tranquil retreat. Overseen lovingly by the warm and hospitable Griet and Philippe, La Grand Veyière's 11 acres cater to campers of all persuasions, with space for tents, caravans and even a scattering of mobile homes and glamping abodes.

Quiet and intimate on the one hand, the site can also be a hive of activity, with an array of games, creative workshops and even the odd spot of live music in the evenings. Kids will certainly not be bored. The lagoon-shaped swimming pool is the focal point of all manner of shenanigans, and an all-round air of bonhomie prevails; you'll likely leave with more than a few extra contacts in your address book.

Beyond the campsite grounds, this château-studded land can be visited all year round, but in truth the summer months are something special. Take a stroll in the countryside and marvel at the countless species of wild flowers. The diverse landscape is truly a camper's dream, with shaded streams that are perfect for canoeing, five-star

mountain biking trails, prehistoric caves ripe for discovery, not to mention rock climbing and horseriding. With this sort of heart-stirring countryside, and delectable regional food, it's very easy to see why the region is a particular favourite of re-locating Brits. So why not join them? Even if it is only for a day or two.

COOL FACTOR A Périgord paradise, particularly for families.

WHO'S IN Tents, caravans, campervans and dogs – yes. Large groups – no.

ON SITE 45 pitches arranged in well-shaded rows (most with electrical hook-ups), and 10 mobile-homes. 5 fully-equipped tents for rent. Communal facilities include 8 showers, 8 toilets, family bathroom and laundry facilities. Small shop, bar (with 2 spacious terraces), table football, pool table, board games and a 150m lagoon-shaped swimming pool.

OFF SITE The nearby town of Sarlat is a charming labyrinth of passageways, sandstone buildings and secluded squares, showcasing some of Europe's best-preserved medieval architecture. You may find it hard to enjoy the town's beauty amongst the sharp elbows of sightseers during the busy summer months. But its cathedral, originally built in the 1100s, and redeveloped in the early 1500s, is a marvel – a real mix of architectural styles.

FOOD & DRINK There's a small shop onsite offering fresh bread, and the bar offers takeaway snacks. Eating out, head to Restaurant de l'Abbaye in Cadouin (0033 553 634 093) for an experience in pure French gastronomy, or follow the river east to Beynac (40 mins) for the romantic La Petite Tournelle (0033 553 299 518) – mains from €16.

GETTING THERE Coming from Perigueux (via Le Bugue) or Brive (via Sarlat) cross the railway in Le Buisson and follow the D25 to Cadouin. Continue towards Beaumont and after 3km turn right on to the D27 (to Molières) and follow the signs. Coming from Bergerac, take the D660 to Sarlat. In Port de Couze turn right, following the D660 towards Cahors (passing through Bayac) and after 3km turn left onto the D27 towards Cadouin; pass the Molières crossroad and drive a further 500m.

OPEN Mid June–mid September.

THE DAMAGE Pitches €6.50–€8.80; adults €5.50–€6.70, children (7–12) €3.70–€5, young children (2–6) €2.70–€4. Electricity €3.90.

le capeyrou

24220 Beynac-et-Cazenac, Dordogne 00 33 5 53 29 54 95 www.campinglecapeyrou.com

In the heart of the Périgord Noir region, along one of the most jaw-droppingly perfect stretches of the Dordogne Valley, is the village of Beynac-et-Cazenac. Nestled under the vigilant gaze of the Château de Beynac, this magical little village clings to the hillside as if it's been flung there by a giant. With its turreted witch's hat buildings and storybook red-tiled roofs, it's clearly medieval, although people have lived here since the Bronze Age. Pull up a chair at a riverside café, order a cool beer and ponder Viking longships prowling up-river as they penetrated the valley in the 9th century. Head upstream to La Roque-Gageac to hire a kayak, then float downstream past cliffs and castles peeking through the vernal river bank.

Situated in this 'five castles valley', in the heart of the Périgord Noir, Camping Le Capeyrou sits beneath the fortress of the Château de Beynac. Waking to the sound of the nearby Dordogne River it's hard to imagine a more enchanting view. The site itself is well catered for, with a generously sized swimming pool, volleyball court and a homely bar, with 120 pitches enjoying plenty of mature shade. Pitch up by the river banks or in the meadow, away from civilisation. Come evening, the bar, with its exposed stone walls and outside patio, is a pleasant spot for sundowners. Inside the recreation room, its walls festooned with old bicycles, there's a huge hearth and grill where people bring their own meat to BBQ (there's a butcher a few minutes from the site). Hey, for homesick Brits, there's even a dartboard!

COOL FACTOR Huge, lush grounds beside a gently flowing river and one of the best castle views in the south of France.

WHO'S IN Tents, campervans, glampers – yes.

ON SITE 120 pitches, the best of which are by the river. Three safari tents recently added. Two shower blocks, disabled facilities, baby rooms. No food on site, but a bar and an inviting swimming pool, toddler pool, kids' climbing area and trampoline. Volleyball court plus table tennis tables and laundry facilities. Campfires are not allowed but BBQs are fine.

OFF SITE The surrounding area is famed for the presence of Cro-Magnon Man some 20,000 years ago. Within a 30km radius there are plenty of troglodyte caves to explore, including world-renowned Lascaux. There are also more than 100 castles to visit. Fishing is a must, with local rivers chock-full of trout, salmon and pike. If horseriding (€16 per hour) and canoeing from Canoe Dordogne (0033 553 295 850) don't grab you, why not take a gentle river ride in a traditional gabarre from neighbouring La Roque-Gageac (€8.50 adult/€6 child)? Hot-air ballooning can also be arranged.

FOOD & DRINK There's a little supermarket by Le Capeyrou's entrance, beside which is a pâtisserie; it might not look like much, but their walnut cake is exported all over the world. In Beynac head for the impossibly romantic la Petite Tonnelle restaurant (0033 553 299 518) up a higgledy-piggledy street. Try the grilled duck, and the chocolate cake is pretty sumptuous, too. Prices from €16.

GETTING THERE Head towards Sarlat-la-Canéda; Beynac-et-Cazenac is 8km south-west of the town, off the D57. Coming from Bergerac, follow the River Dordogne.

OPEN May–September.

THE DAMAGE Tent (2 persons) per night €14.60–€25.80, children €3.20. Electricity €3.50–€4.40.

domaine de soleil plage

Plage de Caudon, Vitrac, 24200 Sarlat, Dordogne 00 33 5 53 28 33 33 en.soleilplage.fr

Slither into your swimwear, tuck a towel under your arm and start to spin. Yes, spin. Now close your eyes, keep spinning and point. Keep spinning. Keep spinning… aaaaaand stop! This is the best way to start your experience at Domaine de Soleil Plage, where water-based activities are as extensive as the campsite's restaurant menu. Hemmed inside a meander of the Dordogne, a beach beyond your tent flaps offers fishing, swimming, canoeing and kayaking, with an onsite rental service that allows you to daytrip downstream past clifftop châteaux and medieval *villês*. If you find your finger pointing away from the river, then it's probably the aquatic area you're heading for. The stylishly designed indoor swimming pool with adjacent hot tub is ideal on cooler days, while the paddling pool, water slides and spa are divided up by tree-dotted patios and tiny wooden bridges. If you haven't grown gills by the time you leave this campsite then you're doing something wrong.

This may all make the the site sound a bit full-on, and when you factor in the mini golf, three playgrounds, tennis court and indoor games room, there's certainly no shortage of things to do. But it's a family-run site with years of experience, and the range of activities is little more than a reflection of the area. The Dordogne Valley is a magnet for cyclists, fishermen and waterborne explorers looking for somewhere to take a break and enjoy a plethora of other sports in a sun-kissed setting. For the adventurous, paragliding and horseriding are a different way to see the region, while beautiful medieval villages like Sarlat, Beynac-et-Cazenac and Les Eyzies (to name but three) are close by, and the prehistoric caves of the Perigord Noir are also just a short drive away.

Back at the campsite, lounge on the beach or relax beneath the shade of the trees. The site is divided into three hedge-lined spaces. Furthest from the river are the fully-furnished chalets, while the other two sections house camping pitches, each with a well-maintained sanitary block, washing area and chemical disposal point. Not all pitches enjoy a riverfront position, but every spot has a good amount of space, easy access to the beach and a prime location in one of the most beautiful regions in France.

COOL FACTOR Riverside fun with water all around.

WHO'S IN Tents, caravans, motorhomes, pets – yes.

ON SITE 128 camping pitches (all with electricity and water tap), 119 rentals (chalets, mobile homes and cabins on stilts). 3 washblocks with showers, sinks, toilets and disabled facilities. Riverside beach, heated aquatic park with indoor and outdoor pools and hot tub. Tennis court, table tennis, mini golf, a sports pitch and 3 children's playgrounds. Restaurant with regional specialities, pizzas and takeaway plus a small shop selling fresh bread and croissants. Bicycles and canoes for hire. Wi-Fi.

OFF SITE Situated on the Dordogne riverside, hiring a canoe from the campsite and heading downstream is highly recommended. Canoe organisers will pick you up in a minibus at the end of the trip. Sarlat (see p.117) and Domme, are 6km away, while the villages of Beynac-et-Cazenac, Castelnaud-la-Chapelle, Les Eyzies de Tayac, Sireuil and Rocamadour are all worth a visit for their timeless beauty and commanding châteux. The prehistoric Lascaux Caves are just under 40km from the campsite and the brand new International Centre for Cave Art (Lascaux IV) has also just opened nearby.

FOOD & DRINK There's an onsite restaurant serving regional specialities, pizzas, snacks and takeaway food. It is located in the centre of the site. There is also a mini-mart that serves fresh bread and croissants. Paddle across the river to La Maison Du Passeur (0033 553 288 420) which enjoys a fine location and serves tasty grub.

GETTING THERE From Sarlat-la-Canéda follow the D46 south to Vitrac. After entering the village take the second left, signed Carsac. Follow this road for 1.5km then turn right signed Soleil Plage. From here you can follow the campsite signage.

OPEN Mid April–end of September.

THE DAMAGE Pitch with electricity for 2 people: €25–€41.50. Deluxe riverside pitch with 2 people: €33–€63.

la blanquette

Route du Cambord, Le Cambord, 24200 Sarlat-la-Canéda, Dordogne 00 33 6 32 04 90 45 www.la-blanquette.com

Oh to live on a French country estate! To throw open one's windows and breathe in dawn's mist before it fades away in time for morning birdsong. To see herds of deer frolicking among ancient woodland... (sigh). Luckily for all Gallic-bound glampers, such rural delights are not any longer exclusively the preserve of the landed gentry.

Enviably situated in the quintessential Dordogne hamlet of Le Cambord (just 6km from Sarlat-La-Canéda), La Blanquette Glamping nestles within the grounds of a sprawling country pile. Two ultra-luxurious, ultra-spacious twin bell tents, christened Chêne Vert and Truffe Noire (that's Green Oak and Black Truffle for us *rosbifs*), sleeping four-apiece and situated within their own spot of tranquil woodland. The tents are decked out with proper double beds (Truffe Noire's is a king, Chêne Vert's is a double), jute matting, hand-painted bedside tables and dreamy fairy lights (as if the air of enchantment needed adding to). Bedding is also provided.

While most of the accommodation is a dog-free zone, Truffe Noire is suitable for your four-legged friend. Set in its own large pitch, it is completely fenced in with a grassy area for dogs to play and relax in. A large fenced-in off-lead grassed exercise area in the heart of the woods is also in the works, so that dogs can run around to their heart's content!

The newest addition to La Blanquette is the lovingly restored 1974 Castleton caravan named Chestnut. Complete with a comfy double bed and fridge/freezer, plus an adjoining timber cabin housing a shower room, cooking area and sofa, this cosy vintage lodging is ideal for couples looking to go glamping in France in cool, retro style.

Outside, the thoughtful attention to detail continues. Each tent has its own private shower room located a handy but respectful 80m away. Each private shower hut has a loo, shower and handbasin and there are electric sockets for hair dryers or electric razors. Next to the shower rooms is a water fill-up point, a washing-up point and a shared-use washing machine. Each tent also has their own kitchen hut next to the tent, with a fridge, hob, grill and an outside dining area with BBQ. A shelter is provided for outside dining for the occasional summer rain shower.

COOL FACTOR Small scale, personal and wonderfully luxurious.

WHO'S IN Glamping only. Dogs by arrangement.

ON SITE There are 2 bell tents and 1 vintage caravan. One of the tents, Truffe Noir, is dog-friendly. All 3 have use of Wi-Fi, a private well-equipped kitchen with hob, grill and fridge; personal large shower rooms with electricity points; a private outside dining area with BBQ; jute matting inside; super comfy beds (linen provided); solar-powered lighting in tents and outside areas; shared swimming pool and sunbathing area. Welcome pack on arrival including local wine, milk, bread, butter, tea, coffee and biscuits. Kayak, bike and canoe hire available on site.

OFF SITE The beautifully preserved 14th-century town of Sarlat is a unique and spectacular place, and well worth a visit, though be warned it attracts hordes of day-trippers during summer (see p.117), particularly around the Cathédrale St-Sacerdos. 17th-century Château de Marqueyssac in Vézac is also within easy driving distance – the gardens are fabulous.

FOOD & DRINK You can't do the Dordogne without sampling some of the famous local cuisine, and luckily there is a restaurant, a farm shop (with freshly baked bread) and a health food store within walking distance (approximately 30 minutes' walk). Sarlat also has a wide range of restaurants, bars and cafés.

PUBLIC TRANSPORT Sarlat train station is 5km away. From there you can take a taxi or pre-arrange a pick-up with La Blanquette.

GETTING THERE Detailed directions are provided on booking. It takes about 8 hours to drive from the Channel Tunnel.

OPEN May–September.

THE DAMAGE £350–£550 per week for 2 people. Add £150 per extra person per week, up to a maximum of 4 people per tent. The caravan sleeps a maximum of 2.

domaine la chapelle

D162e1, 19360 La Chapelle aux Brocs, Corrèze 00 33 5 55 24 48 74 www.chapelle-en-correze.com

With its vacant valleys, deserted forests and seldom-visited villages, Limousin might just be France's most overlooked region. It's not nearly as popular as the Loire to the north or the Dordogne to the south, but it's a neglect that can only add to its appeal, as Limousin offers something all campers crave – the opportunity to get off the beaten track. Hiding in the region's rural depths, Domaine la Chapelle is a small, welcoming campsite with only six pitches. Throw in some nearby historical sights, picture-postcard villages and endless miles of walking trails, and you've stumbled upon a very cool campsite indeed.

This family-friendly site caters to the canvas contingent, glamping and the self-catering brigade, with a selection of apartments, eco-lodges and traditional farmhouses also available. Roland and Angelique are thoughtful owners and have limited their field to only six pitches, so there's ample room for everyone to relax. What's more, the facilities (hot showers and proper loos) are sparkingly clean, with campers rarely having to queue. As an accomplished chef, Roland takes care of the cooking, specialising in Correzienne cuisine. In the onsite restaurant guests can order fresh bread rolls and croissants for breakfast, whilst a tasty evening feast can be enjoyed on the large terrace, with sweeping views over the hilly surroundings.

There are plenty of sights in the vicinity. France's most famous prehistoric cave paintings, in the Grotte de Lascaux, were sealed for years until discovered in 1940 by four boys out searching for their lost dog. Often referred to as the prehistoric equivalent of the Sistine Chapel, this vast network of chambers are renowned for their artistry, with animal figures depicted in shades of yellow, red, brown and black. An hour's drive north-west, the grand Chateau de Hautefort enjoys an enviable position overlooking the Auvézère Valley and Hautefort village, surrounded by formal gardens.

During the summer at Domaine la Chapelle, children play in the swimming pool or playground, while parents sit out in the sun pretending to keep an eye on them. With these kid-friendly facilities, the site attracts plenty of families seeking a summer holiday, and you might find the 'family vibe' here isn't for you, especially during the school holidays. But otherwise, if you're a fan of rambling, horseriding and cycling through unforgettable and often deserted landscapes, you'll be dialling those digits already. *Bon Voyage!*

COOL FACTOR Scenery and serenity in the peaceful hills of Limousin.

WHO'S IN Tents, small caravans, campervans and families – yes. Large groups and dogs – out of season, by request only.

ON SITE Six grass spaces (sun, shade and a bit of both available), all with beautiful views. Wooden eco-lodges (wooden chalets) also available, as well as self-catering cottages. Sanitary block with 2 warm showers, 2 toilets, and 3 washbasins. 2 washing-up sinks, chemical toilet disposal area and laundry facilities (washing machine and dryer at extra cost). A fridge for communal use with freezer compartment. Swimming pool, picnic tables, playground with trampoline, boules court, volleyball, badminton, table tennis, small gym (extra cost), Wi-Fi access, restaurant with terrace – and resident sheep and goats.

OFF SITE The nearby Colette Gardens (0033 555 867 535) are an imaginative interpretation of all things floral relating to the French writer, Sidonie-Gabrielle Colette, best known for her novel *Gigi*. The gardens offer a stroll through literature and botany, presented through a series of 6 landscapes that reflect the 6 regions which marked Sidonie-Gabrielle's life. A wander through the huge butterfly labyrinth is a must. Children will probably prefer the Wizz' Titi (0033 678 195 345) adventure park, where little ones can swing from the trees, practice archery or walk the barefoot path. The charming villages of Collonges-la-Rouge, Turenne, Curemonte and Beaulieu-sur-Dordogne are all a shortish drive away, whilst the Saturday morning market in Brive, is one of the most popular and well-attended in the entire region.

FOOD & DRINK The site has its own bar-restaurant downstairs in the farmhouse where they serve breakfast each morning and dinner in the evening, while a lunch menu runs from June–September. The interesting menu changes daily, with a variety of local and international dishes as well as vegetarian options. Alternatively you can relax with a drink or ice cream on the terrace, in the bar, or by the fireplace. Offsite, the charming little town of Brive-la-Gaillarde, 5km away, has some excellent restaurants.

GETTING THERE From Paris, head south on the A10 to Orléans. From here take the A71 to Vierzon, then follow the A20 until exit 49 'USSAC'. Head straight over 2 roundabouts, then turn right in the direction of 'Malemort sur Corrèze'. Follow the D44 to Malemort, turn left on the roundabout (direction Tull), then turn right at the first traffic lights to Lanteuil, Argentat, Beynat. Straight on for 2 roundabouts then a left on the next roundabout (direction Lanteuil-Argentat-Beynat). Follow the D921 untill you see the sign 'La Chapelle aux Brocs'. This road goes upwards to the village and you turn left on the second road following a little sign that says 'Le Bos'. The campsite is at the end of this road.

OPEN Camping May–September. Eco-lodges end of March–November.

THE DAMAGE A pitch and 2 people from €17.50. Children (aged 2–6) €3.50, additional adults €5.50. Electricity €3.50.

camping belle vue

La Contie, nr Hautefort, 24390 Boisseuilh, Dordogne 00 33 5 53 51 62 71 www.dordogne-camping.org

Camping Belle Vue is well named. What at first might seem like a modest-sized campsite – a mere eight pitches – soon wins you over with its intimate ambience and views over the fields to the local chateau: a grand old building crowning the village of Hautefort that was once lived in by a countess who survived a number of husbands. By night it lights up like a chandelier, and should you visit on a Wednesday evening you'll find people in period dress strutting around its ornamental lawns to the accompaniment of classical music. Sitting in the northern tip of the Dordogne, just below Limousin, Hautefort is a charmingly low-key village, with a clutch of antique shops, galleries and rustic bars.

The campsite is a rustic and comfortable oasis of calm, with just eight pitches, a couple of pre-erected tents and two rental caravans. It's well catered for with its cosy Stable Dining Room, decked out in blue-checked tablecloths and exposed brick walls, and a little shop selling basics where in the evening you can place an order for mouth-watering fresh pastries and bread to be delivered piping hot next morning. Owners Cal and Simon, originally from the UK, wanted to escape the rat race and find a slower pace of life, and they certainly did that. As well as welcoming hosts they're also great cooks and serve up delicious local dishes made with their homegrown veg. Admittedly there's not much to do, but the surrounding area has a smorgasbord of potential activities. Settle back and savour the honeysuckle perfume in the air and feel your pulse lowering by the minute.

COOL FACTOR The terrific valley views, peaceful vibe and friendly hosts keep visitors coming back.

WHO'S IN Tents, campervans, caravans, motorhomes, dogs (on leads) – yes.

ON SITE Just 8 pitches, most with a super view of the Chateau d'Hautefort (lit at night). Two 6-berth, fully-equipped tents and a pair of 3-berth rental caravans. Wash-block with toilets, showers, sinks and a washing-up area. Communal freezer. Swimming pool. Campfires not permitted on site, though there is a barn for larger parties and BBQs.

OFF SITE Oodles of things to do, from riding the Velo Rail (pedal karts) on disused railway tracks, to horseriding and hot-air ballooning (0033 683 433 601), which will set you back around €200 but is unforgettable. You might want to head for the river and hire a kayak. The prehistoric paintings of Lascaux are also just a short trip down the D704.

FOOD & DRINK The cuisine onsite is typically French; Cal whips up dishes like Provençal beef casserole and mains are just €10. The onsite shop sells drinks and ice creams. The Auberge du Parc in Hautefort (0033 553 508 898) has affordable French fare (mains €13), while Le Troubador is more upmarket, with specialities such as wild boar. A 2-course meal starts at €22.

GETTING THERE East of Périgueux, pick up the D5 through Cubjac and Tourtoirac to St-Agnan; head south on D71, keeping an eye out for signs to Hautefort. From the village square (opposite the tourist office) take the D72 for Boisseuilh, cross 3 bridges and then take the left fork in the road; Belle Vue is 500m along on the right.

OPEN May–end of September.

THE DAMAGE A pitch, 2 people and electricity from €18; children (13 yrs and over) €4. Dogs €2.

camping du bas meygnaud

24310 Valeuil Brantome, Dordogne 00 33 5 53 05 58 44 www.basmeygnaud.fr

There's something special about Camping du Bas Meygnaud. Normally if you mention a campsite in France with a pool, onsite restaurant, bike rental, badminton court and a pair of mobile homes, your head begins to swim with the sound of screaming children and the clapping bingo-wings of morning aqua-aerobics sessions. However Camping du Bas Meygnaud could not be further away from this.

Run by potentially the friendliest hosts on the continent and situated in countryside that is sun-floweringly typical of rural France, this is the traditional family camping site that everyone this side of the channel is searching for. A blanket of tall pine trees casts a cooling cover of shade over half of the campsite, the skinny trunks reaching high above, spilling their shadows across the grass pitches underneath. This brown and green scene is given colour by the glorious summer sun splintering through the canopy, as well, of course, as the peppering of colourful family tents. Out in the open there is also ample camping space away from the trees, ideal for those wanting to camp closest to the amenities – modern, clean and well equipped.

The real pleasures here, though, come in the homely little touches that give Camping du Bas Meygnaud that friendly local feel. An organic herb garden looks at first glance a little overgrown, but venture closer and you'll find a treasure trove of produce waiting to be plucked and thrown into your evening meal. The busy worker bees that fly to and fro from the vegetables are also on your side, stockpiling their goods in a beehive that provides honey to campers with a sweet tooth. Some of this produce can be brought in the small grocery shop by reception. Or, if you fancy the night off, enjoy some tasty slap-up regional food and wood-fired pizzas in the campsite's restaurant.

There's also plenty to make active campers feel thoroughly at home. The outdoor pool is a pleasure in the heat of midday, but hiring a bike and cycling the four kilometers to Brantôme – a beautiful little town with excellent eateries and ice cream to cool you down – is more rewarding. When you return to the campsite the pool will still be waiting and all the more satisfying as a result.

COOL FACTOR Quiet and shady camping in the heart of the Dronne Valley.

WHO'S IN Tents, caravans, campervans and pets – yes.

ON SITE 50 pitches on grassy, sloping ground, some with shade and some without. 2 furnished chalets, 2 mobile homes and tents available to rent. Modern and clean bathroom facilities (showers, sinks, flushing loos) and a baby-changing room. Swimming pool, bike rental, playground, volleyball court, badminton, table tennis and boules. Grocery shop, bar, restaurant, BBQ and Wi-Fi. Organic garden, herb garden and beehive.

OFF SITE Sometimes known as the 'Venice of the Dordogne', Brantôme is a lovely little town near the northern edge of the region with a charming mix of medieval and Renaissance architecture. On the banks of the River Dromme (just outside Brantóme) lies Les Jardins Tranquille, a lovely garden which offers exactly what it says. The garden's 9 acres have large, English-style borders, shady wooded areas and a lovely stretch by the river.

FOOD & DRINK There's an onsite restaurant, serving regional food, pizzas and a variety of snacks and fresh bread from the local baker is delivered each morning during July and August. Nearby Brantôme boasts plenty of excellent eateries, including Hostellerie Du Perigord Vert (0033 553 057 058), Cote Riviere (0033 553 466 030) – which has tables over looking the river – and La Recre Gourmande (0033 553 457 704), where friendly Colette and Yann welcome you to their beautiful 17th-century home.

GETTING THERE From Paris take the A20 to Limoges then the N21 to Thiviers. In Thiviers follow the signs to Brantôme (D707, D78). From Brantôme follow the signs to Périgueux (D939) and 4kms after Brantôme turn right at Laserre. From here you can follow campsite signs all the way to the entrance.

OPEN April–September.

THE DAMAGE Adult €5, children €4 and caravans, campervans and tents all €8. Chalets €460 per week, mobile homes €490 per week and rental tents €425 per week.

belair le camping

Maucité, Champagnac de Belair 24530, Dordogne 07766 771611 www.belairlecamping.com

The tiny hamlet of Maucité may be rural – a band of trees wraps around the houses in a green embrace while the River Dronne skirts along one side – but the settlement is not entirely lost to the world. In fact, remote as the place may feel, it boasts two particular assets that the rest of France can be truly jealous of. The first is Moulin Du Roc, a Michelin-starred restaurant, less than a kilometer down the road. And the second is Belair Le Camping, a newly renovated and regenerated riverside campsite.

Bought by the Pantry family in 2016, Belair is a fresh, enthusiastic enterprise that has started small and keeps things on a personal scale. The site currently has just six bell tents, pre-pitched and kitted out with double beds and dainty wooden furnishings, and regular camping is not permitted. The lucky glampers that do bag these spots have acres of space to explore. Bikes are available to hire, so you can whizz along the riverside or pedal your way to Moulin Du Roc for that slap up meal, and there's a raised, over-ground swimming pool where you can while away the sunniest hours.

There are many other ideas in the pipeline, too. Talks of a treehouse are afoot, or perhaps a cosy log cabin, tucked among the trees in the far corner of the site. Some plans remain further in the future than others. There's also an old caravan parked up from the campsite's previous owners. The Pantry's are removing the van for 2017 but keeping its adjacent wooden shack and converting it into a warm communal space with a kitchen area, chiminea, tables and chairs.

The cobbled avenues of Brantôme are the nearest real attraction of note, its Benedictine abbey a particular highlight. But the real joy of Belair is the peace of the more immediate surroundings. Birds chirp a sing-song soundtrack each morning and the hedgerows bulge with fruit as the end of summer approaches. The Pantry family moved here from the Essex countryside – not exactly an urban metropolis – but still site the tranquility of the place as the main attraction. That and the weather of course.

COOL FACTOR Rural charm but modern glamping comfort, and all with a top notch eatery on the doorstep.

WHO'S IN Glamping only. Tents, campervans, caravans – no. Dogs – yes.

ON SITE Six furnished bell tents, 2 showers (1 male and 1 female), 3 toilets; washing-up area. Electricity in all accommodation. Bedding provided, but not towels. Communal fridge/freezer available. All accommodation has a gas cooking stove; charcoal BBQ; wood-burning stove; a double bed (or bigger). Honesty shop for basic items such a milk, cooking oil, canned goods, etc. Decked swimming pool with sunbathing area. Covered social area, for dining and socialising. Pool table, table tennis and other games and bikes available to rent.

OFF SITE Brantôme is 6km away, a beautiful town dubbed the Venice of the Perigord. Encircled by the River Dronne, it's a popular starting point for boat trips and kayaking. The Plus Beaux village of Saint Jean de Cole is only 7km away – the Chateau de la Marthonie (0033 553 621 415) and Romanesque Byzantine church sit overlooking a charming market square, with the River Cole nearby. There's also a market in Brantôme on Friday mornings and another in Thiviers on Saturday mornings. The village of Champagnac de Belair has a public open air swimming pool during the summer months if the on site pool isn't good enough for you!

FOOD & DRINK It's all self catering here. The nearest boulangerie is in Champagnac De Belair (less than 1km away) where there's also a Michelin starred restaurant called Moulin Du Roc (0033 553 028 600), a local favourite. Large supermarkets and further bars and restaurants can be found in Brantôme.

GETTING THERE From Brantôme, take the D78 for 5km until you reach Champagnac de Belair. Turn right onto D82 then left onto D83 and stay on this road for 1km. The campsite is on the right hand sign, signposted Belair le Camping.

OPEN All year.

THE DAMAGE Bell tents for 2 people for 2 nights £125–£200.

le domaine vert

Les Magnes, 19230 Troche, Corrèze   00 33 5 55 73 59 89   www.ledomainevert.nl

Le Domaine Vert is the sort of campsite that makes you want to simply up-sticks, yank the kids out of school and take off to France to start a new life abroad. It has all the whimsical charm of a classic children's storybook, and it's impossible not to be instantly won over by the campsite's rustic, farmyard entrance and miles of open space. There's no doubt that the almost two decades owners Anne and Gerard have been here have involved a lot of hard work – much of the farm's character has been brought out by careful restoration and they've done a vast amount of planting. But why should we let hard work get in the way of our dreams? From your pitch in the long grasses of Le Domaine Vert you too will soon be conjuring up your own plans to live a magical Limousin lifestyle.

It's a well-managed site, for sure, as evidenced by the sheer amount of space on offer. Anne and Gerard's smallholding comprises a magnificent 17 acres, yet they limit the pitches to just nine in total. It doesn't take a mathematician to work out that that's a serious amount of space for each pitch. From most pitches you can't even see any of the other tents in the campsite, which creates a real sense of privacy while also leaving ample room for little tykes to run around and play games in the grass.

The camping area is roughly centred around the couple's house, and this only accentuates the homely, family-run feel of the place. In the courtyard outside, a cluster of tables offers the perfect space to enjoy an evening meal – homecooked with veg from the garden (of course) – and, if the weather turns sour, Anne and Gerard

have an atmospheric cellar space inside as an alternative. It's quite an unexpected discovery and a wonderful place to dine.

Their other magical conversion is inside one of the farm stables, where Gerard has spruced up a former cattle pen and crafted his unique 'cupboard beds' out of old wooden surfaces and doors. The enclosed wooden bedsteads are particularly popular with late arrivals or early departures, or just those who fancy a night without the faff of assembling the tent – with a double bed in one and a bunk inside the other. Together they make a handy family combination.

To a certain extent the campsite is really a reflection of its surroundings. The old farm is spritely and young compared to some of the ancient towns and villages in the region, and a 15km cycle to Uzurche – 'the pearl of the Limousin' – quickly shows you how beauty comes easily to this part of France. Le Domaine Vert is the perfect name for the campsite: simple, honest and spot on. A green place, indeed.

COOL FACTOR Endless space, a dreamy farm setting and affable owners.

WHO'S IN Tents, campervans, caravans, dogs — yes.

ON SITE Around 9 pitches. Electricity available. Bathrooms housed in converted stables, with toilets, sinks, showers, a washing-up area and a washing machine. Wi-Fi by the farmhouse. Three 2-person cupboard beds in the stable and a bunk-bed cupboard bed (for children) in the cattle shed. Log cabin also available to rent.

OFF SITE It's a pleasant 10km cycle to Arnac-Pompadour to the east, renowned for its magnificent chateau (0033 555 985 547), famously gifted by King Louis XV to Madame de Pompadour and also home to France's national stud farm. A similar distance to the west of the campsite lies Uzerche (15km), described by the English writer Arthur Young as 'the pearl of the Limousin' in 1787 — an apt description of the picturesque, riverside settlement. Built on top of a rocky outcrop, surrounded by the river Vézère, Uzerche has a rich heritage and is well worth exploring (see also p. 144).

FOOD & DRINK Anne and Gerard prepare meals in the farmhouse. Dishes are cooked with their own, homegrown produce, whether it be vegetables from the garden, freshly picked fruit or meat reared on the farm. Depending on the weather, they offer dinner in the courtyard, in the 'Bodega' — an atmospheric wine cellar — or the main, covered terrace overlooking the adjoining fields.

GETTING THERE Leave the A20 at exit 45 — Vigeois, Uzerche and at the roundabout, take the third exit (Vigeois). Just after the roundabout, turn left to Vigeois. Drive all the way through Vigeois, keeping right, past the village square and follow the sign 'Troche'. Leave the village, driving through the railway tunnel, across the River Vézère and back uphill again. After about 1km take the road to the right (D50). Follow this for about 5km, and then follow the signs for 'Le Domaine Vert'. Turn right to 'Les Magnes'. It is the second farmhouse on the right.

OPEN April–October.

THE DAMAGE Nightly: €10 per pitch ; €5 per person; €3 for electricity; €1.50 per dog.

moulin de la geneste

19140 Condat sur Ganaveix, Corrèze 00 33 5 55 98 90 08 www.lageneste.net

Uzerche isn't known as 'the pearl of the Limousin' for nothing. It's cluster of ancient, turreted buildings, clambering up towards the steeple of its hilltop church, creates one of the most scenic townscapes in all of France, while the languid pace of the River Vézère imbues a sense of calm and serenity across the entire settlement. Slithering around the town in a tight loop, it's as if the river has squeezed the old centre upwards, the grey-stone buildings crowning the surrounding valley with their spikey rooftops and rows of classical arches. Were you to climb the church tower and peer from the narrow windows, it would be a struggle to pick out the neighbouring village of Condat sur Ganaveix. Though just six kilometers away, the flanks of trees and numerous shallow valleys disguise it among the countryside, but it's on the edge of the village, nestled among such lush surroundings, that Camping Moulin de la Geneste is found.

Spread across 10 acres but with only around 45 camping pitches, Moulin de la Geneste is a country campsite as naturally suited to its surroundings as the birds in the trees and the trout in the river. Much of the site is made up of unmanaged pockets of woodland and long grasses, while three specific camping areas provide space where tents can be pitched or motorhomes parked up for the night. The attitude is pretty relaxed.

Events are suitably spontaneous and homemade – be it floating candles on the lake, a treasure hunt, storytelling in the fairy garden or feeding and brushing ponies – but there are plenty of happy constants to keep you busy through the day. Boules and basketball courts entertain in the warm summer evenings, while managed footpaths lead you through the trees to quiet picnic areas and streams perfect for kids to dabble and splash about during the midday heat.

When you do head elsewhere, though, there is plenty to do. Uzerche itself has a wealth of important heritage – the central abbey is a sign of its influence during the 1100s and the surrounding fort-shaped buildings that were a style of the time led to the French saying: 'He who owns a house in Uzerche has a castle in the Limousin'. It's not a place for fast-paced modern life, of course, (though join the local canoe outfitters and you'll certainly find some speed on the downstream rapids), but for a little casual exploration there are few better spots – tailor-made for aimless ambling.

When you slide your rook across the chessboard back at Camping Moulin you can't help but feel the timelessness of the Limousin area – its mature woodlands and ancient settlements, and the age-old lure of camping out beneath the stars. "Beware", their website warns, "You may find yourself staying longer than you planned". Quite.

COOL FACTOR Wild yet well-organised camping in a top location.

WHO'S IN Tents, campervans, caravans, campers, glampers, dogs (on a lead) – yes.

ON SITE 25 grass pitches, 20 with electric hookups; 3 bell tents; 4 chalets and 3 mobile homes. 2 shower blocks with showers, toilets, sinks, a disabled room, a family room, 2 washing-up rooms and 2 washing machines. A boules pitch, table tennis, basketball net, football area, badminton, 2 outdoor chess tables and free Wi-Fi. Communal fridge for ice-packs. The trout river and large lake are well stocked with fish and the lake has 2 small rowing boats. Animals to pet include ponies, sheep, goats, pigs, chickens and the owners' 2 bouncy springer spaniels. Donkey trekking available. There is also a fantastic 'fairy garden' with a decked platform, wishing well, chimes, tree swing and hidden fairies for children to find!

OFF SITE Uzerche is a charming town with a Friday market brimming with the finest Limousin produce. For something a little more active, visitors can take to the Vézère and do some white-knuckle canoeing with trained instructors at the Base de la Minoterie (0033 555 730 284).

FOOD & DRINK Bread is delivered from the local bakery 6 times a week during July and August. A local farmer also visits selling his fruit and veg. There's always a small stock of food in reception, plus beers, wines and ice creams. Once a week, the site host an authentic Indian feast for all campers. Uzerche boasts several excellent eateries including Le Charmant (0033 555 981 780), Hôtel Joyet de Maubec (0033 555 972 060) and Brasserie Vézère (0033 651 644 048).

GETTING THERE Exit the A20 at Junction 44; at the first roundabout take the exit to Uzerche and continue for 3km to a crossroads. Take a left turn to Condat sur Ganaveix, and continue towards the village, crossing over a railway bridge, and then coming to a T-junction with a church opposite. Turn right, take the second left and follow the signs to the site.

OPEN April–end of October.

THE DAMAGE Tent plus 2 people from €14.

camping la chatonnière

Jumilhac-le-Grand 24630, Dordogne 00 33 5 53 52 57 36 www.chatonniere.com

Never has a campsite harnessed so much power of nostalgia. Like the city image of a handsome, sun-tanned Parisian cycling around beneath the Eiffel Tour, La Chatonnière represents perhaps the archetypal vision of the French countryside, all parcelled up into family campsite form. Imagine, if you will, the perfect French country campsite and then get out your checklist… send us a postcard if anything's not ticked off.

For starters there's the river, glistening in the sun as it flows languidly in long, sandy meanders – perfect for paddling, swimming and cooling off from the midday heat. Along its edges the grass has been systematically worn down by picnic blankets and sun towels or grows in shrub-shaped patches beneath the dappled shade of trees. Then there's the fantastic number of tents, giving a real traditional feel to the place. Campervans and caravans are welcome, but the apron of grass at the very bottom of the site (where cars are not allowed) mean it's still the old-school camping clan that rule the roost here.

The atmosphere of the site is its most memorable feature. Utterly relaxed and laid-back, the place has a plethora of excellent facilities, yet none of that Euro Camp feel that's become more common in recent years. There's badminton, boules and table tennis, bikes for hire and boats you can borrow to mess about on the water, plus a small shop where they sell ice creams and deliver fresh, pre-ordered bread each morning. It's both remarkably casual yet wonderfully well organised. Precisely what you want in a campsite.

The surroundings are, in fact, all part of a designated nature reserve – the Parc Naturel Regional Perigord-Limousin – an added reason why the focus here is on keeping things simple and natural rather than artificial and commercial. Even their facilities are suitably green; the toilet flush uses water from the river and the shower heating is all aided by solar panels on the roof. And any leftovers from the shop? They get fed to the owner's goats of course!

So with the atmosphere in top order, facilities to boot and surroundings green enough to be given 'Parc' status, it surely leaves just one more box on the checklist – a little *culture française*. How about a spectacularly grand, 12th-century château within easy walking distance? Big fat tick for that one too!

COOL FACTOR The ultimate in French country camping: a peaceful riverside location, chilled-out atmosphere and a romantic château within strolling distance.

WHO'S IN Tents, campervans, caravans, small groups (10 max), families, couples, dogs – yes.

ON SITE 43 pitches (all with electricity), 7 wooden mobile homes and 6 rental tents. 2 modern wash-blocks, including disabled facilities, a family bathroom, washing machine and dryer and a covered washing-up area. Wi-Fi zone, public telephone, fresh bread each morning, a small shop and tourist information. Badminton field, table tennis, table football, playground and bikes, canoes and kayaks all available to rent. Small children can play on the nearest river beach (depth 50cm), while 'real' swimming for big kids is accessible in the rest of the river. Communal campfires every 2 days.

OFF SITE Jumilhac-le-Grand (0033 609 617 840) is the closest of several nearby castles, also known as 'the black pearl' of the Perigord-Vert due to its distinctive black roof. The campsite's location within the Parc Naturel Regional Perigord-Limousin means there are lots of outdoor activities on offer, including (300m from the campsite) a riding school with ponies for children.

FOOD & DRINK You can grab ice creams, drinks, homemade takeaway pizza, chips and snacks from the small shop onsite, plus there's fresh bread to order each morning. Offsite, on the main square in Jumilhac-le-Grand, try the traditional French cuisine served at the lovely little restaurant of Lou Boueiradour (0033 553 525 047). In nearby La Coquille, the hotel Les Voyageurs (0033 553 528 013) is another excellent choice worth visiting.

GETTING THERE From the roundabout in Jumilhac-le-Grand (there's only one) take the D79 north in the direction of La Coquille; after 500m take the left turn and the campsite is 100m further on.

OPEN Late May–mid September.

THE DAMAGE Tent plus 2 people €14–€26 per night; mobile homes €345–€795 per week; furnished tents €295–€595 per week.

la jaurie

6 Impasse de la Jaurie, 87500 Ladignac Le Long, Haute-Vienne 00 33 5 55 00 52 23 www.lajaurie.com

If you like your camping accompanied by the sound of bleating sheep and an eco-conscious ethos, then point your motor to the French south-west and seek out the eight and a half charming acres of La Jaurie. This small farm campsite is run by Marcel and Madelinde, whose passion and enthusiasm for the land inspires a camping experience focused on nature and good homegrown grub. Set on a hill overlooking enchanting woodlands, La Jaurie boasts a lovely collection of old buildings and barns. The camping field is bordered by beehives and an orchard of walnut trees, all set alongside a small meandering river. Chickens roam freely, as does Woef the dog, not to mention Pockie and Rhino, the resident cats. There's even a friendly donkey to meet, so be sure to save a carrot or two.

La Jaurie's scattering of camping pitches come with plenty of space. Take your pick from spots by the vegetable patch, the orchard or down by the stream – the waterside pitches are perfect for campfires. While this is fancy-free camping, there are still all the facilities you'll need for a comfortable stay, plus some bonus extras including a solar-powered cooker and a salt-water swimming pool.

Eating at La Jaurie is very much a social affair, with guests welcome to join their hosts for evening dinner. Every Friday, a five-course family-friendly feast is dished up using the wealth of delicious produce grown and reared on the farm itself. The restored traditional bread oven is put to work on Tuesdays with tasty pizzas served up at the communal dining table.

There are plenty of onsite activities to enjoy, including crafts for kids, painting, yoga and even panning for gold. If you want to really get involved you can lend a hand on the renovation of the old farm buildings using traditional building methods and materials. This is also ideal hiking territory, with numerous trails to be found around the rolling landscape of the Limousin. Alternatively, take to two wheels and cycle the *'Voie Verte'* track along the old railway line.

History buffs will no doubt know this region as the land of the Crusades. Richard the Lionheart met his maker with an arrow through the arm at nearby Châlus, while the prominence of 12th-century architecture stands as a testament to the region's historical past. The landscape is dotted with unspoiled villages with oodles of Gallic charm. The closest you'll get to big city living round here is the historic town of Limoges (35km away), though we'll wager you don't make it much beyond the tranquil surroundings of this gorgeously idyllic campsite.

COOL FACTOR Camping, campfires and an eco-conscious ethos in the rolling hills of the Limousin.

WHO'S IN Tents, caravans, tourers, dogs (on leads), small groups – yes. Large groups (20+) welcomed in low season.

ON SITE 20 pitches, 6 with electric hook-ups; 3 separate spots for caravans. Some of the stream-side pitches have campfire areas. 5 toilets, 3 showers, laundry with dryer and washing lines, fridge, solar cooker, microwave, covered picnic area with tables and Wi-Fi. Salt water swimming pool, table football, donkey rides, treasure hunt walking trails, nature workshops, gold panning in the river (weather permitting).

OFF SITE Mapped, circular walking routes from the campsite range from 3km to 18km in length. One route takes you to the the first European elephant sanctuary (elephanthaven. com), just 2km away. Espace Hermeline (0033 555 788 612), 4km away, is an activities centre with velo-rail (small lightweight bikes on a train track), tree canopy adventure trails, zip lines, tennis, BMX trails, swimming and a charming miniature railway.

FOOD & DRINK A small shop sells produce from the farm as well as apple juice, vegetables, jams, cold drinks and ice cream – and there is a BBQ to borrow. Campers can enjoy a home-cooked *table d'hôte* meal from €16.50 pp. Breakfast is also served daily. Every Tuesday night in July and August you can enjoy pizza baked in the bread oven. There's no shortage of local restaurants serving tasty, authentic French cuisine – try La Feuillardière (0033 555 786 146) in Bussière-Galant, the Ferme Auberge de Bellevue (0033 555 583 898) in Rilhac Lastours, or Le Sax'o (0033 555 785 029) in Châlus.

GETTING THERE From Bussière-Galant follow the D901 towards Ladignac-le-Long. After 4km the campsite is signposted on the right.

OPEN April–October.

THE DAMAGE Pitch and 2 people €14–€23.

la ribière sud

Haute-Vienne, Limoges, Châlus, Haute-Vienne 00 33 5 55 78 58 62 www.la-ribiere-sud.com

Known as France's Lake District, the Limousin is celebrated for its wonderful rolling hills, fox-red cattle, and hordes of Brits trying to escape their compatriots from the Dordogne. It's also an area integrally tied to the history of the Crusades and Richard the Lionheart, who met his end in the village of Châlus.

Camping de la Ribière Sud is just a few minutes away from there, set in 22 acres of sleepy woodland and meadow on the former site of a tree nursery. It's a relatively new site run by two British ex-pats from the north of England – Ann and Harry. Harry's an electrician by trade, so everything works like clockwork; Ann is gaining repute as a mixed media painter and her work appears in the local gallery as well as back home.

The site's centrepiece is a wonderfully painted, genuine Mongolian yurt. Inside it's a hobbit hole of gypsy chic, wooden struts delicately illustrated by the hands of nomadic craftsmen; outside, a wonderful canvas dome bound in camel hair. But you don't have to stay in here if you've brought your own canvas – there are plenty of pitches in the shade of mature trees, all with electricity shoud you need it.

Wild boars sometimes pop in for a sniff around, as do the local deer, beneath the ever-present shadows of buzzards who silently soar up above. By night you'll be sung to sleep by the soporific hoot of owls and calmative coos of wood pigeons. The nice thing about La Ribière Sud is the scale of the grounds – you can wander in wild glades and prairie grass without meeting a soul.

COOL FACTOR Mongolian splendour and comfort meets woodland serenity in this simple, immaculate campsite.

WHO'S IN Tents, campervans, caravans, motorhomes, dogs (on leads) – yes.

ON SITE Six large pitches each with electricity. Wash-block with eco-friendly power showers and disabled facilities. Campfires allowed if conditions permit. Enjoy wandering around the garden which is open to the public once a year to raise money for charity. There are flower-filled borders, trees and shrubs and a large pond. During May, join Ann for painting days – €50 for 5 hours (materials provided).

OFF SITE Limousin's capital of Limoges is famed for its pottery and gastronomy, and is a short drive away. North-east of Limoges (between Guéret and Bourganeuf), the Forêt de Chabrières is not only a wonderful place to go walking and picnicking but is also home to Les Loups de Chabrières (0033 555 812 323), where you can see wolves close up. The area is dotted with lakes – some of which have beaches with swimming and picnic areas – and there is kayaking in Aixe-sur-Vienne and Brantôme.

FOOD & DRINK The Hôtel du Centre in Châlus (0033 555 785 862) does great daily specials such as escargots, quiche Lorraine and salads and steaks. Plat du jours cost €13. There's also an Intermarché supermarket, butcher and bakery in town for all your self-catering needs.

GETTING THERE From Limoges head south towards Périgueux on the N21; go through Séreilhac and Camping de la Ribière Sud is 8km further on, on the left, just past the Domaine de la Ribière fishing lake .

OPEN April–end of October.

THE DAMAGE Yurt (max 4 people) €55 per night for 2 people; for each extra person add €10 per night. Tents and campervans €20 per night for 2 people, including electricity. Extra people €3 per night. Dogs €1.

manzac ferme

Manzac, 24300 Augignac, Dordogne 00 33 5 53 56 31 34 www.manzac-ferme.com

Listen... can you hear it? No? That, camping compadres, is the sound of silence. Unadulterated peace and quiet in the heart of the tranquil Dordogne. That, people, is the sound of Manzac Ferme.

Nestled smack-bang in the middle of the sprawling Perigord Limousin National Park (eight scenic hour's drive from Calais), Manzac Ferme is the very epitome of rural seclusion. Fringed by thick woodland, it is a true oasis of tranquility, accessible via near-deserted roads which snake their way to this herbaceous hideaway. This adults-only, dog-friendly site caters to the canvas contingent and the motorhome mob alike but the conscientious owners have thoughtfully limited their field to just 10 pitches, so there's ample room for everyone to relax. What's more the immaculately clean facilities (proper loos, laundry and hot showers) are more than able to cope.

Manzac Ferme and the surrounding Perigord Vert are abuzz with all manner of wildlife. From vibrant butterflies and patrolling eagles to abundant trout and grayling in the nearby River Bandiat, and the deer emerging at dawn from the thick forest pines, a stay here offers a real back-to-nature experience. Despite the sense of remoteness, Manzac Ferme lies just 7km from one of the Perigord Vert's loveliest towns, Nontron – home of the famous folding knife and a number of other great attractions and culinary gems (the region is renowned for crêpes and *confiture*). It's also just an hour away from the legendary Cognac. And without any kids to worry about at camp, it would be rude not to indulge in a tipple....

COOL FACTOR A tranquil, adults-only, woodland hideaway in the beautiful Dordogne region.

WHO'S IN Tents, trailer tents, motorhomes (up to 9m), caravans, well-behaved pets – yes. Sorry, no kids – this is an adults-only site. Maximum 4 to a pitch so group bookings subject to availability.

ON SITE Six hard-standings for caravans, motorhomes and those who wish to park alongside their tent. A separate woodland camping area by the River Bandiat offers 4 secluded and large tent areas, with a separate car parking area 30–50m away. All pitches (hard-standing and grass) come with 6amp hook-ups. Free Wi-Fi across the site. Free hot showers, UK-style toilets, wash-up, a book swap, information area, plus a dump-point for septic tank friendly loos/grey water. Laundry available for a small fee. Campfires and charcoal BBQs not permitted as this is densely wooded area, but gas BBQs are fine.

OFF SITE The Périgord Limousin National Park is brimming with excellent walking and cycle trails – your hosts can provide maps. Just 25 minutes' drive away lies the stunning town of Brantôme, where you can take a boat trip or hire a canoe to cruise down the River Dronne. Nearby, the ancient network of caves at Villars are home to some remarkable prehistoric paintings. The village of Nontron (home of the famous folding-knife) is well worth a visit. If visiting in July, be sure to find out where in Périgord the annual Félibrée will be taking place: this celebration of Occitan language and culture is a huge occasion for the region, with the chosen town decorated with vibrant flowers, as revellers enjoy traditional music, dancing and singing along with Occitan dishes and drink.

FOOD & DRINK There are plenty of excellent eateries just a short drive from the site. Your hosts are full of decent recommendations and are more than happy to call ahead for reservations. Nontron, 10 minutes away, is home to 3 large supermarkets that are open all day, while you can stock up on some of the region's celebrated produce at the Piégut market, which takes place every Wednesday morning. There are also 2 excellent bakeries within a 5-minute drive for fresh croissants in the morning.

GETTING THERE Detailed directions on the website. GPS co-ordinates are: 45.56199, 0.71948 (decimal) or 45deg 33'43.07"N 0deg 43'10.05"E – but they recommend guests take a look at instructions as GPS devices have a habit of taking guests through towns that may not be caravan or motorhome suitable!

OPEN Mid May–mid September. If you would like to visit outside of these times, please contact for availability.

THE DAMAGE A pitch and 2 people €24 (including electricity). Extra people cost €8, up to a total maximum of 4 people per pitch. Pets free.

camping marco de bignac

2 Chemin de la Resistance, 16170 Bignac, Charente 00 33 5 45 21 78 41 www.marcodebignac.com

Situated in the midst of the beautiful countryside of Charente, we love this big, spacious, rural campsite – a large 20-acre site with just over 80 large pitches set on one side of a pretty lake and with all the amenities you could wish for. It's family-owned and run, which just serves to underline its greatest assets – pure, homespun tranquility, yet with enough in the way of facilities and activities to make you never want to leave.

You can camp with your own tent, campervan or caravan, opt for the pre-pitched 'canvas lodge' or book one of two mobile homes. Pitches are flat and grassy and most have electrical hook-ups, with the choice between full sun and shadier spots, set beneath the rows of mature, leafy trees. There are drinking water points dotted around the place and one of the two shower blocks has been recently refurbished, with brand-new showers, washbasins and toilets, plus a separate accessible bathroom with family-friendly facilities. The result is the provision of services you'd often expect on larger scale site, though with a much nicer, twist, owed mainly to the family-run vibe. Freshly baked bread and pastries can be ordered each evening for next day collection at reception – a French camping must – plus there's plenty of tourist information leaflets stashed alongside the main desk, along with local walking and cycling maps, board games and puzzles. To top it off, there is even a mobile beauty therapist who drops by from time to time.

It's a convivial place, with regular events during summer, including live music evenings, dedicated food nights focused on things like moules-frites and BBQs, and a popular boules tournament every Sunday afternoon. Plus there's fishing on the lake and an abundance of wildlife around the site. The neighbouring village of Les Bouchauds is worth a visit, home to the well-preserved ruins of an ancient Roman amphitheatre surrounded by a thick shield of trees, while the regional capital town of Angouleme is only a 20-minute drive away.

COOL FACTOR Family lakeside camping with top-notch facilities and beautiful countryside surroundings.

WHO'S IN Tents, caravans, campervans, couples, families, groups and dogs all welcome.

ON SITE 84 grass tent pitches, plus 2 mobile homes, and 1 canvas lodge. 2 sanitary blocks, one of which has been recently renovated and is heated. Both have toilets, showers, washbasins, an accessible bathroom, a family bathroom with baby bath and baby-changing, chemical disposal, dish-washing and clothes-washing sinks. There's also a freezer, electric hook-ups, a washing machine/tumble dryer, a small shop, fresh bread and pastries every day, a small library and free Wi-Fi in the bar. There's also an outdoor swimming pool, tennis and volleyball courts, boules, fishing on the lake, a children's playground and table tennis.

OFF SITE It's a 20-minute drive to the city of Angouleme, capital of the department of Charente, where you'll find an alluring old district of narrow streets and small squares, ancient ramparts, a cathedral and castle – and lots of appealing pavement cafés and restaurants too. Closer to the site, you should visit the abbey at St-Amant-de-Boixe, the ruined ancient Roman amphitheatre at Les Bouchauds, and, to the north, the lovely old chateau and mill town of Verteuil-sur-Charente. In the opposite direction, consider making the short trip to the river beach and water sports area of St Yriex, where you can go swimming, canoeing and sailing. There's also the old town of Cognac. There's good swimming in the river here but it's most famous, of course, for its cognac producers, where you can sign up to guided tours and tastings.

FOOD & DRINK There is a bar and restaurant on site, which also does takeaways. Otherwise, nearby restaurants include the traditionally French Le Taillefer (0033 545 397 039) in Montignac, 5km away; Les Nymphéas (0033 545 215 296), a simple, good-value brasserie in Marcillac Lanville, 10km away; or, in Angouleme, Angolo d'Italia (0033 545 905 174), an excellent local Italian, or Chez Paul (0033 545 900 461), which serves good (mainly French) food and has a garden.

GETTING THERE Heading north on the N10 from Angouleme, take the D11 turn-off (signposted 'La Touche D'Anais and Vars'); at the roundabout head towards Vars and stay on the D11 through Vars, la Portal and Basse; go under the new railway bridge and take a right towards 'Camping and Bignac'. Follow the road for 3km as far as the village of Bignac and make a (signposted) right towards the campsite. Coming from the west on the A10, turn off at St Jean d'Angley on to the D939 and follow the signs to Roulliac; turn left beyond Rouillac on to the D117 (signposted 'Camping Marco de Bignac') and just before Basse turn left before the new railway bridge (signposted 'Camping and Bignac') and follow the road for 3km as far as Bignac, where you turn right to the campsite (signposted).

PUBLIC TRANSPORT The nearest train station is at Angouleme, a 20-minute drive from the campsite; buses run from there to a bus stop 2 minutes walk from the site.

OPEN February–November.

THE DAMAGE Camping €25 per night; extra people €2–€5.

camp laurent

Le Fournet, St-Laurent-de-Ceris, 16450, Charente 00 33 6 02 22 37 15 www.camp-laurent.com

The River Charente may not be the longest or most famous of French rivers; nor does it have the same iconic status as the mighty Loire and its vineyard-filled valley. However, this languidly meandering waterway has its own unique charms. Once decreed by no higher authority than French monarch François I as 'the most beautiful stream in the kingdom', La Charente snakes its way through some of south-west France's most ancient counties. It is also where visitors to this enchanting corner of the country can find one of the region's loveliest campsites in Camp Laurent.

When expat Tracey first laid eyes on the Poitou-Charente, it was love at first sight. Setting up camp (quite literally) in the summer of 2013, Tracey's vision was of a tranquil retreat – easily achievable due to the adult's only admittance policy. Nestled in eight unspoiled acres just outside the sleepy village of St-Laurent-de-Ceris, Camp Laurent has ample room for just 10 pitches with six hook-ups. They overlook the river and valley below, while butterflies, rabbits and the odd roe deer dominate the scene. Facilities are more than adequate, with wet-room style bathrooms featuring hot showers, modern toilets and a laundry adjacent to the 200-year old stone barn. With the river on your doorstep, you could be forgiven for neglecting the brand new, open-air, wood-panelled pool – just the ticket for cooling off in France's second sunniest region.

With 400 metres of river frontage, the site makes an ideal base to fish for the Charente's abundant trout, carp, pike and eels. A lazy paddle in a canoe or a cruise in one of the numerous pleasure boats makes for a great way to explore the river, taking in such famous names as Angoulême, Saint-Savinien and Cognac – yes, the very same. Just be sure to appoint a designated skipper for the cruise back to camp!

COOL FACTOR Idyllic, peaceful, riverside camping for adults.

WHO'S IN Tents, caravans/motorhomes, dogs – yes. Kids – no (sorry nippers, it's adults only).

ON SITE 10 grass pitches. Swimming pool with seating area. Electric hook-ups available. Wash-block with disabled facilities in wet room-style bathrooms, hot showers, toilets, a laundry and washing-up facilities. Free boats and canoes to borrow and fishing on the Charente possible.

OFF SITE Plenty of cycling and walking routes in the surrounding area, including route 48 which is on Camp Laurent's doorstep. The Charente offers a wealth of great activities including canoeing, fishing or simply taking a leisurely barge cruise. The Lacs de Haute Charente and River Vienne offer similar waterside fun, including a beach. If you're visiting in August, the nearby town of Confolens hosts its annual world music festival, a 5-day summer event that attracts around 30,000 visitors. Confolens itself is beautiful, intersected by the idyllic River Vienne and two historic bridges. The Château de Rochechouart and the castle at La Rochefoucauld are well worth a visit, and the Futuroscope (0033 549 495 906) theme park and La Vallée des Singes monkey park (0033 549 872 020) also make a great day out. The camp is also ideally located to explore Bordeaux, Dordogne, Limousin and La Rochelle.

FOOD & DRINK The nearest bar/restaurant is Le Marronnier in St Laurent de Ceris, about 4km away. There are also lots of surrounding villages that offer an authentic French culinary experience. Several large supermarkets can be found in Roumazieres-Loubert and in Confolens. About 40 minutes' drive away, the regional capital Angoulême has an eclectic mix of places to eat and drink. La Ruelle (0033 545 951 519) is an eccentrically-decorated restaurant in a converted transport depot that serves refined French cuisine with a contemporary twist. No visit to the region could be complete without sampling Cognac's famous brandy and the town's lesser-known aperitif, *pineau*. Try some Limousin beef too if you get a chance.

GETTING THERE For Sat nav, type in coordinates N 45.96126 E0.52819; postcode 16450 and the commune name Le Fournet. This will bring you straight to the doorstep. If Le Fournet does not come up on your Sat nav, type in 16450, then D345 (selecting the anywhere option on this road). This will bring to within about 100m of Camp Laurent.

OPEN Mid May–end of September.

THE DAMAGE €20–€29 per pitch per night, based on 2 people sharing.

chez yurt

Peytaveau 87320 Bussière-Poitevine, Haute-Vienne 00 33 5 55 60 70 58 www.chezyurt.com

It's a time-honoured tale: UK family discover rural French paradise; said family move to said paradise in pursuit of 'the good life' and live happily ever after. And that's pretty much how it happened here. When Cathy Wills first discovered the Limousin farmhouse that now hosts Chez Yurt, she knew she'd soon be kissing goodbye to dear old Blighty. Secluded in a small hamlet in the Haute-Vienne department of the French south-west, this bewitchingly idyllic glampsite is tailormade for a blissfully fuss-free vacation.

The yurt itself – varnished wooden flooring, vibrant, ornately-painted woodwork, latticed walls – seamlessly marries luxury with authenticity. It's well-insulated, bright and airy – cool in the height of summer and cosy during chillier nights. There's also a renovated stone barn ('La Petite Grange') handily fitted with washing facilities, a fully-equipped kitchen and a games room. The cultivated veg patch also bears lots of lovely organic seasonal treats. The air is rich with romance too. Picture the scene; sat beneath an ancient oak, fragrant wildflowers strewn below, the evergreen expanse of the Gartempe Valley before you. If you aren't here on honeymoon, you may well be proposing before you leave.

Venture forth from this herbacious hideaway and you'll soon discover the region's many hidden gems, from the antiques markets and *vide greniers* (car boot sales) of charming Saint-Yrieix-la-Perche to the rolling pastures and tranquil swimming lake at Saint-Mathieu, or the well-preserved 10th-century village of Mortemart.

Cathy really has discovered 'the good life' here

in the French Lake District. Swaying lazily on the hammock, with a post-dinner glass of local *pineau* in hand, you too may well find the call to leave it all behind just a bit too hard to resist.

COOL FACTOR Small-scale yurt glamping with the most amiable of hosts.

WHO'S IN Groups, couples, families, one well-behaved dog (by prior agreement) – yes.

ON SITE One yurt (sleeping 4) with one double bed and 2 singles. There's additional accommodation for 2 in La Petite Grange, plus space for 1 tent pitch. Shower, laundry, children's playground, swimming pool, games room with pool, ping-pong and exercise equipment, trampoline, boules and badminton. Sun terrace. Free Wi-Fi. Campfire permitted (according to season). Bikes available to borrow.

OFF SITE Beautiful, medieval Limoges boasts some stunning Gothic architecture, including the Cathédrale Saint-Étienne de Limoges and the Roman bridge of Saint Martial. For souvenir-hunters, pick up some famous Limoges porcelain – just be sure to have it bubble-wrapped for your journey home. Poitiers, capital of the Vienne region, hosts France's oldest church (the Baptistère Saint-Jean) as well as some stunningly well-preserved Romanesque buildings. There's also a couple of award-winning wildlife experiences nearby, including the thrilling La Planète des Crocodiles (0033 549 918 000).

FOOD & DRINK Cathy offers guests the option of a home-cooked meal twice a week. Best of all, guests can use some of the home-grown produce from Cathy's veg patch. Bussière-Poitevine has a bakery for morning pastries and a butcher's for BBQs back at base. There are plenty of cafés, crêperies and restaurants in the local area, ranging from a simple lakeside pizzeria a few minutes away to the organic gastronomy of Les Orangeries (0033 549 840 707) in Lussac-Les-Châteaux.

GETTING THERE Travelling south from Poitiers, take the N147 towards Bellac, past the signs for Bussière-Poitevine, and turn left onto the C5 heading towards Peytavaud.

OPEN April–October.

THE DAMAGE From £450 per week for 4 people, from £550 per week for 6 people. Short breaks of 3 or 4 nights possible in the low season (from £215).

les quatre saisons

Chignat, nr Bourganeuf, 23250 Soubrebost, Creuse 00 33 5 55 64 23 35 www.les-4-saisons.com

Ah yes, the Four Seasons. Do you mean the global hotel chain? No. The Vivaldi concertos then? No. Er, is it a pizza? No, no, no! Les Quatre Saisons campsite, of course. There's been a campsite here for ages, but it's only in the last nine years, since it was taken over by Andrew and Bernie Carnegie, that it's really taken off. The new owners dug flat pitches into the sloping field and turned one of the barns into a games room and campers' shelter for the occasional spells of inclement weather (ah, so that's why it's called the Four Seasons!).

In making these changes they've produced a great little getaway in the heart of the Creuse region of Limousin. Situated amid rolling hills, Les Quatre Saisons lies just 4km east of the little town of Bourganeuf, which was supposedly founded by the Knights Templar and was one of their favourite French hang-outs. The main camping area is fairly open and fringed with trees but with a couple of hidey-holes if you want to keep out of sight of the neighbours. Off to the side are a couple of smaller, more discreet areas behind the farm buildings for the Howard Hughes and Greta Garbos among you. But if you are happy to show your face, you could do worse than sign up for one of Bernie's evening meals. She's a qualified chef and when the weather's nice will serve up a three-courser on the lawn. Just don't ask for a *quattro stagioni...*

COOL FACTOR Discreet, serene hideaway in the heart of the Creuse region of Limousin.

WHO'S IN Tents, campervans, caravans, dogs (for a fee and notified in advance) – yes. Large motorhomes – no (they get stuck on the steep drive).

ON SITE 25 level pitches (all with electricity) on 5 acres of meadow, with a special area in July and August for quiet camping. There's 1 central facilities block with 3 showers, 3 toilets and 1 disabled toilet and shower. There's also a washing machine (€4), a barn for shelter, table tennis, fridges for campers' use, grazing for donkeys and free Wi-Fi.

OFF SITE The site's on the GR4 walking trail and there are over 150km of trails around the region. There's also horseriding, biking and fishing and slightly further afield the huge Lac de Vassivière; which is one of France's top water sports venues.

FOOD & DRINK Evening meals are available on site at €25 per person for 3 courses, wine €6 a bottle. Homemade bread and croissants in the morning (order the night before). The nearest places off site are in Bourganeuf, where there are 2 small brasseries in the square opposite the church: Le Central (0033 555 640 567) and La Mezzanine (0033 555 643 117), which both serve standard French fare.

GETTING THERE From the N145 between Guéret and La Souterraine, take the D912 for Bourganeuf. At the roundabout in Bourganeuf follow the D8 towards the Lac de Vassivière. After 3.5km turn left on to the D37. From here follow the blue campsite signs that will lead you all the way to the entrance.

OPEN Officially April–September, but by arrangement you can probably stay any time.

THE DAMAGE Pitch €8; plus €4 per person, children up to 6 yrs €2. Electricity €4. Dogs €2.

le monteil revolution

Le Monteil Revolution, Le Monteil, 23250 Sardent, Creuse, France 00 33 5 55 54 93 24 www.lemonteilrevolution.com

The thick forests around Creuse, a department in the very centre of France, were once awash with the country's native wolf population. European greys dotted the woodland here until as late as 1937 and, in the last decade, have been re-introduced – albeit in the fenced safety of Chabrières forest. The same forest once spread all the way south, in a vast green rug across the region, encircling the tiny hamlet of Le Monteil. While the trees are fewer in number now than the days when wolves roamed free, the place is still blessed with a magical closeness to nature. Deer, owls and badgers thread their way among the woods at night, while flora and fungi abound.

Set on the fringe of the woods, a 15-minute drive from the wolves of Chabrières, Le Monteil Revolution is a site that seems to boast as much history as the trees themselves. Built during the midst of the French Revolution in 1792 (hence the campsite name) the farm cottage that owners Charley Tysler and Calum O'Connor are currently restoring wears the date, imprinted on a section of chunky stonewall, like a badge of pride. It has withstood the test of time, even through its more worn and crumbling years.

Just as the wolves have been re-introduced in Chabrières, Charley and Calum are re-introducing life to this old dwelling and, since early 2016, have been restoring not just the cottage but the land around it too. The eight acre smallholding today plays host to two luxurious glamping domes, kitted inside with king-sized beds, wood-burning stoves and enough bedding to keep you snug and warm whatever the weather. Semi-circular bay windows in the dome-sides allow you to look out into the trees and keep watch for wildlife of the non-wolf kind, while within, battery and solar powered lighting adds some extra function to the off-grid setup.

Explore the campsite and you quickly find extra treats. In particular, the Japanese-style bath among the trees surrounded by rocks and with a superb view out across the valley. The hot, clean water is completely chemical-free and you can sit and wallow in the warmth to your hearts content (or at least until your fingers turn to wrinkled prunes). The tiny pool is wood-fired and only a short walk from the domes. It's not the sole bathing spot though, as each dome has its own private bathroom facility with hot showers, but it is the spot with the best views. It's difficult to leave.

Elsewhere around the smallholding, pigs nuzzle among roots and geese waddle around the driveway. There are also chickens that supply the daily eggs and the owner's have a small honesty shop allowing you to buy their fresh fruit and vegetables when in season. On hand to give any advice on the area or lend you maps if needed, Charley and Calum are also keen cyclists and plans are already afoot to offer two-wheeled holiday packages to guests in the coming seasons. For now they make do with recommending the local footpaths, with routes starting right from the campsite entrance. Take some sturdy shoes and binoculars for the wildlife. Oh, and keep your eyes peeled for those wolves!

COOL FACTOR An ancient home and a modern glampsite, with space to unplug and a laid-back ambience.

WHO'S IN Glamping only. Tents, campervans, pets – no.

ON SITE Two geo-domes, sleeping up to 2 adults and 2 children. Each has a wood-burning stove, beds (bedding and linen provided) and a private bathroom with a shower, sink, toiletries, hair-dryer and sockets. Washing machine, dryer and a covered outside hanging space. Wood-fired outdoor bath in the forest. Free Wi-Fi. Access to a fully-equipped kitchen. Chickens, geese and pigs on the smallholding – guests can be 'hands on' if they wish. Individual campfires not permitted but there is a communal fire pit by the kitchen area.

OFF SITE There are several great walks from the doorstep (maps available on request), or head a little further to the Monts de Gueret for the best forest routes, as well as the opportunity to try mountain biking or horseriding. If you really want to stretch your legs, you can go get lost inside the world's biggest hedge maze, the Labyrinthe Geant (0033 442 221 915), a 10-minute drive away. You could be stuck in there for hours. It's just 15 minutes to the Loups de Chabrieres (0033 555 812 323), the 32-acre public wildlife park where the wolves are found.

FOOD & DRINK Homegrown produce from the farm is available to buy (seasonal), including fruit, veg and meat. Restaurant Influence (0033 555 819 832) is a 7-minute drive away and the campsite even offers a taxi service for guests who would like to sample the wine menu!

GETTING THERE From Gueret follow signs to the Loup de Chabrieres on the D940. Continue on this road and, after 8km, you will see a sign on the right for the D940A Chapelle-Taillefert. Follow this for 10km until you reach Coeurgne and crest the hill. Turn right at the sign for Le Monteil. Drive for 700m, then turning left following the signs to Le Monteil. Pass a barn on the left and house on the right, Le Monteil Revolution is signposted on the left after these.

OPEN All year.

THE DAMAGE From €550–€700 per week per dome. Long weekend and other duration rates available on request.

domaine la mathonière

03350 Louroux-Bourbonnais, Allier 00 33 4 70 07 23 06 www.lamathoniere.nl

Don't you just hate it when you turn up at a campsite and the owner whips out a red marker pen and a site map of numbered pitches and plonks a big fat cross on No.127? It's usually way down the far end, between the fence and the bins and with a long, desperate walk if nature calls. It's really not what you want. How much nicer when instead a campsite owner stands in front of a green field, opens his arms out wide and says 'Anywhere you like. Just don't scare the donkeys.'

Thankfully that's more the kind of welcome you'll find at Domaine La Mathonière, a campsite set amid the forests and lakes in the heartland of the old Dukes of Bourbon. Behind the fine old rustic farmhouse there's an expanse of green field, broken up here and there with the odd hedge and tree, but essentially an open area where you can pick a pitch to suit your mood. There's a large tree in the middle, which provides a heap of shade, and there's a large (heated) swimming pool too. Elsewhere, closer to the farmhouse, there's a great little café-cum-bar with a sheltered seating area. Here you can enjoy a café au lait or something stronger if you prefer, while the owners can cook a three-course *table d'hôte* meal for you. Once a week they also organise a fabulous BBQ for every camper on the campsite.

It's a tried-and-trusted French formula. A few old farm buildings converted into a lovely owners' home, some *gîte* accommodation, an open field for the camping and the cooking of communal meals.

No worries if you'd rather do your own thing, but it's good to meet the neighbours. There's also another common feature of these kinds of places: large, luxury safari tents with an en suite bathroom inside and views to die for. If you want something more basic, you can book a large bell tent instead. Closer in style to camping but still allowing you to travel light.

This may all make Mathonière sound a little formulaic, but honestly, it's not. It's a simple, wholesome, unpretentious place – brilliant for kids to run wild but with enough space to stretch out if you don't want to be pestered.

The region around is dotted with forests and copses and has loads of interesting old towns and villages to explore. While it is possible to get to places on foot, by bike, or by donkey, the farther-flung destinations are really only accessible by car. There's a lake with sandy beach in the vicinity and loads of forest trails that are great either on foot or by bike. Just don't get lost. Perhaps it's best to lay a trail of breadcrumbs behind you and hope that you manage to find your way back before the birds eat them. Because you'll want to find your way back to La Mathonière, and probably more than once. It may be based on a simple formula, but then all the best formulae are simple. Like E=mc2. At least in theory. But then, making things look effortless is often the hardest trick in the book. And you really don't need to be Einstein to figure that out.

COOL FACTOR Middle-of-nowhere peace and quiet and a great safe haven for the kids.

WHO'S IN Tents, campervans, caravans, dogs – yes.

ON SITE In addition to the usual facilities of hot showers, WCs, and washing facilities, there's a great little café-cum-bar with a sheltered outdoor seating area, where communal meals are served and where you can sit and play some of the games available, from chess to board games. Next to this is the lounge area with free Wi-Fi. Then there are the animals, the pool, and a large kids' playground to keep the little ones happy. And if none of that works, the site is big and secluded enough just to let the kids run amok on their own.

OFF SITE Where to start? There are some great little towns and villages in the vicinity, such as Hérisson and Bourbon L'Archambault. In the former, there's a wonderful ruined 14th-century castle with a crumbling keep. For something a little more adventurous head to the Plan d'Eau de Vieure, a T-shaped lake just north of Vieure that boasts a small section of sandy beach and also offers kayaks, canoes, and pedalos for hire. In the opposite direction is the 27,182-acre Forêt de Tronçais – so old that Julius Caesar is said to have passed through it. Today it contains oaks that are hundreds of years old.

FOOD & DRINK If you don't fancy partaking of the onsite *table d'hôte* meals or the BBQ, head into Cosne-d'Allier where you'll find a large Carrefour supermarket with everything you need to cater for yourselves. Unfortunately the town's not that hot on restaurants or bars. For those you're better off going the extra miles to Montluçon or Moulins, where there's a much better choice.

GETTING THERE The site is off the D16 north of Cosne-d'Allier. Come off the D16 on the eastbound D251 and go through Louroux-Bourbonnais, keeping left and then heading along the D57 for Theneuille. About 2km beyond the village, turn left at the crossroads. There's a small sign for the site, but if you're heading south you can't see it. Follow the road up the hill and the site is on your right. Parking is past the house. If you go to the Mathonière website there's also a handy link to Google Maps with a pin right on the site.

OPEN May–October.

THE DAMAGE Adults €7–€10; children (up to 13 yrs) €4–€6. Dogs €2. Hook-up €4. Gîtes per week (starting saturdays) €345–€515 and safari lodge tents €250–€925. Large bell tents (max 4 pers.) €265–€475.

domaine les gandins

1 allée des Gandins, 03140 St-Germain-de-Salles, Allier 00 33 4 70 56 80 75 www.domainelesgandins.com

Un gandin, you may or may not know, is a dandy or aristo – the kind of guy who lost his head to the guillotine when the French Revolution rolled into town. There were loads of them who lived lives of quiet luxury on little estates, just like this one, until the Revolution came along and recommended that that kind of thing ought to come to a stop.

The estates, of course, remained, even though their owners went the way of Louis XVI and Marie Antoinette. Of course, once the dust had settled and the cobbles had been hosed down, most of them eventually found their way back into the hands of a new aristocracy, as is the way with so many revolutions, but thankfully some are now hotels, B&Bs, gîtes and campsites, open to everyone, including the *sans coulottes*.

Of all the domaine-style campsites in France, this one, at Domaine les Gandins, is surely the dandiest of the lot. A magnificent house, dating back to long before the Revolution, sits at the centre of a glorious little estate comprising various gîtes (including one in a converted pigeon loft), a stretch of sleepy river, a fantastic treehouse and – this is where you come in – a spacious and leafy camping field.

The main house, with its red-tiled roof and deep-green shutters, is postcard-perfect, and the grounds are all immaculately kept by the friendly French family who own and run the site. With all its attendant facilities, Domaine les Gandins is really something of a one-stop-shop of a campsite, so much so that you might be forgiven for pitching your tent one day and staying for a whole week without ever venturing beyond the confines of the site.

For a start, the river of La Sioule is a minute's stroll through the meadow behind the complex of buildings and past the treehouse. It's not the raciest of rivers, so it's perfect for a paddle or just for cooling off on a hot summer's day, and there are plenty of shady places in which to lounge around and listen to the birds or the gentle sound of the water. That's assuming you can block out the sound of the kids splashing about. Then there's the busy kitchen, which is at the heart of the site and always seems to have steam and smells emanating from inside. Whether you just want a morning cuppa to go with your croissant or fancy taking part in the communal *table d'hôte* meal in the evening, you'll find that the kitchen is the social hub around which everything else revolves.

If you do venture off the site while you're here you could do worse than head down to Vichy, the sulphurous old spa town that gained notoriety during the Second World War when it became the seat of Marshal Pétain's government. It's now just a thermal spa town next to the wide Allier River, where folk come to take the waters in search of a cure for rheumatism or gout, or just to stroll through the leafy riverside parks. You could, however, just take the waters at the campsite. It might not have the same kind of sulphurous healing powers, but the peace and tranquillity will surely have much the same restorative effect.

COOL FACTOR Really dandy camping in upper-class surroundings by a sleepy river.

WHO'S IN Tents, campervans, caravans, groups, dogs – yes.

ON SITE 35 grassy camping pitches. There's 1 large chalet-style block tucked off to the side of the site, with a row of toilets, showers and laundry facilities. There's a great treehouse between the estate and the river, and down at the riverbank there's a communal firepit and some wooden furniture for lazing about. BBQs permitted off the ground.

OFF SITE The site is rather out in the boonies, and the nearest town of any note is Vichy, which is worth a visit if you're a fan of thermal waters. Otherwise, if you're looking for inspiration, you could do worse than check out Les Gandins' website, where you'll find suggestions of things to do in the local area listed under 24, yep 24, separate headings, ranging from parachuting and where to browse the best bric-a-brac shops, to thermal bathing in Vichy and bike hire. It's an impressive list – it even has a volcano – so if you can't find something useful to do with yourself after browsing that, then take a walk along the river and give yourself a stern talking to.

FOOD & DRINK You can pick up bread from the van that visits the site and there are coffees and ice creams available from the kitchen during the day. Or why not treat yourself to a 4-course *table d'hôte* meal in the evenings (€26 for adults, including wine and coffee). For a real treat, head into Vichy to Maison Decoret (0033 470 976 506); a kind of French-fusion restaurant with set menus from €40 and up to €165 for a multi-course meal with selected wines for each course.

GETTING THERE Midway between Gannat and St-Pourçain-sur-Sioule on the N7/D2009, turn left on to the D36 heading for Étrousset. Just over the bridge, turn left at the red and white houses; follow the road straight and over the old railway track and the site entrance is on your left.

OPEN Late April–early October.

THE DAMAGE Pitch €6–€10; adults €5–€8, children (up to 9 yrs) €4–5. Pets €7.50. Electricity €4.60.

cosycamp

Les Ribes, 43800 Chamalières-sur-Loire, Haute-Loire   0033 471 03 91 12   www.cosycamp.com

Picture the scene; a French summer's evening at dusk, the heady scent of wild herbs and flowers lingering in the soothing air, a glass of chilled Chenin blanc in hand and the gentle lapping of the nearby river soundtracking this idyllic scene. Throw into this picture an array of quirky accommodation options alongside plenty of pitches for traditional tent camping and you have one seriously super, luxury campsite.

Opened in May 2013, CosyCamp has already become one of the Loire Valley's best eco-sites. Occupying an enviable riverside location in the picturesque village of Chamalières-sur-Loire, this is a place positively charged with history – the most evident example being the 12th-century Roman church. Surrounding the peaceful villages which adorn the lush valley floor are highland plateaus and rocky gorges which attract no end of walkers and enthusiasts of all things outdoors. You can hike, bike, trek or climb your way around

this unspoiled, under explored region of Central France. Ask on site for routes and rental prices.

With safari and Canadian tents, gypsy caravans and treehouses to choose from, it really doesn't matter where you decide to lay your head. The main draw, however, is still the wonderful riverside surroundings and the more back-to-basics atmosphere of the place. Campfires on the terrace draw families together every evening – inevitably culminating in a mountain of molten marshmallows – while the 'no-vehicles in the camping area' rule means little ones are safe to run wild without much supervision. It's just another little sign that your considerate hosts have designed the site with relaxation in mind. From the various gardens (flower, vegetable, orchard, botanical garden, labyrinth, even a 'garden of fragrances'), to the onsite bird sanctuaries and wellness centre, a stay at CosyCamp will definitely recharge the batteries.

COOL FACTOR Real riverside camping and glamping on the banks of the beautiful and historic Loire.

WHO'S IN Tents, caravans, vaccinated pets, large groups – yes.

ON SITE 63 camping pitches, 1 gypsy caravan, 2 treehouses, 10 safari lodges, 10 Canadian tents and 5 cottages. 2 shower/toilet blocks (one heated during the cooler seasons). Laundry and baby-changing facilities. Electrical hook-ups. Indoor swimming pool, heated outdoor pool and a paddling pool. Fishing equipment can be rented onsite. Campfires in designated area in the evening.

OFF SITE The picturesque village of Chamalières-sur-Loire and its Roman 12th-century church are well worth a visit. Besides the countless river-based activities to whet your whistle, the region is also brimming with lots of other outdoor pursuits. There's a rock-climbing site in Chamalières-sur-Loire itself while for the more intrepid, the Via Ferrata des Juscles in Pertuis is 19km from the site. Les Ravins de Corboeuf, known as 'Le Petit Colorado de l'Auvergne', is a geological curiosity of coloured clays. There's also a leisure park in Neyrial, Yssingeaux, (17km away) with quad bikes, trampolines, mini-golf and archery amongst other activities. There's also the remarkable town and cathedral of Le Puy-en-Velay, a UNESCO World Heritage site, which is also well worth a visit.

FOOD & DRINK An onsite snack bar serves up simple, local dishes, using organic and fairtrade products whenever possible. There's also a daily specials menu dinner and the likes of 'pancake family party', plus burgers from the grill. Special breakfasts and picnics can be arranged by request. There are many local markets during the day and in the evening in the summer. Chamalières-sur-Loire boasts 3 decent bars and restaurants, while Le Puy-en-Velay has numerous places to eat and drink.

GETTING THERE Follow the N88 beetween Saint Etienne and Le Puy and exit at Bas-en-Basset. Follow the 'road of the river Loire' up to Retournac, then cross the bridge and turn right to Chamalières-sur-Loire.

PUBLIC TRANSPORT Chamalières-sur-Loire train station is just 300m from the campsite.

OPEN Start of March–early October.

THE DAMAGE Basic tent pitch + 2 people €15.50–€27; extra adult €3–4, extra child (3–6yrs) €2–€3. Pets €3. For comfort pitches and glamping units see the website for details.

auvergne naturelle

Le Cros, 43440 Laval-sur-Doulon, Haute-Loire 00 33 4 71 76 38 53 www.yurtholidaysfrance.co.uk

Deep in the heart of the protected Parc Naturel Régional Livradois Forez, hidden from view up the pine-clad slopes of Laval-sur-Doulon, Camping Auvergne Naturelle is earthy and magical. The sound of the babbling brook at the bottom of the wildflower meadow here conspires with birdsong and wind chimes to create a symphony of peace.

Imagine, if you can, leaving the majesty of your Genghis Khan yurt in the brilliant-blue dawn to gaze down the valley, birds of prey circling overhead. This campsite is truly off the beaten track, and, with its alpine feel, the area reminds you more of Switzerland than France. A campfire burns throughout the night, inviting story-telling and bread-making for nocturnal kids, plus the chance for you to get to know your fellow guests. That's easily done, for although the site has its own forest and is anything but small, the facilities themselves are all within close proximity. They include a funky wood shower block, which has been designed to maximise the mountain view. While soaping yourself down, you can look out of the open-slat shower on to the woods beyond.

The days stretch out lazily here. After your morning croissant and *café au lait*, you can head off to explore the forest and surrounding meadows for the lengendary Beast of Gévaudan, or simply put your feet up and watch the littl'uns run wild. Children, in particular, love it here, perhaps because the owners have laid on as many child-friendly enchantments as possible. For a start there are child-only trails; one leading into a little glade strung with bells, hammock and fairies. Kids especially enjoy whittling their own walking sticks in the morning bushcraft sessions and learning how to build the perfect fire. Adults who feel those wildman genes stirring can explore their inner bushman too. There are courses for all age groups, along with a few more colourful pastimes – from yoga to axe-throwing.

The yurts themselves, of which there are four, have been subtly positioned to create maximum privacy and give you the finest views. Inside they look like a summer shoot from an edition of *Homes & Gardens*, with cream throws, wood floors, fresh wildflowers and rustic furniture. A communal barn, charmingly tumbledown, is decked with fairy lights, candles and a huge beamed ceiling, with a self-catering kitchen at one end. Combined with the long dining table, it gives the impression of a Viking longhouse. The space also doubles as a playroom for kids on rainy days – there are creative materials and stacks of board games in the corner.

Another favourite aspect of the place, apart from the comfy yurts, killer views and soporific pace of life, is the owners – Rob and Kathryn, from Manchester, who make for perfect hosts. He's a joiner who also studied bushcraft under Ray Mears, while Kathryn turns her eye for detail to the interiors of the yurts and is also a great cook. Her continental breakfasts are an ideal way to start the day, however late you lie in.

All in all, Camping Auvergne Naturelle is intimate, amazing value for money, and destined to become one of the best sites in France for making your great escape to.

COOL FACTOR Natural heaven. This is one of the most relaxing and beautifully isolated campsites in central France.

WHO'S IN Glamping only. No tents, campervans, caravans or pets.

ON SITE Four yurts. Each has solar-powered lighting and a luxury en suite toilet plus a washbasin outside. The yurts are also family-friendly, with 2 extra camp beds per yurt for the kids. Campfires are tended by Rob, who, according to his dad, has been building fires ever since he was little. The shower block is simple but sparkling clean, and perfectly located just a short walk from your yurt, close to the communal barn. Each yurt is allotted its own personal hot shower. For babies there's ample room for nappy-changing in the yurts. Other facilities include a self-catering kitchen, fridge, fairy trail, swings, wild meadow and 20 acres of woodland to lose yourself in. Morning bushcraft courses are available (adults €20 and kids under 12 years €10).

OFF SITE Donkey walks and horseriding can be organised. There are markets in Brioude every Saturday morning (8am–1pm). The magnificent countryside is begging for you to hire a mountain bike from Oléon Motoculture, Brioude (0033 471 501 007) and ride around like the Von Trapps. Half-an-hour up the mountain, La Chaise Dieu is famed for its beautiful abbey and bijou antique shops, cafés, and restaurants. A world-famous classical music festival takes place here in August. It's also just a 30-minute drive to the River Allier – a fabulous place for canoeing and arguably even better than the renowned Ardèche given how quiet it is even in peak season. An hour-and-a-half away are 80-odd dormant volcanoes, the most dramatic of which is Puy de Dôme, a mecca for hiking and paragliding.

FOOD & DRINK Kathryn makes homely grub three times per week including dishes like boeuf bourguignon, chicken chasseur and sausage and mash local-style. Dinner costs €16 and includes delicious homemade desserts like tarte-aux-pommes. For supplies there's a supermarket in nearby Brioude (half-an-hour away). If you fancy exploring the local area for foodie delights try Auberge de Chassignolles, a 20-minute drive, which serves excellent authentic Auvergne cuisine.

GETTING THERE Get off the A75 at Junction 20 and head for Brioude, from where the D588 wiggles to Laval-sur-Doulon. Keep following the signs for La Chaise Dieu, and in Laval-sur-Doulon take the D562 towards St-Didier-sur-Doulon; the campsite is located approx 1km along this road.

OPEN Mid May–end of September.

THE DAMAGE Prices per yurt per night based on 2 people sharing: 1–2 nights from €110 per night; 3–6 nights from €90 per night; 7+ nights from €80 per night. Extra €10 supplement per child, per night.

camping terre ferme

386 Chemin des Baisses, Le Petit Condal 71480 Condal, Saone-et-Loire 00 33 3 85 76 62 57 www.terreferme.eu

The owners of Terre Ferme, Matthijs and Renske Witmans (yep, they're Dutch), bought this place years ago while they were still living in the Netherlands, and over years of long-distance commuting have slowly and painstakingly turned what was an old maize farm into a new and stunning campsite.

They restored the magnificent long farmhouse and designed and built a facilities block in the local rustic style. Eventually, a few years back, the place was finally ready to make the big move south and it was 'so-long Holland' and '*bonjour La France*'. Now that all the works are complete Matthijs and Renske can sit back and admire what they've achieved, which is a really charming little *aire naturelle* campsite.

Terre Ferme is situated in Le Petit Condal, a tiny *hameau* in rural Burgundy that is as small as the name implies. Condal itself is pretty small, but this place is so tiny that it hardly features on the map at all. Mind you, the property here covers 17 acres, of which some has been cleared to make the camping field, some penned off to keep donkeys, sheep and chickens and others left as natural woodland and a spring-fed pond. The two-and-a-half-acre camping field has only 20 pitches and cars are kept off the grass, so you can imagine how much space there is to stretch out. If you don't fancy sticking up canvas yourself you can always hire a pre-erected safari-style tent in the field. This sleeps four and has its own cooking facilities and fridge. Or there's a compact wooden chalet, which sleeps four in a double bed and two bunks set off to the side behind the facilities block.

Most of the immediate area is given over to maize farming, and the quiet back roads are a maze, too – perfect for idling around on a bike. These are available to hire from the farmhouse, including a tandem. This is also the *terroir* which breeds the famous *poulet de Bresse*, the most famous chicken in the world. These beauties are reared outdoors on small, dedicated farms and are protected by the same kind of *Appellation d'Origine Controllée* that governs the production of wine. They don't come cheap, but let's face it, half the reason you come to France is for the food and drink (the other half's probably a combination of the weather and the scenery), so it's worth giving one of these especially edible chooks a spin around the rotisserie. They are to your standard cellophane-wrapped supermarket chicken on its little plastic tray what a filet mignon is to a burger. And much the same can be said for the delicious little site at Terre Ferme, which is certainly a class apart.

COOL FACTOR A blissfully quiet rural hideaway – all a convenient couple of miles from the motorway.

WHO'S IN Tents, campervans, caravans, dogs (for a fee) – yes.

ON SITE 20 pitches, all with electricity available. 1 facilities block, built in the local rustic style, with showers and toilets (both unisex) and a urinal tucked round the back for the chaps. Washing-up sinks, a washing machine (€4.50) and a terrace with tables and chairs. A minute's stroll down the hill from the main camping field is a quiet spring-fed pond surrounded by trees and there are various domesticated animals to pet.

OFF SITE This is a fairly remote farming area but that's the attraction. You can hire bicycles from the site at €9 per day. If you can make it that far (10km) it's worth visiting St-Amour, a little town of narrow, colourful streets, ivy-clad houses and an impressive old church.

FOOD & DRINK There are various facilities (fridge, coffee-maker, for example) on the terrace, and all kinds of goodies on sale from the farmhouse, along with wine and beer, and you can order up fresh bread for the morning if you ask the night before. The bread oven is also used on Wednesday evenings, when campers can make their own pizzas, and an old Citroen campervan is currently being transformed into a chip van. In Varennes there's a bakery and butcher and a small Proxi supermarket, plus a decent little restaurant, Le St-Saveur (0033 385 746 559), specialising in local grub.

GETTING THERE Come off the A39 autoroute at exit 10, between Lons-le-Saunier and Bourge-en-Bresse, and, just after the péage booths, take the first right at the roundabout. Follow the road towards Petit Condal. Just before the village turn left – the campsite is a few hundred metres on your left.

PUBLIC TRANSPORT The closest public transport hub is the railway station at St-Amour. You can arrange for the campsite owners to pick you up from here.

OPEN May–October.

THE DAMAGE Pitch €4–€6, plus €4.70 per person over 6 years. Dogs €1. Safari tent €260–€295 per week. Wooden chalet €100 for 2 nights or €325–€395 per week.

huttopia plage blanche

3, rue de la Plage, 39380 Ounans, Jura 00 33 3 84 37 69 63 www.huttopia.com

You don't have to be a good swimmer to have a good time at Huttopia La Plage Blanche, but water-loving campers will get the most out of this well-equipped campsite on the banks of the Loue. Stretched along the river's edge, the grassy tent pitches here have easy access right down to where the languid waters flow – safe, slow and thoroughly refreshing. If you don't like the thought of the soft, silted riverbed oozing between your toes then you can retreat to the onsite swimming pool or the bubbling L-shaped Jacuzzi. Sounds like a tough life, eh?

Indeed, with 188 camping pitches, Huttopia La Plage Blanche is not the sort of site that does things by halves, and it certainly doesn't fall into the 'small and intimate category'. Yet what it does offer is facilities by the bucketload, along with a surprising ability, despite its scale, to retain a personable feel. It has all the essentials of any self-respecting French campsite – fresh baguettes and croissants in the morning, bottles of the local wine in the campsite bar and a boules court where the fiercest of family duels take place – while its riverside location means the best pitches have a great sense of space, with the open river on one side.

Offsite, the best bet is to bring a bike (or rent one from reception) and head across country towards the beautiful village of Dole, built up around the banks of another river – the Doubs – and partly populated in the summer by hordes of tourists who chug through in their narrow boats. Perhaps the main highlight of the place is some of

its tiny restaurants and bars (including an excellent converted space around the old water mill). It's also the birthplace of Louis Pasteur, and the small museum inside his old family home offers a fascinating insight into his monumental legacy to the world of science.

Further afield, dramatic Besançon to the north-east is a must-visit. Located on the inside of a remarkable tight meander in the river, it seems to denote a shift in geology where France becomes mountainous and forested. The hilltop citadelle and the town centre's haughty cathedral are particular highlights, although walking up to the former can be tough on the legs – particularly after all that swimming.

COOL FACTOR Riverside camping with space and facilities for kids to go wild.

WHO'S IN Tents, campervans, motorhomes, caravans, families, groups, couples, pets... everyone!

ON SITE 188 camping pitches and 20 pre-pitched wood and canvas tents. 3 washroom blocks (toilets, sinks, and hot showers), 2 of which have disabled access and 1 with baby facilities. There is a small indoor swimming pool and a much larger outdoor one, plus a paddling pool for younger children and, of course, the river itself. There's a playground, boules court, table tennis, table football, volleyball, basketball and bikes available for hire. The central lodge has internet and free Wi-Fi, there's a shop for essentials, a library and tourist information in reception. Activities for children are also organised during school holidays.

OFF SITE At the campsite entrance there is an excellent activity centre (0033 384 377 204) offering high-wire tree trails and a zip-wire from one side of the river to the other. The centre is also where you hire a canoe or kayak to paddle down the Loue for the day and get picked up later. You can also hire mountain bikes for exploring the Val d'Amour and Chaux forest. Further afield, it's 20km to the pretty town of Dole – a great place to go for evening drinks and a meal.

FOOD & DRINK The campsite has a bar-restaurant that overlooks the river and pizzas available from a stone oven. Traditional fresh bread and pastries are available every morning, if ordered the evening before.

GETTING THERE From Dijon, follow the A39 towards Dole and take the first junction after the airport onto the D905. At the first roundabout turn right, then continue on the D905, bearing right after 1km. At the next roundabout take the first exit onto the D472 and follow it to the village of Ounans. In the village turn left on the D71; the campsite is on your left.

OPEN Late April–mid September.

THE DAMAGE Pitch + 2 people from €15 per night; additional adults €5.50–€5.70; children under 2 years free, children 2–7 years free in low season, €4.20 high season. Electricity €4.30. Pets €2.30–€4. Glamping from €41 a night.

camping divonne les bains

Quartier Villard, 2465 Vie de L'Etraz, 01220 Divonne-les-Bains, Ain 0033 4 50 20 01 95 www.huttopia.com

There's an irony to all the facilities at Camping Divonne Les Bains, situated right on the Swiss-French border. Set on the edge of a thick forest that tumbles down one of the highest mountains in the Jura range – La Dôle – it has a magnetic location for all outdoorsy types. Yet, geared to accommodate families too, there's a complete spectrum of onsite options: a heated swimming pool and volleyball, tennis and pétanque courts, which can leave you wondering why they have created such elaborate onsite activities when the continent's natural playground is right there on your doorstep?

The campsite is certainly large, with almost 200 different pitches massed among the trees, but each spot still retains its own privacy, and multiple wash blocks mean you'll never have too far to walk to spend a penny. With so much on offer, the campsite has a diverse mix of guests: backpackers, rock climbers and mountain bikers, along with family groups, lounging by the poolside or warming up on the tennis court. But it's away from your pinecone-scattered pitch that the real benefits of this campsite are found, with trails leading right from the entrance into the trees and up the angular sides of La Dôle – summit 1677m. If you're feeling lazy, you can drive into Switzerland and up the paved road in Gingins to Chalet de la Dôle just below the peak. From the top, you can see the Alps to the East, while Lake Geneva spreads below – where you can also spend your days, boating, bathing and generally having a ball.

COOL FACTOR Camping at the foot of the Jura mountains with Lake Geneva on the doorstep.

WHO'S IN Tents, campervans, caravans, groups, dogs – yes.

ON SITE 181 camping pitches and 80 glamping units (wood and canvas tents and chalets). A heated outdoor pool with surrounding decking and a snack bar and pizzeria during peak season. Reception lodge with Wi-Fi, a small shop, library, board games and tourist info. Playground, tennis court, boules pitch, table tennis, table football, volleyball court and bike hire.

OFF SITE The nearby adventure course (0033 676 642 031) in the trees of Divonne is a great spot for children, while the Château Voltaire (0033 450 405 321), 17km away in Ferney-Voltaire, is best for a little culture. The Swiss border is just moments away in the car and it's a short drive to the shore of Lake Geneva.

FOOD & DRINK The onsite bar-restaurant serves homemade pizzas along with other snacks and drinks. It's only open over the May public holidays and through July and August but there are plenty of good eateries in Divonne-les-Bains.

GETTING THERE From Dijon follow the A39 south, leaving it 30km south of Dole and following sings to Poligny where you join the N5. Follow this for 50km, and 10km after Morez, in Cure, continue onto the D105. Continue on the D105 to Gex (around 30km). Follow the main street through town and out past the intermarche supermarket; after 4km look for the camping signposts.

OPEN April–October.

THE DAMAGE Pitch and 2 people from €14.50 per night. Additional adults €3.70–€6.20, children (2–7 yrs) free in low season, €5 in high season. Electricity €4.30. Dogs €2.20–€4.50. Glamping accommodation from €41 per night.

camping les dômes de miage

197 Route des Contamines, Saint-Gervais-les-Bains 74170, Haute-Savoie 00 33 4 50 93 45 96 www.camping-mont-blanc.com

There are not many campsites out there that can rival this one for views. Elevated 900m high in the Haute-Savoie region of the French south-east, Camping Les Dômes de Miage boasts unparalleled, truly breathtaking vistas of the mighty Mont Blanc and the spectacular surrounding Rhône-Alpes.

Managed and maintained by charming multi-lingual hosts Stéphane and Sophie, this Alpine Eden is a veritable institution. It's been welcoming campers for more than 50 years (that's three generations), and doesn't go for the bells and whistles ('no noisy swimming pools, no static-caravans... no animation programs' – whatever they may be!) and why would it need to with a setting like this?

It's a site of happy contrasts – sprawling yet remote; wild yet well-managed. Kids can ride their bikes with abandon, unencumbered by the tents and caravans occupying the spacious, shady (if you prefer) pitches which sit along the site's wooded fringes. Facilities are first-rate, free and open 24/7 (with the shop and reception open till 8.30pm). Unlike many of the purpose-built ski resorts round these parts, Saint-Gervais-les-Bains also has a uniquely authentic Savoyard heritage and charm. And then there's the view: the sublime mountainscape that launched a thousand brush strokes and stanzas of Romantic verse. A campsite on the roof of Europe? We think that's a height worth scaling...

COOL FACTOR Breathtaking views of Europe's highest peak.

WHO'S IN Tents, campervans, caravans, dogs (on a lead) – yes.

ON SITE 150 pitches, 100 with electricity. 2 facilities blocks, with showers, baby-changing room, disabled facilities, washing machines and dryers. Chemical waste disposal. 2 play areas, basketball area, volleyball area, table tennis, TV room, library. Free Wi-Fi. Small shop. Free ice for cool-boxes.

OFF SITE Mont Blanc literally looms over everything. Hop on the Mont Blanc Tramway (0033 450 532 275) from Saint-Gervais-les-Bains-Le Fayet station to savour the views from Nid d'Aigle (2380m elevation), in front of the Bionnassay glacier. Nearby Saint-Gervais-les-Bains has an ice rink (0033 450 935 002) and leisure centre with swimming pools, tennis courts and crazy golf. There's also a market every Thursday.

FOOD & DRINK The onsite shop sells bread, wine, snacks and other basics and there's a supermarket around 7km away. There's also the Hotel Restaurant les Dômes de Miage (0033 450 935 562) a stone's throw from the site entrance.

GETTING THERE Follow the A40 and take exit 21 in the direction of Le Fayet, and then Saint Gervais. In Saint Gervais, follow the D902 in the direction of Les Contamines. The campsite is 2km down here on the left.

PUBLIC TRANSPORT There's a bus stop at the campsite entrance and the free St-Gervais shuttle during the high season. The Tramway du Mont-Blanc station is 2.5km away, while the TGV railway station is just 5.5km away.

OPEN Mid May–mid September.

THE DAMAGE A tent and 2 people €21.20–€26.60, caravan with hook-up €25.80–€31.20. Extra people €4–€6.20. Children (under 10 years) €2.90–€4.80. Dogs €2.

ferme noemie

Les Sables, 38520 Bourg d'Oisans, Isere 00 33 4 76 11 06 14 www.fermenoemie.com

Mention Bourg d'Oisans and most travellers will think of Alpe d'Huez, the world-famous ski resort that sits 21 hairpins above the bustling town. Advanced cyclists are likely to froth with excitement; they view these mountain bends the same way that Catholics view Lourdes, harbouring lifelong desires to visit. It's not for the actively-challenged, however: the climb is steep and it can take three hours to pedal to the top (under an hour for the pros), but once there you can buy a certificate testifying that you've conquered what was the first Alpine climb introduced to the Tour de France, in 1911.

Alpe d'Huez may also boast the longest black ski run in the world, the 16km 'La Sarenne', but as thrilling as the snow-covered mountain range is, summers here are truly special. Regardless of whether cycling is your bag or not, time spent sprawled on the lawns of Bourg d'Oisans' outdoor swimming pool will do wonders for your limbs. It will bronze them at the very least; and after a *tartiflette* lunch in town, you can march off the frighteningly calorific local dishes on the 680km of walking trails at Ecrins National Park. It's the largest of France's six national parks, with a landscape that's a helter-skelter of peaks and valleys, visible in all their glory from the Ferme Noemie campsite at Les Sables, just up the road from Le Bourg d'Oisans.

Ferme Noemie has 20 numbered pitches, in homage to the Alpe d'Huez hairpins. The owners Melanie and Jeremy are great skiers. They met working for a UK ski-holiday company in the late 1980s and basically never returned home. He's good with his hands; the chalet shower block and loft apartments are all his own work. And Melanie is a consummate hostess. Should the nights turn chilly at this high altitude, warm blankets are handed out. An office reception is crammed with information leaflets, a coffee-making machine, microwave and fridge. If you've run out of beer, the couple will lend you theirs; they won't want anyone to go dry. In fact, they give away the cider made from their own apples for free.

The adjoining cliff face is striking and majestic. Caravans have to park on the right of the driveway so that they don't spoil the alpine serenity. 'Camping for softies' is the couple's latest project: bell tents with beds, duvets, wine glasses and a sheltered cooking stove. So successful are these tents that there are now four on site, cosy and contemporary in green and cream.

The nearest places of interest are all pretty niche – various museums celebrating minerals, hydro-electricity and crystals. But you could spend a day perusing the Domaine de Vizille's exhibitions on the French Revolution, set in a stunning deer park. Then, perhaps, you could try a spot of rock-climbing, rafting, horseriding or, er, 'parapenting', which involves running off the side of one of the mountains with a large gliding canopy attached. This certainly isn't a campsite to be idle – you'll be fighting fit and ready to tackle those hairpins yourself by the end of your stay!

COOL FACTOR The location, the view, the British owners, the fresh air.

WHO'S IN Tents, campervans, caravans, dogs, large groups, young groups – yes.

ON SITE 20 pitches and 4 part-furnished bell tents (sleeping 4 each). 1 chalet-style wash-block, gorgeous inside and out, with showers and disabled facilities. In reception there's a coffee machine, fridge, freezer and microwave. Bread and croissants can be delivered to your pitch in high season. Washing machine and dryer €4. Badminton net. Free Wi-Fi. Communal BBQ, no campfires.

OFF SITE Cycle the Alpe d'Huez, a 13km climb from Bourg d'Oisans to Alpe d'Huez, renting a bike from town – road bikes, mountain bikes and electric bikes all available (reserve online or at the campsite). There are also 2 riding centres nearby, if you fancy exploring on horseback. For info on the Domaine de Vizille 18km drive visit www.domaine-vizille.fr.

FOOD & DRINK La Muzelle (0033 476 795 802) in Bourg d'Oisans is highly recommended and there's a pizzeria just at the end of the campsite road. For something different, make a detour to the Hôtel de La Poste in Corps-la-Salette (0033 476 300 003), a bonkers art-deco restaurant that you'd expect to see on a film set, which serves a 5-course set lunch that you'll not forget in a hurry.

GETTING THERE The 'Romans route' is very easy, most of it is a long, straight, fast road that leads you onto the Grenoble bypass, the Rocade Sud, and up to the Oisans Valley. Follow the A48, A41or A51 into the region and the take the D91/D1091 to the town. More windy, but with spectacular scenery, is the route de Napoléon via Corps-la-Salette.

PUBLIC TRANSPORT Plane or TGV to Lyon or Grenoble, from where buses run to Bourg, then take a taxi 4km to Les Sables.

OPEN April–October.

THE DAMAGE A pitch and 2 people €22–€44, bell tents €400–€450 per week, children from €2.50. Dogs free. Electricity €4.50.

camping le gouffre de la croix

1050 Route du pont de vezor, 38680 Châtelus, Isere 00 33 4 76 36 07 13 camping-vercors-choranche.fr

A gleaming stream of tranquillity, the River Bourne slithers through the heart of Vercors Natural Park at its own calm and languid pace. Set within deep mountain valleys, where the western edge of the Alps merges into the green and abundant Presles Mountains, the river is an inevitable focal point of most things around here. And nothing less is true of Camping du Gouffre de la Croix, a waterside paradise for every type of camper. Below the pitches, banks have softened into sandy beaches and the shallows have become a haven for kids, frolicking safely in the clear waters. If you like a site that lets the setting do the work, you're in for a treat.

It's unfair, of course, to say that the backdrop is everything. There's a fair degree of management that benefits this site too. The facilities are excellent, there's a playground and table tennis for the kids, a reception shop where you can order fresh bread and loan a book from the library, and an excellent little bar that offers the perfect spot to while away the evening. Yet with all these man-made additions they have been careful to simply enhance the natural setting, with the site lurking subtly beneath the dappled shade of the trees.

The pitches themselves number fifty in total, spread over terraces that stagger their way down to the riverside, ideal for tents and small campervans, with spaces for a few caravans at the top of the site. For glampers there's also a new safari tent-style lodge mounted on a wooden floor and stocking everything you need for your holiday, minus the

bedding and towels. Ideal for five people, it has two bedrooms and a living space with kitchen.

As for days out, walkers can grab their fresh croissants from reception as they head out into the surrounding mountains: the area is renowned for its spectacular gorges, especially on the eastern side where it's squeezed through hard-rock valleys. Families, meanwhile, can enjoy the magnificent caves of Choranche, carved underground by tributaries of the river and pooled throughout with green-blue pockets of water. Stalactites droop from the ceiling on their way to meet their centuries-old partners poking up from the floor and walkways lead you through the vast grotto – a natural wonder not to be missed.

COOL FACTOR Riverside relaxation and a location hidden among the greenery of the Presles Mountains.

WHO'S IN Tents, campervans, caravans, couples, families, dogs (on a lead) – yes.

ON SITE 50 pitches (all with electricity), 2 mobile-homes and 1 tent lodge for rent. 2 wash-blocks with toilets, sinks and showers, one of which has laundry facilities (a washing machine and dryer). A small grocery shop in the reception area also serves fresh bread and croissants every morning, plus there is a bar serving drinks and snacks open every evening. Wi-Fi in the bar. Playground and trampoline for children. 2 river beaches with access for swimming and playing.

OFF SITE Miles of well-marked footpaths lace the Presles Mountains, where you can see wildflowers like chamois and orchids plus the local waterfalls to the east – there are maps and other information in reception. Canyoning is also popular, with some of the best spots just a few kilometres east of the campsite. Mountain biking, fishing, kayaking and climbing are also all possible – again there's plenty of info in reception. An attractive hour's walk from the site, the caves of Choranche (0033 476 360 988) are the main local highlight. The stream that winds through the caves feeds a stunning, emerald underground lake, and there's a sound and light show that takes you through its history.

FOOD & DRINK There's a small bar onsite and fresh bread in the morning, and it's just a short walk to Choranche where there is a small restaurant in one of the hotels (0033 476 361 262). Or you can drive to Pont en Royans (8km) where there's a clutch of bars, restaurants and cafés along with the essentials – a grocery, chemist, doctor and post office.

GETTING THERE Leave the A49 at exit 9 (St. Marcellin) and take the D5181 to Pont-en-Royans, then Villard de Lans. From Choranche, at the Hotel Jorjane turn right and cross the bridge. Gouffre de la Croix is on the left.

OPEN Mid April–mid September.

THE DAMAGE A pitch and 2 people €15–€25.50.

le grand bois

Col de Boutière, D233, 26460 Le Poët-Célard, Drôme 00 33 4 75 53 33 72 www.le-grandbois.com

Peek through the trees of this nature reserve woodland and a cluster of humungous safari-lodge tents loom into view. Close to the limestone scenery of the Parc Régional du Vercors, this settlement has pioneered next-level glamping, with a set of sturdy canvas homes perched on wooden decks hidden in woodland behind an 18th-century inn. These constructions are simply huge; you'll stretch your legs just fetching a glass of water and families can hang out here all day without feeling claustrophobic. Choose between a covered or uncovered terrace porch, then tie back the front flaps to create an open-plan abode filled with double and bunk beds and full-sized wardrobes. Look out towards a view of arboreal wilderness.

But it's not all about luxury glamping: you can also book a tunnel tent sleeping four, with awning, bedding, and gas stove; a small 90s caravan for two, or just pitch a tent in the meadow near the pool, snack bar, dining patio and wash-block. Once acclimatised, you can explore the park by bike or on foot; or just enjoy your place in the woods; it's too special to leave for too long.

COOL FACTOR Taking camping in the woods to a whole new level, this campsite is too special to leave.

WHO'S IN Campervans, caravans, tents, dogs (except during peak season), large groups, young groups – yes.

ON SITE 10 fully-equipped luxury safari-lodge tents as well as 40 sheltered pitches all with electric hook-ups for tents, caravans and campervans. A few pitches are available in the sunny meadow; most are located in the woods and offer plenty of shade and privacy. *Table d'hôte* dinners, pizzas, breakfasts available. Swimming pool, playground, volleyball, Wi-Fi, bread service. Bar 4pm–10pm. No BBQs or campfires.

OFF SITE Mountain bikers can take on the challenge of Mont Ventoux and the Vercors, infamous climbs on the Tour de France. Bike storage on site.

FOOD & DRINK Stuffed ravioli is a local speciality, and the Auberge de l'Estang in Saoû (0033 475 760 570) is a good place to try it.

GETTING THERE Take exit 18 off the A7 to Montélimar Sud and follow the D540 to Dieulefit, then Bourdeaux. Follow the signs Vers Pascalin and Le Grand Bois on the D233. The campsite is at 250m on the D233.

PUBLIC TRANSPORT TGV to Valence or Montelimar, train to Montelimar or Crest, bus to Dieulefit.

OPEN Start of May–mid September.

THE DAMAGE 2 adults with tent €21, children (2–7yrs) €5, extra adults €7. Safari lodge €385–€770 per week, €55–€110 per night (not July/Aug). Tunnel Tent €315–€560 per week. 90s Caravan €315–€560 per week. Dogs €4. Hook-ups €4. Breakfast €6–€8. Table d'hôte dinner €25. Gîtes €560–€805 per week, €85 per day. B&B rooms €55–€85 a night.

camping la source

05140 Saint Pierre D'Argençon, Hautes-Alpes 00 33 4 92 58 67 81 www.lasource-hautesalpes.com

There's something very wholesome about Camping La Source. Firstly, there's the air. Clean, pure breezes roll off the mountains and filter through the trees to fill every inch of the expansive sky that dominates this charming campsite. Second, with a manageable 25 plots, it's never crowded, which explains the tranquillity. Birdsong and crickets provide a steady background chatter, adding to the all-natural ambience. A walk through the campsite's woods reveals a surprising variety of trees, including pine, cherry, lime and walnut, but the stars of this woodland show are the giant sequoias. These towering trees are genuinely impressive, their thick trunks rising from the pine-needle-strewn ground so high that you risk cricking your neck just trying to see the top.

Whether you're just relaxing or using the campsite as a base for hiking from one picturesque village to the next, the view is what makes this site special. Whichever plot you pick, you're overlooked by mountains close enough to glide from – a fact that some regulars take advantage of by hang-gliding down from the peak to land right back at their tents. As for nightlife? Well, you won't find much, but there are bars and shops in Saint Pierre D'Argençon (2km) and Aspres-sur-Buëch (7km), or a little further afield in Veynes or Serres (about 15 minutes' drive). The sleepiness of the local settlements perpetuates the calm back at La Source, where there's not a jot of light pollution. It's the perfect patch for stargazing. Stock up with wine, lay out in the open spaces and enjoy the blanket of stars above.

COOL FACTOR Peaceful, spacious tranquillity with a spectacular backdrop. You half expect Julie Andrews to come running out of the woods in a habit.

WHO'S IN Tents, caravans, campervans, dogs (under control) – yes. Noisy folk between 11pm–7.30am – no. Groups must be pre-booked.

ON SITE 22 pitches and 3 luxury woodland tipis. A cute wash-block has 2 showers with sinks, 3 bathroom sinks (2 with private cubicles) and 3 washing-up sinks. A separate block for toilets. Washing machine from €3. Badminton and boules courts, a kids' play area and a communal BBQ. No campfires or charcoal BBQs allowed, but electric or gas BBQs are fine. Tipi guests have a shared outdoor Jacuzzi.

OFF SITE It's all about the Great Outdoors. Nearly 7,000km of walking trails cover the Hautes-Alpes region, so pack your hiking boots.

FOOD & DRINK La Source has its own restaurant offering breakfast, afternoon tea and cakes and evening meals. At Aspres-sur-Buëch (7km), Christian Breton sells everything from creamy local cheeses to regional wine, and there's a small supermarket, bakery, butcher and café-bar. For eating out, try Auberge de la Tour (0033 492 587 108) or Pont La Barque (0033 492 538 010), both within 10 minutes' drive.

GETTING THERE Leave the N75 at Aspres-sur-Buech and turn onto the D993 towards Valence. Follow the windy road, continue past the turning for St-Pierre-d'Argençon and soon you'll see signs to 'La Source (Camping, Chambres d'Hotes)'. Turn right into the campsite.

OPEN Mid April–mid October.

THE DAMAGE Pitch €4.50, adults €4.50, children (under 10 yrs) €2.50. Dogs £1.50. Electricity €4 per night. Extra tent €1, extra car €1. Tipi for 2–4 people €60–€80 per night, €300–€500 per week.

camping du brec

Le Brec, 04320 Entrevaux, Alpes-de-Haute-Provence 00 33 4 93 05 42 45 www.camping-dubrec.com

If the French Alps boast some of Europe's most awe-inspiring scenery, then the Maritime Alps in the country's south-eastern corner are truly a sight to behold. The southernmost tip of the mighty mountain range, they straddle the border between France and the Italian regions of Piedmont and Liguria, an undulating landscape of lush, craggy mountains and vast gorges scything each valley in two. Great pools have formed from melted glaciers and ancient sparkling lakes now await the would-be swimmer, and it's beside one of these that you'll find one of the region's most enviably-located campsites.

Managed by English-speaking hosts Clare and Eric Rondeau, Camping du Brec is an idyllic 7.5 acres of family-camping space. With a mixture of shady pitches catering to tents, campervans and caravans, it's big on facilities but has a refreshingly low-key slant, and it's in fact the gorgeous lake and beach that really mark it out. A hive of swimming, fishing, canoeing and general aquatic escapades, this private waterhole is the focal point of campsite life, helped in no small measure by the lakeside bar.

As if the lakeside locale wasn't enough, Camping du Brec is also mere minutes from some of the best southern France has to offer. There's the sprawling Mercantour National Park (home to wild boar, golden eagles, and wolves); the heady vineyards and perfumed lavender fields of Provence; the picture-postcard town of Entrevaux – its citadel a marvel of medieval construction; and it's not a huge distance to the considerably less rustic Côte d'Azur. But it's the natural wonders that dominate here: Le Gorges de Daluis, Lac d'Allos – there's an epic scale to everything. And for those brave or foolhardy enough, there's always cycling the Col de la Bonette, Europe's highest road and the bane of the world's greatest cyclists during the Tour de France.

The price to pay for it all is dizzying, serpentine roads that snake their way around the mountains and along the meandering River Var. But as the sun descends over the peaks, its glinting rays dancing on the lake, and you kick back with a beer on the lakeside terrace, you'll be glad you made the journey.

COOL FACTOR Family camping by the side of a private lake, set in the magnificent Maritime Alps.

WHO'S IN Tents, campervans, caravans (not double-axle), well-behaved dogs – yes. Groups are welcome during the low season but must make prior contact for group rates and availability (no stag or hen weekends).

ON SITE 88 pitches (all with electric hook-ups) including 79 pitches for short-stay campers (of which 3 are tent-only pitches). 6 self-contained bungalows and 3 pitches for year-round campers. 2 shower blocks with ample toilets, showers, washing-up sinks and separate clothes washing sinks. A baby room with a bath and shower, while the newer of the 2 blocks has disabled facilities. Washing machine and dryer (€3 each). Ironing board and iron available at reception. Caravan/campervan service area. Freezers for ice packs; Wi-Fi connection on 80% of the site (€1 for 24hrs); computer with free internet connection at snack bar. European electrical adaptors can be borrowed from reception, as can hiking maps and guides, and table tennis, badminton rackets and boules. Fresh bread service running from Easter to the end of September, and 2 communal wood BBQs available for use.

OFF SITE The site is an ideal base for all manner of outdoor pursuits – rafting, canoeing, kayaking, canyoning, Via Ferrata and climbing trips are all organised by the campsite. Nearby Entrevaux is a charming medieval town with a historic citadel and ramparts. You can also hop on a lovely old restored steam locomotive and explore this stunning region at a more leisurely pace. An hour's drive away lies the Mercantour National Park (0033 492 812 131), with peaks reaching 3000m and the Lac d'Allos, the largest natural high-altitude lake in Europe. The famous Gorges du Verdon is also around an hour away. The 14km Martel Trail follows the course of the River Verdon, taking in some of the country's most stunning scenery. Make easier work of it by setting off from Chalet de la Maline.

FOOD & DRINK There's an onsite snack bar overlooking the lake which serves draught beer, hot and cold drinks, ice creams and light snacks (salads, paninis, chips, etc). There's a choice of restaurants in Entrevaux (1.5km away), among which Auberge du Planet (0033 493 054 960) serves traditional French food as well as pizzas. In Annot (8km), the ever-popular La Table d'Angele (0033 492 838 850) serves a tasty menu and regular plats du jour. For local delicacies, be sure to sample some 'secca de boeuf' – a dried salted-beef speciality from Entrevaux. The region is also famous for its apple juice, which is a great accompaniment to the region's famous sweet *pain d'épice* (ginger bread). There's a well-stocked supermarket less than 2km away for any provisions.

GETTING THERE From Nice, follow the D6202 in the direction of Digne-les-Bains for about 75km as far as Entrevaux. Drive past Entrevaux and stay on the same road for approx. 4km until you cross the River Var. Immediately after crossing the river, turn right down a side road (signposted 'Camping du Brec, Intermarché') and follow the road to the end (approx. 2km). From Digne, take the N85 towards Nice for approx. 17km until Barrème, where you take D6202. Approximately 4km before Entrevaux, and before crossing the River Var, turn left down a side road (signposted 'Camping du Brec, Intermarché'). Drive to the end of this road (approx. 2km).

OPEN Mid March–mid October.

THE DAMAGE A pitch and 2 people from €19.10, adults €5.50, teenagers (13–17yrs) €5.15, children (2–12yrs) €3.45. Electricity €1.60–€3.25. Pets €1.

les eucalyptus

Chemin des Moulins, Plages de Pampelonne, 83350 Ramatuelle, Var 00 33 4 94 97 16 74 www.campingleseucalyptus.fr

It's not the sharp menthol smell of eucalyptus leaves that hits you when you turn off D93 on to chemin des Moulins, but the earthy acidity of rows of bountiful grapevines. This is wine country, and husband and wife team Philippe and Florence Lamon grow the vines that produce the local Les Grimaldines wines made by the local co-operative. Their hard-working enterprise doesn't stop with grapes, however. The industrious couple also renovated part of the farmhouse at the turn of the millennium and converted it into holiday apartments. But their pièce de résistance at Les Eucalyptus is their campsite, Camping à la Ferme, which is just a few kilometres from the beaches of St- Tropez and gives you all the benefits of the beaches and glitz at a much more reasonable price than its neighbours.

The site is a short moped ride away from the farmhouse, beyond the vines and near the working part of the farm, although the grapes are mushed offsite at the co-operative. The occasional sound of a putting tractor is drowned out by the comforting roar of waves beyond the bamboo plantation that backs on to Moorea Plage, part of St-Tropez's legendary Pampelonne sands. You can sunbathe here on the private bit of the beach – and the sunloungers are reasonably priced for the area – but the public beach is just as nice, fringed with cafés, restaurants and various boutiques channelling a French-Reggae vibe. Further towards Pampelonne's world-famous Plage de Tahiti, there's a larger campsite with its own supermarket – perfect for stocking up before retreating to the privacy of Camping à la Ferme. If you're after a spot of glamour, you could walk to the ultra-exclusive Kon Tiki beach huts and Club 55, famous since Brigitte Bardot's first sashay and where megastars such as George Clooney have been spotted more recently.

Although you may occasionally spot a yacht on the horizon, the seclusion of Les Eucalyptus feels miles away the glamorous holiday vibe nearby. The grounds host around 30 pitches and you're more likely to see a vintage Citroën van than a 4x4 parked up alongside the tent. The campsite's pitches are well spaced and there's a well-appointed, if basic shower block. The Lamons promise to update the facilities soon and have added it to their never-ending to-do list. A brick-built BBQ is available mid-season, when there is less wind and not so much risk of fire, but if you're looking to eat out, the stylish hotel-restaurant Les Moulins de Ramatuelle is just a seven-minute bicycle ride away. A visit to nearby Ramatuelle, a quaint medieval town in the mountains with a nocturnal market every Wednesday, is also recommended, and you should also stop by, Les Vignerons de Grimaud, to pick up some of the wine that's made from the campsite's very own grapes. You're also only a short drive from the resorts of St-Tropez and Port Grimaud, and all they have to offer (if you have a spare €2,000, why not hire a yacht for the week). They're certainly worth a look, if only because you know you can return to the peace and tranqulillity of Les Eucalyptus at the end of the day.

COOL FACTOR The proximity to St-Tropez's most famous beach, and the wry humour of Philippe Lamon.

WHO'S IN Tents, campervans, caravans, dogs, small groups, young families – yes.

ON SITE Around 30 pitches with electricity, washrooms with 4 sinks, 2 cold showers, 2 hot showers (€1), 2 women's toilets, 2 men's toilets, 2 outdoor urinals, washing machine (€5). Kids have the beach and bike rides. BBQ facilities. No campfires.

OFF SITE Pampelonne beach stretches over several miles, so it's well worth wandering along. The most famous area is Tahiti, where Brigitte Bardot used to hang out in the 1950s. Exceptional views along the St-Tropez Peninsula. The town is only 5km away if you want to rub shoulders with the rich and famous; try a spot of people-watching at Le Caves du Roy (0033 494 566 800) in the Hôtel Byblos. Port Grimaud offers cheaper thrills, particularly Azur Park Gassin, with its mini-golf and fairground attractions. For the more adventurous, Pep's Spirit (0033 494 968 804) in nearby Grimaud offers guided tours by mountain bike and various outdoor sports.

FOOD & DRINK Les Moulins de Ramatuelle at the nearby hotel of the same name is the place to go for French cooking (0033 494 971 722) and a touch of glamour. St-Tropez has plenty of places to choose from, including Petit Joseph, with contemporary Asian-style food cooked up by the same kitchen as the swisher Grand Joseph next door (0033 494 970 166). There's a market at Grimaud on Thursday, and a bigger one at Port Grimaud the same day and Sunday. St-Tropez's famous place des Lices market happens Tuesday and Saturday morning; plus there's a daily fish market near the old port.

GETTING THERE The D93 runs down the coast from St-Tropez to Ramateulle. Les Eucalyptus is on chemin des Moulins – follow the signs for Moorea Plage.

OPEN End May–mid September.

THE DAMAGE A pitch and 2 people €17–€31.

haut toupian

30630 Goudargues, Gard 00 33 4 66 50 40 71 www.imaginefrance.fr

Just outside the village of Goudargues in Provence, nestled at the end of a narrow lane and signposted with homemade signs, Haut Toupian is exclusive by design. The accommodation is limited – there are only two pitches on the 11-acre site and they come pre-filled with tents. But what spectacular tents they are!

Both of the large, rectangular safari constructions are set on raised timber decks with a terrace out front. From one of the terraces the panorama of trees and mountains is spectacular. The other terrace enjoys a more rustic view, taking in the traditional stone farmhouse, gîte and surrounding woods. There are no busy roads within earshot, so birdsong and wind rustling through trees forms the soundtrack – with the occasional rustle of a nearby boar. Fungus growing on oak trees is testament to the purity of the air (fungus can't grow in polluted air), as is the crystal-clear view across the Cèze Valley's woods, vineyards and lavender fields. The tranquillity here can take your breath away.

Having taken in the view, you need to prepare for more delights as you step into the tent. For a start there's a double bed. Yes, a real bed, draped with a thick duvet and soft, furry chocolate-brown throws. There are also sofa chairs that open into single beds, a wine-and-cheese fridge, a Nespresso machine… oh, and bathroom, tucked away at the back of the tent, with a porcelain loo and basin, jet shower, fluffy towels, dressing gowns and a range of organic toiletries. Already this is 5-star camping, but there's more.

Haut Toupian's owners are Polly and Hans. Polly is a great cook who, with a little notice, will prepare a five-course feast using fresh local produce; in fact your dinner might well be the highlight of the whole trip. Perfectly griddled scallops served with local peach wine, neat stacks of goats' cheese, aubergine, courgette, tomato and Parmesan, *confit* of duck with sautéed veg, cherries poached in Merlot, local cheeses and bread: all bursting with local flavour and accompanied by local red and white wines. Polly also prepares and delivers your morning breakfast daily.

In keeping with the lazy mood that is so easily brought on by good food, great wine, sunshine and a pool, the countryside around Haut Toupian is sleepy. Horseriding, cycling, canoeing and walking are recommended for active types, and for everyone else the region's plentiful wine-tasting tours combine agriculture, history and, of course, regular swigs of velvety reds and crisp whites.

Adventurous foodies will enjoy exploring the culinary treats in Goudargues, also known as 'Venice of the Gard' – an exaggerated title for somewhere with just one canal, but the weekly Wednesday market is well worth a visit. Indeed, between Polly's kitchen talents and the village, a stay at Haut Toupian is a treat for the tastebuds, if not the waistline. It's not a cheap camping break, true, but Haut Toupian's luxurious tents, idyllic location and sublime food set a new standard at the very top of the glamping scale.

COOL FACTOR Luxurious accommodation, fantastic food and beautiful scenery in a remote country location – in fact more of a sublime, al fresco hotel than a campsite.

WHO'S IN Couples, young families, groups (by arrangement) – yes. Tents, campervans, dogs, large groups, young groups – no.

ON SITE Two luxury safari tents with en suite bathrooms. King-sized bed with bedding, bath towels and dressing gowns, 2 single sofabed chairs that fold out to beds for children, a wine-and-cheese fridge, Nespresso machine, kettle, lighting, power sockets, a safe and Wi-Fi. Bathrooms have a loo, basin and excellent jet shower. No cooking facilities on site. All detergents must be organic as waste water is reused on the land. Each tent is on a platform with a terrace out front with table and chairs. A few steps from the tents there's an unheated pool (shared with the gîte) with a resident plastic duck, half a dozen sunloungers, chairs and tables.

OFF SITE The tourist office in Goudargues is a great starting-point for any local adventures. From there, find information on wine tours and tastings, olive-oil mill tours, horseriding – there's a huge paddock with riding tuition on the left as you leave the drive (0033 664 720 370), canoeing, golf, climbing, cycling, and walking routes. Culture vultures will enjoy exploring Avignon, Châteauneuf-du-Pape, Orange and other nearby towns, and for sun-worshippers the sea is just 2 hours away.

FOOD & DRINK Breakfast is included and a bottle of regional wine provided on arrival. Picnic hampers with local produce available (€22) – great for day trips. Some evenings a 5-course 'tent service' dinner is available. Cooked in her kitchen, using fresh local produce, Polly's *table d'hôte* dinners rival the best local restaurants. Offsite, a local vineyard, Domaine La Réméjeanne, hosts Thursday-morning tours followed by wine-tastings and a lunch buffet (0033 466 894 451).

GETTING THERE As you leave Goudargues, take the left marked Uzès and after 150m you'll pass Café des Sources. Follow the road for 3km, then look for the right turn signposted 'Haut Toupian'. From there follow the lane, watching out for the signs marked 'Polly-Hans'.

PUBLIC TRANSPORT Nîmes and Avignon are each a couple of hours from Goudargues by bus but local public transport is limited, so bikes or a car are best to make the most of exploring the area.

OPEN Mid April–mid October (outside high season 2-night minimum stay, based on availability, otherwise weekly Saturday–Saturday).

THE DAMAGE Per tent (2 guests) from €120 per night (min 2 nights) including breakfast. Weekly rates Saturday–Saturday €625–€990 including breakfast, depending on season. Additional guests – up to a maximum of 4 – cost €154 per week, again including breakfast.

mille étoiles

Mas de Serret, 07150 Labastide de Virac, Ardèche 00 33 4 75 38 42 77 www.campingmilletoiles.com

On a shady, wooded hillside overlooking the River Ardèche, Mille Étoiles is easily one of the most beautiful campsites in all of France. The forested land, sitting high above a canyon of sparkling, turquoise waters, is so fairytale perfect, in fact, that weddings are a regular occurrence.

Experienced campers who love the great outdoors will get the most out of a stay at Mille Étoiles. The surroundings are a treasure trove of footpaths and trails, while the wooded setting gives a slight wilderness feel, despite the fact that every little comfort is catered for, from lanterns at night to posh toiletries in the washrooms. If wildlife is all you need, you can bag one of the camping pitches in the main field – known as 'The Village' – or in the woods. But if you're those seeking extra luxury, you can partake of the campsite's growing number of glamping options.

Mille Étoiles test-drove a few yurts in 2003, with no electricity or water, way before glamping in France took off, and cited nature as their star attraction. One look at these nomadic Mongolian yurts and fancy family bathrooms, though, suggests that there's a lot more to the campsite than the enchanting surroundings. Raised on pine platforms, the yurts (now 'electrified') are scattered a decent distance apart, with sumptuous double beds draped with large mosquito nets. Each one is themed and furnished with chunky wooden chests or canvas wardrobes, ethnic pictures and recycled bedside tables. Starched, comfortable hammocks swing outside, while inside a practical kitchenette includes a fridge, stove and coffee machine.

There are a further two safari lodges, which include a well-equipped kitchen and dining area and provide the most space for large families; while everyone has access to the handcrafted pizzeria and café, the kids' playground and campsite library. It's a twenty-minute scramble down a steep decline from the campsite to the water, where, once on the river bed, walkers can follow the river the length of the gorge. If all that splashing about doesn't wear you out then counting the stars certainly will. With no electricity on site, they shine brighter than you'll ever have seen before after dark and sit like a sparkly blanket above the trees. They are the *mille étoiles* that give the site its name and will get you well on your way to a good night's sleep. 1, 2, 3…

COOL FACTOR A forest, a beautiful river – and welcoming young hosts.

WHO'S IN Tents, campervans, caravans, canoeists, nature-lovers, dogs – yes.

ON SITE 33 camping pitches, 11 yurts, 2 safari lodges and 2 tents on stilts. A giant communal yurt in the middle of the woods is available for group hire or for general use (yoga routines, storytelling, hide-and-seek). Tent pitches in the woods and in a field with water points, a few electric hook-ups, picnic tables and hammocks. The self-catering yurts comfortably fit a family of 4. The safari lodges sleep 7 with ample space and have fully-equipped kitchens and en suite bathroom facilities. Otherwise there are 2 shower blocks, one by the yurts with 6 family bathrooms (sink, shower) and another block with 4 shower cubicles and 5 loos, plus laundry. Bath towel hire €4 each. There's a small grocery shop and a library. The bar, pizzeria and pancake house opens mornings and evenings, selling local wines, beers, fresh juices, water, ice creams, pizzas and Ardéchoises specialities. There's a playground and you can rent mountain bikes by the day, half-day or for several days.

OFF SITE Canoe on the Ardèche or Cèze. Hire boats and instructors (0033 426 622 644) to take a 2-hour or 2-day excursion. Park at Sauze; a shuttle bus runs to Vallon Pont d'Arc, so you can pick up your vehicle at the end of the day. Join the throngs at the sandy beach of Vallon Pont d'Arc, or view it from the road above. This stone 'bridge' is one of France's best-known landmarks. Barjac is a short drive away – worth a visit on Friday mornings for the market.

FOOD & DRINK A recent addition to the campsite is an excellent little restaurant with reasonable prices and hefty portions of food. There is a varied menu (including local specialities) and the mussels and chips are a particular highlight. For a special occasion it's around a half-hour walk to La Petite Auberge (0033 475 386 194) in Labastide de Virac, with its enchanting terrace and wonderful view of the vineyards. There is a small farm shop near the campsite; ask for directions.

GETTING THERE Follow the A9 to Avignon/Lyon, then follow the signs for Bollène/Montélimar, taking exit 19 at Bollène and following the D994, D6086 and D901. Turn right on the D979 into Barjac and follow the signs to Labastide; look for a sign on the left to Les Crottes, then Mille Étoiles.

PUBLIC TRANSPORT Avignon or Montélimar are the nearest TGV stations, from where buses run to either Barjac or Vallon Pont d'Arc – from where you'll need to take a taxi. Nîmes, Avignon and Lyon are the nearest airports, 90 minutes' away.

OPEN April–November.

THE DAMAGE Tent campers €15–€21 a night for 2 people, extra people €4, children 3–12yrs €2, under-3s free. Self-catering yurts from €60 a night for 2 people, minimum 2 nights' stay and in high season weekly (€490 for 2 people). Bed linen €10 per bed.

camping le clapas

280, chemin de la Vernède, Salavas, Vallon Pont d'Arc 07150, Ardèche 00 33 4 75 37 14 76 www.camping-le-clapas.com

Le Clapas might sound like the kind of thing you'd do to a Ricky Martin track – but 'clapas' is actually an old Occitan name for a pile of stones, or a building made from a pile of stones. In the case of Camping Le Clapas, the stones come from a beach slap-bang on the River Ardèche – the robust stream of water that forged the beautiful gorges found in this area and which gave the département its name.

A former municipal campsite, Le Clapas was taken over around ten years ago and transformed into something a little more special. Trees were planted and small walls built using the eponymous stones, which still line the river banks and the site's private beach; and facilities were tweaked and expanded to make the site more cosy, imaginative and comfortable. The site's 67 decent-sized pitches sit beneath a swaying miscellany of acacias and pines, and many (though not all) offer views of the river. It's a family-friendly place, with boules, table tennis and volleyball on offer and regular group entertainments, such as BBQs, themed evenings and karaoke. Adults are well catered for too, with a small but well-stocked onsite bar.

Thanks to the river, canoeing and kayaking are the big draws here, with gentle stretches for beginners and feisty rapids for adrenaline fiends. Canoe and kayak tours leave directly from the site and range from a leisurely 8km paddle to a more strenuous 32km river trip. If water-related activities don't grab you, there are plenty of other diversions. The most obvious – the Gorges de l'Ardèche – features limestone cliffs that reach up to 300m

high; one of the most popular sights along the way is the natural 60m stone arch known as the Pont d'Arc, which hogs much of the local publicity material. It's about an hour's pleasant stroll from the site.

Amateur speleologists (that's cavers to you and me) will no doubt be aware of nearby Chauvet – a Paleolithic network of caves containing paintings and engravings thought to be over 36,000 years old. Easily rivalling the more famous sites of Lascaux and Cosquer, the cave's priceless archaeological value means unfortunately visitors cannot currently visit the caverns. However, the excellent Grotte Caverne du Pont d'Arc Cave Exhibition is the next best thing. The local region is also studded with what are known as *villages de caractère* – timeless symbols of the area's rural heritage heavily marketed by the tourist board. Once you see these in the flesh, it's hard to refute their obvious wow factor. Balazuc and Vogüé, in particular, are worth heading to: the former hangs off a steep clifftop surrounded by trees; the latter is a similarly stunning collection of stone houses huddled beneath an imposing 17th-century château.

But where the site really comes into its own is as a chilled retreat from the summertime masses. With over 100,000 tourists descending on the area throughout July and August alone, it can be difficult not to feel a bit smug as you paddle in peace on the river, happily doing Le Clapas. Let the others do Ricky Martin!

COOL FACTOR A killer position right on the Ardèche river with its own private beach.

ON SITE 67 camping pitches, most with electricity, plus 2 'lodge tents' and 16 mobile homes. All the amenities you'll need, except a restaurant. There are 2 modern sanitary blocks with toilets, showers and basins plus washing machines, a grocery store and snack bar.

OFF SITE For *Via Ferrata*, tree climbing and a traverse over the river, try Adventure Camp (0033 475 359 413) in Grospierre 15km away. Kids will love exploring the caves at Aven d'Orgnac (0033 475 386 510). Treat yourself to a stay in a castle in Balazuc, where chic Moroccan tadelakt interiors go hand in hand with medieval fireplaces and Romanesque exteriors at the striking Château de Balazuc (0033 475 885 267). The village of Labeaume (15km) is also a stand-out spot, right on the banks of La Beaume river.

FOOD & DRINK Pizza and frîtes are served on site throughout the summer, but for pukka Provençal food check out Les Tilleuls (0033 475 377 212) in Lagorce. Vallon Pont d'Arc also has a regular market every Thursday and a food market every Sunday in high season.

GETTING THERE From Aix-en-Provence, take the A8 to Salon-de-Provence, then the A7 towards Orange. Continue through Orange on the E15 and turn off towards Vallon Pont D'Arc. Follow the signs to Salavas and then keep a look out for signs to Le Clapas.

PUBLIC TRANSPORT The closest you can get is Vallon Pont d'Arc, which is accessible by train or bus, or to Salavs by bus. From there, the site is a 25-minute walk or a taxi ride (about €13).

OPEN Early April–early October.

THE DAMAGE Pitch for 2 people €15–€29.50, extra adults €4.70–€7.50, children (2–10yrs) €3.20–€5.80, under 2yrs free. Pre-pitched and equipped tents €245–€560 a week, mobile homes €245–€795.

camping chantemerle

Lieu dit La Pontèze, Bédouès 48400 Florac, Lozere 00 33 4 66 45 19 66 www.camping-chantemerle.com

When author Robert Louis Stevenson penned *Treasure Island*, his colourful plot drew on a life peppered with interesting travels. Decades earlier, his adventures around the south of France had inspired *Travels with a Donkey in the Cévennes,* a classic of outdoor literature. Meandering through the tree-clad mountains, Stevenson's idea of cool camping was definitely a little different from ours today, not least because his shabby homemade sleeping bag was so heavy a donkey was required to carry it, but all the same he knew a stunning location when he saw it – 'a smooth sandy ledge... the Tarn below... a thin fringe of ash trees... a faint sweet perfume which pervaded the afternoon air'. The idyllic setting Stevenson found is now a resting-point for travellers, and Camping Chantemerle is the name it takes. Things have changed a little since then, but the Tarn still frolics through its sandy channel, and the ash and Spanish chestnut trees shade a riverside spot that is as unpretentious as it is relaxed – a campsite where time passes you by as gently as the water's flow.

The campsite's pitches – along with a handful of mobile homes for rent – are spread beneath the trees, all with electrical hook-ups if required. Around 25 of the 69 pitches are right by the river, and the rest have easy access to the water, where a private sloping beach reaches down to the Tarn, deep enough for paddling and bathing, though not quite enough for a proper swim. There's also a great swim-hole at the far end of camp that's perfect for proper wild swimming. Choose between sunning yourself on the beach beside an old bridge or hopping along the rocks that cluster on the riverbank as you head upstream towards a deeper gorge. Head this way in the evenings to perch quietly on the bank to catch a glimpse of a resident beaver family, bobbing along in the water pushing branches on their noses.

Back at the campsite there is plenty to keep you entertained, with an outdoor play area, table tennis and a pétanque court, along with an established bar/restaurant that is careful to avoid any holiday parkish car-crashes like karaoke nights or conga trains. Instead they serve good, local food in a simple café setting that reflects the personality of the campsite's owner Nicole and her friendly team, who together make Camping Chantemerle the place that it is. French speaking, half German/half American, and warm, welcoming and full of local knowledge, Nicole is the go-to person when you finally drag yourself away from the riverside and decide to explore the the surrounding area. Ensconced in the Parc Nationale des Cévennes with picturesque rural settlements dotted amongst the hills, it is difficult to go wrong. Like our wayward traveller Stevenson, tie your laces, point your finger and go and explore. A wondrous landscape awaits.

COOL FACTOR Relaxed riverside camping and wild swimming in the beautiful Cévennes mountains.

WHO'S IN Tents, campervans, caravans, dogs – yes.

ON SITE 69 pitches and 8 mobile homes. Riverside pitches are just a few metres from the water. Showers and toilets are relatively old and simple but immaculately kept. Laundry, free Wi-Fi, book exchange, tourist info, games room, swimming pool, playground, table tennis, table football and a pétanque area. Bikes can be rented and campers can even hire a donkey for the day for a spot of Stevenson-style trekking. The River Tarn is ideal for paddling and bathing, with the best swimming from the beach underneath the bridge. The Robert Louis Stevenson hiking trail goes right through the campsite.

OFF SITE The Gorges du Tarn, 5km away, is a tumultuous section of the same river that slides lazily past the campsite – it's perfect for wild swimming. Cévennes Évasion Voyages Nature (0033 466 451 831), based in Florac, arrange *Via Ferrata* walking, rock climbing and *spéléologie* (potholing), while Canoe 2000 (0033 466 485 771) can organise canoeing. Both operators speak excellent English and guests of Chantemerle receive a 10% discount.

FOOD & DRINK Freshly-baked bread and croissants are available at reception (May–September). There is an excellent campsite bar/restaurant (La Bergerie): overlooking the river, it serves regional specialties as well as popular pasta dishes and pizza. For dining out, head to Florac, 4km away, where you can enjoy the best crêpes in the region at Au Pecher Mignon (0033 466 451 428). If you really want to push the boat out, La Lozerette (0033 466 450 604) in Cocures – 800m from the campsite – serves refined French cuisine in a gorgeous setting.

GETTING THERE Leave the N160 at Florac following signs to Bedoues (D998). 2km after leaving the N160 you will cross the River Tarn. The campsite is on the left immediately after the bridge.

OPEN Mid April–mid October.

THE DAMAGE A pitch and 2 people €14 –€20, children €3.50–€4. Electrical hook-up €4.50.

camping la cascade

Salvinsac, 48150 Meyrueis, Lozere 00 33 4 66 45 45 45 www.camping-la-cascade.com

You'd better take a jaw-sling with you when driving to La Cascade along the Gorges de la Jonte. Because if the views along this scenic chasm (especially the part between Le Rozier and Meyrueis) don't make the lower half of your face succumb to the force of awe-inspired gravity, then the fantastic atmosphere at the campsite will. The area around the gorge brims with campsites, but the majority are large and rather characterless places. La Cascade, on the other hand, enjoys a more detached location slightly away from the gorge itself, positioned at an altitude of 750m at the foot of the majestic Causse Méjean.

There's no denying it's a big campsite. But big in a large, open and friendly way, not packed to the gills with caravans. Rather than welcoming motorhomes and building loud discos, La Cascade's hospitable French owners, Anne-Marie and Jean-Noël, have kept it deliberately natural, with just a smattering of wooden chalets (13 to be exact) and a huge amount of space for campers.

There are 50 pitches in total, split between two main fields (plus a couple in a delightful little hidden area next to a stream), and wherever you throw up your tent you get lots of space and lovely open-sky views, either of the handsome Causse Méjean or the fresh, towering pines on the other side. In the morning, the first sounds you're likely to hear are bells and sheep.

Both Anne-Marie and Jean-Noël grew up in the Alps and have a strong appreciation of nature. They bought the campsite from a previously eco-conscious couple and take their cue from the environment – something reflected in the ardent eco-policy of the site: 60 per cent of the energy needed to heat the domestic water is solar, two-thirds of the lightbulbs are low-energy consumption and there's an emphasis on recycling. They are also members of the *Via Natura Association* (the association of ecological campsites in France) and have recently installed an observatory for the newly reintroduced rare bearded vulture.

There's a small restaurant on site, with a shop selling lots of excellent local produce. There's also a fair amount to keep you busy, including a sizeable boules court, a small library with lots of info on the surrounding region, a playground for kids and a badminton net stretched across one field. You can splash around in the spring and waterfall right next door (which is connected to the River Jonte) or take one of their guided hikes during summer.

Since the site is located within the Parc National des Cévennes, there's an abundance of activities off site, too. You have direct access, of course, to the nearby Gorges de la Jonte, which offers plenty of climbing, hiking and cycling opportunities; and the even more spectacular Gorges du Tarn, formed by the River Tarn between the Causse Méjean and the Causse de Sauveterre, is also just a half-hour drive away.

Here you can take walks and drives, enjoy kayak trips or rafting, go fishing, caving, or canyoning. All you need are some wheels, a desire for adventure and of course your very durable jaw-sling.

COOL FACTOR Spacious and peaceful eco-camping in the Parc National des Cévennes.

WHO'S IN Tents, campervans, caravans – yes. Dogs, groups – by arrangement in low season only.

ON SITE 41 camping pitches and 13 chalets. No campfires allowed, but BBQs okay if they are raised off the ground; a clean and well-maintained shower and toilet block with 6 showers, 6 toilets, disabled access and a dry toilet (all free); washing machine available (€5). Boules court, kids' playground, free bikes and table tennis. The onsite shop sells local delicatessen goods and you can also access Wi-Fi if you need to. Binoculars are available to observe the copious birdlife – vultures, short toad eagles, and more – from the site and on walks.

OFF SITE Hiking in the Cévennes National Park is a hugely popular activity and there are hikes available for all levels, such as the breezy 3-hour climb up to the Corniches du Causse Méjean, or a hike up to Le Puech Pounchut (also 3 hours), where fabulous 360-degree views of Mont Aigoual and Causse Méjean are the reward. They have details on these walks and many more in reception. The Dargilan caves in Meyrueis (0033 466 456 020), discovered in 1880 by a shepherd who was hunting a fox, are a beautiful riot of ochres, yellows, saffron, and pinks, and well worth a visit; La Barbote (0033 565 626 626) is a great place to organise canoeing and rafting in the Gorges du Tarn and de la Jonte, as well as other activities such as Via Ferrata and climbing. Les Arts du Vide, run by

Géraud Fanguin (0033 681 063 496) is also recommended for organising canyoning, climbing and bird-watching trips. If you'd like to paraglide over the Gorges du Tarn, try Antipodes Millau (0033 565 607 203), who organise trips from around €70 per person.

FOOD & DRINK The site serves fresh bread and pastries each morning and has a deli shop selling local produce. There is also an excellent snack bar and cute little onsite restaurant. Elsewhere, Meyrueis has lots of pleasant cafés and restaurants such as Le Jardin des Glaces (0033 466 454 375), which serves a delicious aligot (potatoes, crème fraîche, Cantal cheese), and the Hôtel du Mont Aigoual (0033 466 456 561) – one of the best restaurants in the area, elegant but still good value, with a terroir menu for €20 and gourmet menus from €32. Slightly more down to earth, but with consistently good food, is the aptly named Hôtel Family (0033 466 456 002), and there are plenty of smaller restaurants along the river.

GETTING THERE Take the A75 to Millau and come off at exit 44/1. Pass through the Gorges du Tarn, Le Rozier, Meyrueis, and take the D996 towards Florac until you see the sign for La Cascade in Salvinsac. Leaving the A75 at Marvejols, take the N108 to Balsièges, then the D986 to Ste-Enimie– Meyrueis. Follow the directions, as above, to Salvinsac.

OPEN April–September.

THE DAMAGE Tent plus 2 people €12.70–€20, chalets €286–€678.

domaine de pradines

Route de Millau, 30750 Lanuéjols, Gard 00 33 4 67 82 73 85 www.domaine-de-pradines.com

If you like your campsites to come with a healthy dose of history, check out Domaine de Pradines. According to official documents, the site was once owned by a certain M. Cambacères, a key official in Napoléon's government. Indeed, Napoléon is said to have stayed here during the period of his Egyptian campaign, for which Cambacères planted some trees following the outline of the imperial eagle as a welcoming gesture. Not impressed? Well, architectural evidence shows that the site harks back at least to the Knights Templar. Still not enough? Okay – how about the discovery of a 4th-century Roman coin in the grounds?

Today's incarnation of the campsite is in the capable hands of Virginie (from France) and George (from Scotland), who have been in charge of the place, along with their respective families, since 2006. Situated slap-bang in the middle of the Parc National des Cévennes and Parc Régional des Grands Causses, Pradines is as idiosyncratic as they come. It boasts a series of Turkmen yurts, wooden chalets and a multi-storey glamping 'nest', all set on an almost unbelievably large tract of land (370 acres) that's mostly left wild. Around a quarter of the area has been reserved for the main camping field, a vast and fairly unruly space that has a touch of the savannah about it, helped by the African-style BBQ area and tall, blonde grass.

Campers can choose to take one of the huge spaces around the periphery of the field, or lose themselves completely in the woods. Either way, it's unlikely you'll be disturbed by your neighbours unless they're shouting through a megaphone; and unless you have powerful binoculars, you won't be seeing much of them either.

While the owners admit that the rugged feel of the site isn't for everyone, it'll certainly suit anyone with a sense of adventure or those who yearn for nature. Besides, it's not so rough really: amenities include a shower block ensconced in a charming old vaulted stone barn, a kids' playground, a pool, a restaurant and a well-stocked shop. You can even get Wi-Fi if you need to.

The real idea, though, is to get a bit closer to nature. To take a memorable hike or adrenalin-pumping raft trip through one of the nearby gorges – the Tarn, Jonte, and Dourbie are all within easy reach – and other outdoor playgrounds that offer a multitude of activities, from climbing and hiking to kayaking, rafting and canyoning. You can even paraglide if you want to see the area from a bird's-eye perspective. Or explore the forests, granite hills and magnificent caves of the Cévennes. There are places like the charming holiday town of Meyrueis to visit, or Millau, which is home to the marvellous Millau Viaduct, the highest bridge in the world.

Guided walks and maps are available from reception or you can simply head off to explore the campsite's expansive terrain, which includes 30 species of wild orchid among other rarities, birds and butterflies. Maybe you'll find something older than a coin from the 4th century BC. A dinosaur footprint maybe?

COOL FACTOR Spacious pitches and a well-preserved natural environment in the middle of two great national parks.

WHO'S IN Tents, caravans, campervans, cars – yes. Groups by arrangement only.

ON SITE Three communal BBQ areas, 50 huge pitches, 48 of which have hook-ups; some are close to the sanitary block, others further away. Pitches have either sun, shade, a bit of both, or finally there's semi-wild camping for the more adventurous or complete tranquility seekers. There are 9 hot and 2 cold showers (including one with disabled access), washbasins in cubicles, washing-up sinks, a washing machine and dryer. Swimming and paddling pool, 2 tennis courts, boules court, children's playground. Restaurant with a beautiful vaulted ceiling typical of the region, takeaway food options, shop, Wi-Fi, volleyball and badminton courts. No campfires.

OFF SITE An embarrassment of riches awaits. There's the Grotte de Dargilan caves (0033 466 456 020) or the famous Roquefort cheese caves (0033 565 585 600) and the famous viaduct at Millau (the nearest town) and its historical old centre. The Micropolis Insectarium will appeal to creepy-crawly lovers of all ages (0033 565 585 050). Fremyc (0033 658 134 848), in Meyrueis, organises rafting, canoeing, walks, bike rides, caving tours, *Via Ferrata* and more. Airzone Parapente (0033 660 847 623) can organise tandem rides over Millau and the Grands Causses. Randals Bison (0033 467 827 374) offer cowboy-style riding on their bison farm. Great walks and wild river swimming are easy to find and there are a variety of activities such as canoeing down the Tarn river, hiking, *Via Ferrattas*, horseriding and visiting Templar strongholds – all locally accessible.

FOOD & DRINK Pradine's auberge serves food in July and August in an ancient building with an impressive stone vault (formerly a Templar chapel). It has a pleasant grassed terrace or you can take away. There is also a small shop on site which serves fresh bread daily. The village of Lanuéjols has a hotel-restaurant and bar called Hôtel Bel Air (0033 467 827 278), which is informal and family-run. Meyrueis is a bustling village in the summer with a weekly market, shops and a wide range of cafés, restaurants and bars, such as the Hôtel du Mont Aigoual (0033 466 456 561), which has good food and a down-to-earth atmosphere, and Le Jardin des Glaces (0033 466 454 375), which serves up local specialities. For other local restaurants, try Auberge de Cadenas (0033 565 714 270). Farms in the region rear unique Brebis sheep that produce rich milk used to make Roquefort cheese in, yes, Roquefort not far from Millau. For a sample of this famous delicacy, try Au Marché Paysan–Magasin de Producteurs Fermiers in Millau (0033 565 613 935).

GETTING THERE Pradines is 35km east of Millau, and 1½ hours north of Montpellier, 2 hours west of Nîmes, 3 hours' drive south of Clermont-Ferrand.

OPEN Camping officially June–mid September, but sometimes May too depending on the weather. Yurts can be rented April–September. The Nest and bell tents June–September. Gîtes and chalets March–November.

THE DAMAGE Tents and 2 adults €12–€17 (electricity €3); large 4-person yurts €350–€570 per week; small 2-person yurts €240–€280 per week; 4-person-bell tents €55 per night, 5-person bell tents €62 per night; minimum 3 nights high season.

camping goudal

Route de Lacaune, 34330 La Salvetat-sur-Agoût , Hérault 00 33 4 67 97 60 44 www.goudal.com

The glossy magazines may claim Cameron Diaz spends millions washing her hair with bottled spring water but if only celebs like her knew to visit Camping Goudal in the south of France. They'd have everything they need. Burbling from a south-facing slope, natural spring water (bottled and sold nationally as 'La Salvetat') cascades through rocks into a series of streams bound for the River Agout. The streamside campsite is fed by the same waters – its taps, showers and washing machine all use the mineral water – while an oval lake offers guests the chance to bathe in the fresh *eau naturelle*. The Cameron Diaz treatment at a fraction of the cost.

Set in the gentle slopes of the Parc naturel régional du Haut-Languedoc, Camping Goudal is an established site on the estate of an old farm. The main reception and entrance buildings date back to 1839 and set the tone for the style of rustic, rural camping beyond. Grass pitches, all with electricity, spread through mature trees and terraced levels gently descend to the lake, fronted by a small sandy beach.

It's not all back-to-nature simplicity. For luxury seekers, the furthest end of the site has some ready-made glamping options – well-equipped wooden chalets accompanied by smaller, slightly more basic cabins, while pre-pitched tents come furnished with beds, bedding, a kitchen set, gas grill and wardrobe. And whether you pitch your own tent or plump for one of these upmarket options, all guests can treat themselves at the onsite bistro. Surrounded by grey-stone cliffs on one side and an ivy-clad old

building on the other, diners lounge on a quaint, sunny terrace as they wait for pizzas from the stone-baked ovens.

Despite the lake, Camping Goudal also has a large swimming pool, a playground and runs loosely organised activities for the kids – den-building, bug-hunting and the like. It all has a rather homely and homemade feel which suits the place down to the ground. Camping here is about family time and exploring the natural surroundings, an atmosphere only enhanced by stone dwellings that seem to have grown into the slopes of the site itself. Everything is well worn, yet also lush, young and green. There's obviously something special in the water.

COOL FACTOR Homely camping with an informal restaurant.

WHO'S IN Tents, caravans, campervans, trailer-tents, dogs (on a lead) – yes. Pets inside the glamping accommodation – no.

ON SITE 100 pitches with electrical hook-ups, 8 pre-pitched tents (4–6 person), 5 chalets (4 person) and 2 cabins (4 person). 2 sanitary buildings with showers, toilets, sinks, a family/baby shower, washing machine and dryer. Tents and chalets have beds, a complete kitchen inventory, wooden garden furniture and a gas BBQ (chalets also have a bathroom). There is a swimming lake, swimming pool, playground, trampolines, table tennis tables and books to borrow. Children's activities organised in high season, including den-building, crafts and the weekly evening campfire.

OFF SITE Hiking and mountain biking trails lead directly from the campsite, while Lac de la Raviège and the River Agoût are suitable for both wild swimming and fishing. It's a 10-minute drive to the local tourist office in La Salvetat-Sur-Agout (0033 467 976 444) where you can grab information on canoeing, canyoning and horseriding in the local area, or walk the history trail around the village itself.

FOOD & DRINK The onsite bistro is casual but excellent and has a terrace for your evening tipple and stone-baked pizza (you can also take away). There's also a daily bread service. Head to Salvetat-sur-Agoût for more options: La Pergola (0033 467 236 350) is a popular and affordable choice or continue a little further to Hôtel La Plage (0033 467 976 987) with a changing, seasonal menu, located beside Lake Raviège.

GETTING THERE From La Salvetat-sur-Agoût, follow the signs directing you to Lacaune. After 4km Camping Goudal has clear signs you can follow. From Lacaune, follow the signs to La Salvetat-sur-Agoût and after 15km you'll see the signs.

OPEN Mid May–mid September.

THE DAMAGE €15–€30 per night per pitch including 2 people; extra people €3.75–€4.25. Electricity €4.95. Cabins €40–€45 per night. Chalets €415–€775 per week. 4-person tents €495–€650 per week. 6-person tents €515–€670 per week.

belrepayre airstream & retro trailer park

Nr Mirepoix, Ariege (09), Midi-Pyrénées 00 33 5 61 68 11 99 www.airstreameurope.com

A couple of decades ago, Perry Balfour and his wife, Coline, set about transforming a beautiful part of the Ariège countryside into a themed trailer park. They found an impressive collection of 15 Airstreams and painstakingly restored each one to its former glory, then decked them out in 1970s-era fabrics and flea-market paraphernalia. Most of these glistening beauties have come all the way from America, although one, transformed into a distinctive, colourful diner called Apollo Lounge, was discovered sitting under the Eiffel Tower.

Though the exteriors look majestic – especially when winking simultaneously in the Ariège sunshine – the interiors look even better, with cute bathrooms and showers, funky bedrooms and lots of aptly vintage touches including floral curtains, retro crockery, black-and-white TVs and even an eight-track music system. Sliding in a scratchy Sly & the Family Stone cassette and putting your feet up on the sun lounger outside is a pretty cool experience, to say the least. There's not much else on site save for an activities field, a nearby wood to explore and a small store at reception. In the evenings, all the action centres around the neon playground known as the Apollo Lounge, where Coline serves up tasty French food and Perry, cunningly disguised as DJ Bobby Lotion, lives out his pop-star fantasies, spinning everything from Motown to rock 'n' roll and disco on vinyl.

If ever there was a campsite to help you trip back in time – this is it…

COOL FACTOR Europe's first retro Airstream trailer park, in the foothills of the Pyrénées.

WHO'S IN Tents, vintage caravans, camping cars, groups – yes. Pets – not in the Airstreams.

ON SITE 15 Airstreams for rent, each equipped with furniture and kitchen; a slightly old-fashioned but well-maintained wash-block with 3 toilets and 3 showers; field next to reception caters for tenters and increasingly VWs. Sauna, yoga room, table tennis, badminton, bike tracks, outdoor cinema screen, small shop. No campfires.

OFF SITE Hiking and mountain biking are the most popular options. Bikes are rented on site or can be delivered (0033 631 942 491). Medieval castles close by include the marvellous Château de Montségur, a former fortress near Montségur. Discover Ariège by microlight with Partag'air (0033 561 019 200) in Troye-d'Ariège.

FOOD & DRINK The Apollo Lounge serves decent organic food on site in the evenings and is also well stocked with beer and wine. The Airstreams have cooking facilities and nearby Mirepoix has great cafés and restaurants and a good farmers' market every Monday on place du Maréchal Leclerc. Try Le Comptoir Gourmand (0033 561 681 919), where you can feast on mussels and monkfish in a converted barn.

GETTING THERE Full directions on booking. Fly to Carcassonne, or take a train to Pamiers or Toulouse, then hire a car or Perry may be able to pick you up. Or, arrive in your own classic car to get a 10% discount.

OPEN End April–mid September.

THE DAMAGE Pitch and 2 people €20–€30 per night. Airstreams from €90 per night to €990 a week (sleep 2–4). Sheets, towels, cleaning extra.

mas de la fargassa

Mas de la Fargassa, Montalba, 66110 Amélie les Bains, Pyrénées-Orientales 00 33 4 68 39 01 15 www.lafargassa.com

An organic fruit farm that lives off its land – selling plums, apples, strawberries, gooseberries, raspberries, pears and 120 kilos of organic bread each week – needs some assistance, and the Dutch–English proprietors get it by offering work placements to young travellers. In exchange for free accommodation and food, the land is cultivated, the donkeys and horses walked and fed, the bread kneaded every Tuesday (ready to sell at a co-operative of local farmers) and the fires are lit at night.

Watching workers from all over the world busying themselves and relaxing together lends a really cool vibe to this location. Actually, the location is cool enough without them, and turns over as a family-friendly business in the height of summer. But anyone who's trekked to far-off lands will be impressed with the journey to get here. Don't even think of turning back along the windy 9km road that cuts through the mountains: once you've started, there's nowhere to turn around. Some people rate the view of the Gorges du Mondony as their holiday highlight, others will always regret having looked down. On a positive note, the smaller the vehicle, the less your vertigo-induced fear. Mobile homes are a definite no-no.

It took owners Frauke & Johan two years of travelling down never-ending roads to find their dream home. One day 20 years ago, they caught a glimpse of chimney smoke rising through a clearing in the trees. The proprietor of that particular home wasn't selling, but next door they spotted an isolated, dilapidated forge that had been uninhabited since the 1930s. They snapped it up along with the surrounding 600 acres, then set to work transforming rubbles of stone into fully functional, modern accommodation. Today, they hire out a gîte, a chalet and a pigsty (perhaps better described as a two-person, one-room studio). In total they can sleep up to 18 people.

They also have six well-equipped Dutch tents named after the trees they're next to (holly, plum, etc.) – either by the stream or on a raised level overlooking the garden; plus, there's space for you to pitch your own tent. There's a covered eating area where 50 people have been known to crowd around dining tables for the vegetarian evening meals. You can also swim in the river – making dams is apparently the holidaying proclivity of older Dutchmen. It feels quite exciting to be so near to Spain in dense woodland. Go for a long stroll and you feel like a bandit sneaking across the border. Johan, arranges regular group outings where you can hike to a Spanish restaurant for lunch, maybe catching glimpses of wild boar along the way. Afterwards you can return by car to allow some extra eating time. These trips are rightfully popular and it's good to stretch your legs without the worry of getting lost – something all too easy in this ancient wooded and rocky terrain.

With your feet up after a hard day, it's easy to see how the owners fell in love with the place. Today they continue living a peaceful and just about sustainable life with their six homeschooled children: an amazing, feat borne of patience, hard work and assiduous planting. Hats off to them for living the (self-sufficient) dream.

COOL FACTOR Organic living and river swimming in France's sun-baked Languedoc-Roussillon region.

WHO'S IN Tents, glampers, families, couples and sun-seekers — yes. Caravans, campervans and dogs — no.

ON SITE In the summer there are 6 fully-equipped spacious 'De Waard' tents, accommodating 4–5 persons. Until June and again in September you can come with your own tent but to avoid disappointment always contact the site first. The shop sells campsite basics (organic bread, milk, coffee, alcohol). There's a washing machine, internet (by ethernet cable), hot showers, kids' play area and a shared BBQ. No pets are allowed but they have their own cats, dogs, rabbits, chickens, donkeys and ponies. Frauke offers weekly donkey and horse guided rides.

OFF SITE The narrow mountain road has a precipitous drop; it's not for the faint-hearted. Nor is it for those who like nipping out to the shops. Any journey away from the site is a bit of an adrenaline sport in itself, so for something a little more relaxing planning a hiking trip with Johan is recommended — particularly his half- or full-day walks across the border into Spain. Pony- and horse-trekking can also be arranged, with shorter routes for children.

FOOD & DRINK Home-baked bread, cakes, jams, chutney and organic vegetables and fruits are at your fingertips.

GETTING THERE Fly to Perpignan or Girona, then hire a car or take a bus to Amélie-les-Bains. The road is in the eastern Pyrénées mountains, 20 minutes from Amélie-les-Bains by car, 50 minutes from Collioure. Heading south on the D115, after Amèlie-les-Bains, take the first left signposted to Gorges du Mondon, passing Mas Pagris village along a long dirt track (with a precipitous drop!). On its descent, there's a right turn into the driveway.

PUBLIC TRANSPORT You can get a bus from Perpignan to Amélie-les-Bains. It's a two-hour walk from there or they may be able to pick you up.

OPEN Open all year round. May is a great time to see Céret's cherry blossom in full bloom.

THE DAMAGE Please contact Frauke and Johan for prices.

ascou la forge

Camping Ascou la Forge, 09110 Ascou Frankrijk, Ariege 00 33 5 61 64 60 03 www.mountain-sports.net

In the heart of the Pyrénées, close to the Spain–Andorra border, Ascou La Forge is like a family-friendly base camp for a world of European adventure. Surrounded by forest and mountains and a well-spring for all things outdoors, it's a real hub for adventure and extreme sports – exactly the reason that owners Adrie Dekker and Helma Gorter first moved here. Originally from the Netherlands, they moved to France in 1994 and set up Ascou la Forge, driven by their passion for nature and love of outdoor persuits. They certainly didn't choose a bad spot. Footpaths riddle the mountain sides, lakes laze in shimmering pools at the bottom of every valley and peaks spike a dramatic skyline.

The site itself, while surrounded by rich, forested vegetation, retains a surprisingly open feel, made up of 55 large, well-organised pitches, most of which can be provided with electricity. For those looking for a more glamorous option, two yurts are also available, and a few other accommodation options like gîtes and apartments will allow you to convince even your camping-phobic friends to come along.

Down one side of the site, a river spills into a lake where fishing is permitted. Campfires can be lit along its banks, sending thin whisps of smoke across the site, and marshmallows are sold in the site reception (along with basic food, local wine and books about the area), so you can indulge to your heart's content. Not that you need to waste your time crouched around the campfire. A restaurant (open daily from May to September, and again from December to April, for the ski season) serves excellent, locally-sourced food and has a wonderful terrace for admiring the views. There's also a bar with the finest Belgium beer on draft.

The list of things to do in the area is extensive, and caters to every interest. There are a number of fantastic walking trails from the site – Adrie and Helma are more than happy to recommend the best – and if, as the sun begins to set, you decide you're not ready to turn back, you can stop at one of the several gîtes d'etapes in the mountains. Once you set out you'll understand the draw. Each turn reveals a new natural wonder, a field of mountain flowers or a crystal clear lake at the bottom of a deep valley, and the diverse range of route options leaves a nagging sense that you haven't seen it all. Not that you ever can. Be careful though, it's exactly this sense of unfinished business that led Adrie and Helma to move out here. You may just end up wanting to do the same!

COOL FACTOR A tranquil base for exploring the mountains of the Pyrénées.

WHO'S IN Tents, caravans, campervans and dogs – yes. During the high season (July–August) large groups are not accepted.

ON SITE 55 pitches (most with electricity), 3 chalets, 1 apartment and 2 wooden yurts. There are 2 toilet buildings, with 9 hot showers, 9 toilets and washrooms and laundry facilities. A new Sodiac swimming pool is available for all to use. A small river flows alongside the campsite where children can also swim and build dams and there is a lake where you can fish. Campfires permitted on the lakeside and river banks. In the high season an activity is organised every day, from slack–lining to games of hide-and-seek.

OFF SITE The campsite is perfectly situated for hiking and the owners are happy to recommend certain trails. As well as the campsite, the owners also run an outdoor centre, and campsite visitors can participate in various outdoor activities such as kayaking and rock-climbing, all led by English-speaking guides. A little further afield you'll find the underground river of Labouiche (0033 561 650 411) where you can take a cruise through the caves, or visit Montsegur Castle (0033 561 010 694) or the Chateau de Foix (0033 534 098 383) to learn about the area's history.

FOOD & DRINK There are 2 dining options at the campsite: a restaurant (open May–September and December–April), where you can eat à la carte or from the menu of the day; and a small bar, where you can find snacks as well as local wines and Belgium beer on draft. In Ax-les-Thermes (a 10 minute drive) there's a wider variety of restaurants and pubs.

GETTING THERE From the roundabout in Ax-les-Thermes, follow the sign Ascou-Pailhères. After 3.5km turn right towards Ascou; 3km past Ascou you will see Goulours lake; the campsite is on your right, 500m after the lake.

PUBLIC TRANSPORT There is a train station and buses stop in Ax-les-Thermes, from where a lift to the campsite can be organised with the owners.

OPEN All year.

THE DAMAGE A pitch and 2 people from €13 without electricity, €16 with electricity.

camping site et paysages la serre

Camping La Serre, 09600 Aigues-Vives, Ariege 00 33 5 61 03 06 16 www.camping-la-serre.com

It's no surprise to us that one of our favourite campsites from a previous edition of this very book was snapped up by a pair of avid *Cool Camping* fans when it went on sale in 2014. After all, the site is nothing short of a masterpiece and today it continues to be a fully-fledged, award-winning work of wonder. It's certainly not lacking in space, nor is it lacking in stonking views and excellent facilities. So what a joy it is that new hosts Corinne and Patrick are just as welcoming and friendly as the last.

The first thing you notice about Camping La Serre is the sheer amount of room. This is not a congested campsite, but an orderly, manicured place with masses of trees, well-kept grass and wide-open skies. There are 14 wooden chalets on site, as well as an area for caravans, but the high hedges mean they're generally unobtrusive. Plus the 48-pitch tent area is entirely separate and comes with similarly vast, enclosed terraces shaded by ancient oaks, thoughtfully placed so as not to obscure the views. The newly-built Cabane dans le Arbes ('the Hut in the Trees') offers a charming alternative if you're on the hunt for something different. A timber treehouse that comfortably sleeps a family of five, the fully-equipped lodge offers perfect sylvan seclusion and a sweeping panorama of the Pyrénées. The rest of the campsite is connected via large walkways that have their own names, underlining the impression that you're in a self-contained universe here. The reception area is fairly simple – a small cabin with a laundry room, a naturalist's library and tourist information leaflets – and Corinne and Patrick are always on hand to give out advice, maps, cycling circuits and more. Around the corner there's a decent-sized pool, a badminton net, slides and a football pitch, while, on the other side of the reception a huge warehouse is filled with old farming equipment – an eco-museum started by the previous owners and later expanded through local donations. It gives a thorough picture of France's farming practices over the years, and in summer the owners also organise a local foodie evening here, with farmers bringing wine and produce from the surrounding area.

Large and spacious as it is, the campsite only takes up a small portion of the total 170 acres on offer. Much of the remaining space is grazed by skinny sheep, but part has been set aside for a wild nature reserve that houses various species of orchids, birds and butterflies. Campers can head off on foot to walk the well-marked trails, or, if you're looking to head further afield, the surrounding countryside is awash with paths for cyclists and walkers. There are pretty villages to discover and larger cities, such as Toulouse, to visit – though something tells us that you'll be in no rush to get away. After all, we think there's nowhere better.

COOL FACTOR Giant pitches and an onsite nature reserve at this award-winning eco-campsite.

WHO'S IN Caravans, campervans, tents, groups, dogs – yes.

ON SITE 48 very large camping pitches, cabins, safari tents and a treehouse. Swimming pool, washing machine (€5), large children's play area, 4 clean and decent toilet and shower blocks, a nature reserve and eco-museum on site (both free).

OFF SITE Bikes can be arranged through the site, or you can make a call to Vélomondo (0033 631 942 491), who deliver bikes and can advise on routes. Adults and kids alike will love the Parc de la Préhistoire (0033 561 051 010) in Tarascon, which has outdoor installations showing how caves are formed by water flowing over rock, examples of the types of shelters used in Magdalenian times, and replicas and photos of drawings and paintings found in other caves. There's also a restaurant and picnic area. If you enjoyed La Serre's eco-museum, the Forges de Pyrène (0033 534 093 060) in Montgailhard is recommended, with several different areas in a pretty park and exhibitions on sabot-making and horn-comb manufacture, plus an old forge and bakery.

FOOD & DRINK The site sells fresh baguettes, croissants and coffee in the morning, as well as excellent bio-wines from local producer Coteaux d'Engraviès (0033 561 68 68 68). There are food and wine-tastings once a week on site during July and August. In the tiny town of Léran you'll find a very nice British-run bistro called Le Rendezvous (0033 951 424 791), which serves good lunches and evening meals and has free Wi-Fi access and regular music nights.

GETTING THERE The site is accessed by way of the D625, between Mirepoix and Lavelanet. It is well signposted from both of these towns.

OPEN April–end of October.

THE DAMAGE A pitch and 2 people €13–€24, extra people €5, dogs €2. Mobile homes from €100 for 2 people for 2 nights, €330–€490 for a week. The treehouse starts at €256 for 2 nights for a family of 5.

etang du camp

12320 Conques, Sénergues, Aveyron 00 33 5 65 46 01 95 www.etangducamp.fr

Situated on a mountain plateau beside a lake ornamented by a Monet-style bridge, Étang du Camp is a once-neglected municipal site that in 2006 was lucky enough to be rescued. The views are serene, but there are a couple of quirks you might want to prepare yourself for, not least the sight of water buffaloes beside the reed-fringed lakeside – a sight that is all the more real due to the honeyed African light dappling the canvas of your safari tent. Check your GPS and you're actually in Aveyron, and the buffaloes belong to a neighbour. But the lake and the safari tents are real and very alluring, plus the latter come fully-equipped with a real bed and cooking facilities.

Stuart and Christine are great hosts and an excellent source of knowledge on how to make the best of the area. Their organised campfires are an ideal time to share ideas, enjoyed with a glass of wine and *aligot-saucisse* (local-style sausage and mash). A first port of call is the nearby settlement of Conques, a cliff-huddling town which looks as if it's stepped straight out of *The Name of the Rose*. Sit in the peaceful Abbaye de Ste-Foy (best visited in early evening as the light is fading) and listen to choral music before walking the labyrinthine streets. You'll be following in the footsteps of thousands of Santiago de Compostela pilgrims, who've been coming through here since the 11th century.

COOL FACTOR An exotic-tinged mountain-top retreat with views, walks and a medieval town to die for.

WHO'S IN Tents, caravans, campervans, dogs – yes.

ON SITE The site has mature shaded areas and a maximum of 40 pitches. A clean wash-block catering for babies and disabled campers. There's also a washing machine (€4). Ice cream parlour, table tennis and play area. The lake is home to pike, carp and perch, and fishing is free provided you throw it back. Organised campfires. All safari tents have real beds, cooking facilities, a BBQ and picnic table. Fresh bread delivery if ordered the night before.

OFF SITE Aveyron's wooded valleys, poppy-flecked mountain meadows, honey vendors and pottery workshops are the attraction here. One of the loveliest walks is the 7km ramble in La Vinzelle (ask Christine for details and a map). Pick up a kayak and float down the Lot from Entraygues-sur-Truyère.

FOOD & DRINK Christine serves up continental breakfasts (€6.50–€7.50) and evening meals are also available one night each week. The nearest town is St-Cyprien-sur-Dourdou, which has plenty of cafés and grocery shops, incuding Hervé Busset (0033 565 728 477), a 1-star Michelin restaurant in a magnificent historic setting. The Auberge St-Jacques (0033 565 728 636) is cheaper, with 3-course meals starting at €18.

GETTING THERE By car from Brive-la-Gaillarde, head to Figeac on D840, then to Decazeville. From here it's easy to reach St-Cyprien-sur-Dourdou, then follow signs to Sénergues on the D502 then D46; L'Étang du Camp is signposted from the D242.

OPEN April–September.

THE DAMAGE Safari tent (2–4 people) €227–€305 per week. Tent (2 people, electricity) €18.50 per night. Campervan (electricity) €19.50 per night. Mobile home (2–4 people) €260–€490.

camping fans

Lieudit Fans, 12390 Rignac, Aveyron 00 33 5 65 64 49 56 www.camping-fans.com

In the words of Bjork, 'It's, oh, so quiet'. We're in the heart of the Aveyron, one of France's largest, least-populated, départements, and, we might venture, one of its most beautiful. Yet there's hardly a soul to be seen. It's high season, a time when the roads are choked with traffic and café tables permanently occupied by the hungry hordes. Yet Belcastel feels like a slice of France that is still relatively unspoiled by mass tourism.

A fabled medieval settlement, home to some 200 residents, Belcastel sits on the tranquil banks of the River Aveyron. Its 11th-century chateau and spread of ancient houses, set on cobbled streets, nestles on the wooded slopes along the riverbank. The town's humpbacked Gothic bridge, positively demands an impromptu game of Poohsticks. It's easy to see why this has been officially voted one of the most beautiful villages in France.

Just down the road, in the idyllic hamlet of the same name, Camping Fans is set within 55 acres of tranquil riverside valley meadows. This picturesque family-friendly site is the pride and joy of wonderful campsite chiefs Pieter and Marcelline Quartero. Essentially, it's a tale of two campsites: an *aire naturelle* site that caters to the bulk of campers, including a couple of groups in the fully-furnished glamping tents (akin to a miniature circus pavillion on a wooden deck), while The Secret Valley is secluded between the wooded slopes of the valley. To call the pitches spacious would

be an understatement. Even in the height of the summer season, this place never feels crowded and kids can run around the place as they please.

The main draw here, though, is the river. Its gently-flowing waters are safe for all children of swimming/paddling ability, and there's a small sandy beach to navigate your way in. With the summer sun in full beam, there's a steady stream of parched campers lining up to jump of the jetty into the cooling waters of the tranquil Aveyron. The river is also teeming with wildlife, from herons and coypus to trout and the sweet-tasting *écrevisse* (crayfish to you and me) – the perfect addition to a summer salad.

There's a pleasingly lazy pace to life round here. There are no 'animations' for children ('we think children are much more capable of amusing themselves than whatever we as adults may possibly come up with') and Pieter and Marcelline pride themselves on their daily break between 12.30pm and 3pm. Fresh bread and croissants are delivered from the village boulangerie every morning in high season – the perfect accompaniment to the excellent morning coffee to be had in the communal barn.

Camping Fans by name; camping fans by nature – Pieter and Marcelline know exactly what campers want out of an Aveyron holiday under canvas. And no doubt this gorgeous, unspoiled riverside site will be winning a few more fans, season after season.

COOL FACTOR A wonderfully unspoiled riverside site in the heart of the Aveyron countryside.

WHO'S IN Tents, trailer tents, well-behaved groups, dogs (outside of high season) – yes. Caravans/motorhomes, campervans, dogs (in high season) – no.

ON SITE 33 pitches spread over adjoining 2 sites ('The Secret Valley' and the 'Aire Naturelle'). The Secret Valley has a wash-block with 1 shower, 1 sink and 2 toilets for up to 8 tents; the Aire Naturelle site has 2 showers, 4 toilets and 6 sinks for up to 25 tents. There's no electricity in the Secret Valley but Aire Naturelle has 17 hook-ups (2 amp) and also boasts 2 fully-furnished, cotton glamping tents (each sleeping 4). Fridge and a washing machine available. Free Wi-Fi available at the café in the Small Barn.

OFF SITE Aveyron is a dream for the outdoor enthusiast. There's canoeing just an hour from Camping Fans and plenty of great hiking routes, with the GR62B directly accessible from the site. Gorgeous Belcastel (officially among 'the most beautiful villages in France') is just a short drive away. Its quaint cobbled streets, distinctive 15th-century stone houses and medieval castle sit on the tranquil banks of the Aveyron river. Every Friday its night market brims with plenty of stalls offering food, drink and good company. Beyond, Villefranche-de-Rouergue boasts many historic buildings and a famous Thursday morning market. Enchanting old Rodez also boasts a market on Saturday morning. The atmospheric medieval village and ruined twin towers of the château inférieur at Peyrusse le Roc are also an essential visit. An hour's drive away, the Tarn-side city of Albi hosts a UNESCO World Heritage Site around its cathedral and the renowned Musée Toulouse Lautrec (0033 563 494 870) in honour of its most famous son.

FOOD & DRINK Fresh bread and croissants are delivered by the village baker every morning in the high season. Homecooked hot meals are offered twice a week. There's a great little market in Rignac every Tuesday morning –

perfect for basic and artisan produce. You can also order takeaway pizzas from the village. L'hôtel restaurant du Vieux Pont (0033 565 645 229) in Belcastel offers stunning views and impressively refined French cuisine. For something a little less grand, Chez Anna (0033 565 639 561) serves simple food from its delightful terrace. The famous wine region of Marcillac is just 20km to the north-west of Rignac: be sure to visit for the Sunday morning market and pick up a nice bottle of red to accompany the local specialty, *tripoux* (stuffed sheep's tripe).

GETTING THERE Coming from Paris on the A75, follow the signs for Clermont-Ferrand. Continue in the direction of Montpellier and leave the motorway at Sévérac-le-Chateau. Follow the signs to Rodez on the N88. In Rodez follow the D994 and the signs for Montauban at all the roundabouts. Then, after almost half an hour of driving, you will arrive at a roundabout named 'Giratoire de Rignac-Centre' which is actually the first roundabout after leaving Rodez. Turn left onto the D997 in the direction of Colombiès and Belcastel (do not go into Rignac). After about 5km you will arrive at Le Pont Neuf; just before the bridge you will see a small and narrow road turning sharply to the right with signposts indicating Fans and Camping de Fans. Follow this small road, with the river on your left-hand side for about a kilometre to the first buildings. You have arrived at the farmhouse. If you find that you have crossed the river you've gone too far!

PUBLIC TRANSPORT The nearest train stations are in Rodez and Villefranche-de-Rouergue. But as public transport is very bad in the region and taxis quite costly, you really need a car to get around – if only because the closest shops are 6km from the site.

OPEN May–end of September. The Orchard Barn is open April–October.

THE DAMAGE Pitch €6, adults €6.50, children under 9 years €3.25. Small supplementary tent €3. Electricity €2.50. 'Circus' Canvas Tent €450–€500 per week. Old Orchard Barn €390–€550 per week.

le camp

82330 Varen, Tarn-et-Garonne 00 33 6 11 94 33 68 www.lecamp.co.uk

If there's a better feeling than that of gliding smoothly through a crystal-clear natural swimming pool while eye-to-eye with frogs perched nonchalantly on rocks, then we've yet to experience it. The chirp of crickets, the buzz of dragonflies, birdsong, and, of course, the croaking chorus of those ubiquitous frogs provide the soundtrack to a wonderfully wild swim which proves the perfect introduction to Le Camp, a secluded south-west campsite set in leafy surroundings and combining 5-star facilities with a truly relaxed atmosphere.

The site is owned and run by Sally and Stephen O'Hare, a British couple who in 2007 gave up high-flying jobs to set up the sort of site that they would want to stay at. They were looking to create something small, personal, comfortable and natural, especially with children in mind, as it's well known that kids don't like 5-star hotels, even if their parents do. Here, nippers can run around in a safe, beautiful setting while mums and dads can relax and feel as if they too are having a treat.

These treats, as the visitor will discover, are many and varied. From the fluffy towels in each of the tents and yurts, to the large handmade double beds and clever en suite composting toilets, this is camping with the rough edges smoothed off. Take breakfast, for example. Whereas most sites might see people struggling to fire up a gas stove, Le Camp takes the strain out of *le petit dejeuner* by providing fresh pastries, local cured meats, cheese, yogurt, baguettes and proper lattes from a machine that wouldn't look out of place in Starbucks. Naturally, it's all included in the price.

Don't worry, though, the essential spirit of camping still remains. The central cooking area lets different visitors meet and chat while they prepare dinner, but there's none of that cringeworthy group action. Sure, there's a little court set up for an impromptu game of pétanque and a badminton net hangs between two trees, but there are no chalked-up league tables or happy-camper types urging you to join in the fun. The vibe is as natural as the surroundings.

Perhaps most impressive is just how different it could have been. Sitting in the stunning Aveyron Valley in the Midi-Pyrénées region, this formerly run-down campsite used to have some 38 camping pitches, but the current owners have allowed the surroundings to flourish, shrinking it down to just three safari-style tents, two woodland yurts, and one 'giant' yurt, with the latter boasting its own sandpit, firepit and shaded seating area. The eco-credentials, too, are impressive. 'Grey' water is recycled, solar lighting is used and the pool is cleaned naturally by gravel and plants. Local, organic products are used as much as possible, and most of the furniture has been handmade by Stephen himself. His transformation from high-flying Google exec to man-of-the-woods type is one that he clearly relishes. It's an incredible place to bring up children, he says, and every day is an outdoor adventure.

COOL FACTOR The most refreshing campsite pool you'll ever swim in, plus thoughtful touches of luxury throughout.

WHO'S IN Kids, large groups, young groups – yes. Tents, campervans, caravans, dogs – no.

ON SITE Six tents, all with wide beds, solar lighting and, in all but the 2 woodland yurts, dry composting toilets. Shower block with 3 shower rooms and a disabled room. Full range of kitchen appliances, crockery, utensils and condiments. Snug block with a wood-burning stove, a book exchange, magazines, games, power sockets, Wi-Fi – and free breakfast served. Free laundry. BBQ and salad/herb garden to help yourself to. The natural, fully-fenced swimming pond does not have a lifeguard, but has a wristband-operated alarm system. Trampoline, sandpit, rope-swing, boules and badminton. Excellently equipped for toddlers and babies – just ask.

OFF SITE There are over 1000 climbing routes around the Gorges de l'Aveyron and the landscape is criss-crossed by waymarked walks. Head to the nearby St-Antonin-Noble-Val to enjoy a spot of kayaking, hiring your boat for the day from Kayman canoes (0033 568 429 681). Alternatively, buy a fishing licence from a local newsagent and do some angling for trout from one of the area's many bridges. Further afield, the Forêt de la Grésigne offers the chance to experience the largest oak forest in Europe. If it rains, take a short drive to Albi and check out its Toulouse-Lautrec museum (0033 563 494 870). Sally and Stephen are happy to suggest ideas and book things for you, so just ask.

FOOD & DRINK In the nearby medieval town of St Antonin Noble Val, characterful La Corniche (0033 563 682 695) is exellent and the views are knock-out. Or seek out the riverside Manjocarn Café (0033 563 682 585), hang out of choice for all the local climbers and so laid-back it's unbelievable.

GETTING THERE Advanced bookings required. Detailed directions provided once booking is confirmed.

OPEN June–September. Minimum stay of 7 nights in July & August, 4 nights in June & September.

THE DAMAGE Yurts and tents from £165 per night (includes breakfast, bedding and use of all facilities free of charge).

the midsummer retreat

Nr Saint-Antonin-Noble-Val, Tarn-et-Garonne, France   00 33 6 04 19 88 11   www.themidsummerretreat.eu

There's something wonderfully organic about the way the yurt at The Midsummer Retreat is set into its landscape. In the grounds of an old French farmhouse, the surroundings are wild and slightly disordered yet without feeling overgrown. Flowers fight among lush, long grass to be seen and potted daisy's spill over the tops of their containers. The wooded slopes around the garden give the sense that it is almost sunken into the landscape, yet the lawns themselves are neatly mown. Combine all this with the timber frame of a manmade kitchen area and the earthy-colour of the single, glampers' yurt and it's almost as though the place simply grew, like the garden, from the ground beneath it.

The site has, in fact, been a labour of love and many years in the making. The hard work here has been worth it. With just one yurt for guests – sleeping up to four people – The Midsummer Retreat has a truly personal feel and it's only right that something so small should be extra special. The attention to detail is impeccable. The private bathroom, for example, features recycled 16th-century terracotta tiles found in an ancient, local forge in the River Aveyron gorge, while the kitchen and living space is furnished with vintage finds from local markets. The rustic, old-country vibe it creates mirrors the setting but it still retains some modern functionality – there's a fridge, oven and electricity for charging your camera or mobile phone.

Nearby St-Antonin-Noble-Val is the reason for the camera. The tiny medieval town has everything you need – cafés, boulangeries and postcard shops – all crammed into a picturesque labyrinth of tiny alleyways and tall stone houses. It boasts one of the oldest town halls in the country. Visit on Sunday to catch the bustling market, where you can stock up on local cheese before heading further along the river for a picnic and a swim. The River Aveyron is as beautiful as it is calm and perfectly safe for a good paddle.

Once you're well worn out, you can retreat back to camp for a nice lie down and a chance to soak in the view. The best of it is sometimes comes when darkness falls. The middle section of the canvas roof can be completely rolled back and, sunken in the hollow of the landscape, there's no light pollution to spoil the stars. Kick back and enjoy the show, you've got the whole place to yourself.

COOL FACTOR Peace, privacy and acres of natural space. Saint-Antonin-Noble-Val is a stone's throw away and the accommodation itself is finished to the finest detail.

WHO'S IN Glampers only. Tents, campervans, caravans, pets – no.

ON SITE Yurt (sleeping 4) with wooden floor, antique rugs and decor, double bed, additional box-bed/sofa-bed, books, games, mosquito nets if needed. Linen, towels and soaps all included. Self-contained bathroom space with shower, hand basin, toilet. Kitchen area with cooker, fridge/freezer, crockery, cutlery and utensils, electric sockets, table, chairs and high chairs if needed.

OFF SITE Maps and guidebooks on local walking routes are found on the bookshelves at the campsite. This is real walkers' country and there are suitable footpaths for all levels. Swim in the river which starts a short drive away at St-Antonin-Noble-Val. Those too chicken to go in the wilds of the river water can use the outdoor pool there instead, complete with with dramatic views of the Gorge de Ayeyron. Canoes are also available to hire along the waterside in town, or follow the river's course from St Antonin past the ancient chateaux of Penne and Briuniquel by car, stopping along the way to swim in the water – there are a few natural beaches (not sandy though) and some great rocks to jump in from.

FOOD & DRINK If you fancy whipping up a storm in the campsite kitchen (cupboard basics are supplied), head to Saint-Antonin-Noble-Val where there's a thriving local market on Sundays. The town also has 2 wonderful bakeries and 2 good small supermarkets for anything else. In terms of restaurants and cafés, Café De La Halle is the best for ice cream, cold drinks and people watching in town. Go in the evening (after 7pm) for pizza.

GETTING THERE This is a small, private glamping site so you only get the exact location and directions when you make your booking.

OPEN Late May–end of September.

THE DAMAGE From £750 per week.

country camping

Lieu dit Louise, 31550, Gaillac Toulza, Haute-Garonne 00 33 5 61 08 45 37 countrycampingfrance.com

A healthy tan, a nice dose of vitamin-D – there's much to be said for sun-seeking. And if you're the sort of person who needs an excuse, just look to nature. It's a part of our natural evolution. Like a field of sunflowers in the Midi-Pyrénées turning from east to west as the day goes on. Or like the leaves of the fig trees tilting in the afternoon light as they bring themselves to fruit. As the hippies would say, 'it's all natural man. It's all natural' So while during the winter months Country Camping may close the gates for a little shut-eye, come the beginning of April campers seem born to trickle back again – human sunflowers coming down from the north to catch those revitalising rays.

Nonetheless, that the Midi-Pyrénées is often dubbed 'Toulouse and the Midi-Pyrénéan Desert' is something of a misnomer – a reference not to the heat but to the relative absence of activity in these parts compared to the bustling city an hour's drive away. There's a definite rural feel, a landscape that is home to more farms than any other region in France. And it's this quiet rusticity, this peaceful countryside charm and pastoral *joie de vivre* vibe that Country Camping is very much a part of.

In springtime, you can catch the last of the colourful blossoms as they're replaced by cherries dangling appetisingly from the trees. In autumn, it's the peaches, like soft, velvety fists, ripe for the picking. Whenever you come, the shady trees that enclose the twenty grassy pitches provide a natural, green feel that's in keeping with the pastoral

French surroundings. The best spots are actually those with the slightly lower hedges, the gaps revealing views across the neighbouring field and partially wooded valley.

Those looking for a little more luxury can rent one of the pre-pitched bell tents, bag the bijou wooden chalet or try one of three, fully-furnished safari tents onsite. All allow plenty of space and save you the hassle of packing up the car with heaps of camping gear. Yet the real comfort of this campsite is the easy-going atmosphere it affords. A small outdoor swimming pool sloshes around under the energy of younger campers, overlooked by a chilled-out bar terrace where quieter kids are setting about a nerve-racking game of giant outdoor jenga. After that, try the neighbouring stretch of woodland, somewhere to build dens and search for dragons and gruffalos – though the ones around here are French-speaking, so kids may have to brush up on their vocab before any unexpected encounters.

It's these simple pleasures that make Country Camping such a great campsite, independently of the many pleasant attractions nearby. It's an easy cycle to the old military village of Saint Ybars, while a drive to the spectacular natural Pyrénées Ariégeoises park provides an endless list of outdoor activities to try. But while these exploratory day-trips reveal the place to be anything but a desert there's something just as charming about a lazy afternoon back at base, frolicking in the pool and enjoying the ever present necessity of the sun.

COOL FACTOR Fresh fruit and chilled camping in the sunshine. What more could you need?

WHO'S IN Tents, caravans, motorhomes, campervans, trailer-tents, dogs – yes.

ON SITE 20 grass tent pitches and 12 hardstandings all with electric hook-ups. 8 bell tents for rent, 3 large, 2-bedroom safari tents, a wooden chalet and mobile homes also available to rent. All pitches have electrical hook-ups and each safari tent has a living kitchen area with a gas hob and refrigerator, a shaded veranda, and can accommodate up to 5 people. Bed linen and cooking utensils are provided. There are 2 shower and toilet buildings, washing-up facilities, a disabled shower and toilet and a washing machine (€6 per wash). The campsite has a swimming pool with decked sun terrace, a boules court, bar and terrace, BBQ area, volleyball court, children's playground with outdoor table tennis and Tarzan rope swings. Childrens' activities include painting, clay modelling, treasure hunts, boules competitions, glass painting and jewellery making. Wi-Fi is available.

OFF SITE The region has a host of interesting cities, towns and villages to visit – lively and beautiful Toulouse (1hour's drive) and historic Foix (50mins), overlooked by an ancient castle (0033 534 098 383) – are amongst them. Closer at hand, the nearby fortress villages such as Saint Ybars (10mins away) and Carla-Bayle (25mins away) are also worth a trip. Take the family white-water canoeing on the Garonne, challenge yourself to climb the aerial walkways of Sequoya adventure park (0033 561 685 151) or try horseriding through the local countryside. For the best of the scenery, head to Parc Naturel Régional des Pyrénées Ariégeoises (0033 561 027 169), a half-hour's drive away and the most scenic spot for outdoor pursuits and wildlife watching.

FOOD & DRINK Country Camping has a cheerful bar that provides a variety of drinks. On Saturday's there's a BBQ held on the terrace overlooking the swimming pool and Thursday is pizza night, with pizzas cooked in their outdoor wood-fired oven served in the bar or under the sunshades outside. Elsewhere there are nearby markets in Auterive and Carla-Bayle, the best places to go for fresh local produce.

GETTING THERE Country Camping is located near the village of Gaillac-Toulza, which is situated in the Haute-Garonne, 39km from Toulouse, the department capital. It is approx a 9–10 hour drive from Calais, a 4-hour drive from Bilbao, 6 hours' drive from Santander.

PUBLIC TRANSPORT It is an hour and 15 minutes' drive from Carcassonne airport and 45 minutes from Toulouse airport – served by Easyjet and Ryanair. The nearest train station is in Saverdun (approx. 10mins by car) and Auterive (approx. 15mins by car). The nearest transport link via bus is Saint Ybar (approx. 20mins walk away).

OPEN April–October.

THE DAMAGE 1 person tent/caravan pitch €12–€18; 2 person tent/caravan pitch €16–€22.50; extra people €6, children (1–15yrs) €4. Electricity €1.50–€4. Dogs €2.

camping pré fixe

Route de Saint Gaudens 31 420 Cassagnabère-Tournas, Haute-Garonne 00 33 5 61 98 71 00 www.camping-pre-fixe.com

Covering a region of over 45,000km², the Mid-Pyrénées is the largest departement in France. In an area bigger than the Netherlands, visitors could be forgiven for feeling a little bit, well, overwhelmed, especially in the shadow of such imposing mountains. But fear not, cool campers, for this is also one of France's most sparsely populated regions. Daily life seems to breeze along round these parts, with the locals renowned *gourmands* and unashamed exponents of that quintessential *joie de vivre*. We're happy to report that this laid-back atmosphere has extended to the local camping fraternity and in particular, the wonderfully easy-going Camping Pré Fixe.

Nestled next to the ancient foothill village of Comminges – the historic regional capital – Camping Pré Fixe positively oozes peace and tranquility. Campers are spoilt for choice with a number of accommodation options on offer, including traditional tent pitches, luxury lodges and chalets as well as the cute little Canadian cabin on stilts, complete with double bed and kitchenette – perfect for camping couples. With an onsite swimming pool, tennis courts and more activities than you shake a baguette at, there's plenty to keep you occupied (and that's not even mentioning the wealth of outdoor pursuits that await in the surrounding mountains). The camp's own bar – *Le Bistro* – is a labour of love for resident sommelier and owner Cyril who stocks some of the finest vino courtesy of a carefully selected band of local producers.

So with good wine, good entertainment and even better views, Camping Pré Fixe ticks all Cool Camping boxes. When it comes to glamping in France, the decision has never been easier.

COOL FACTOR A perfect family site with a homely, welcoming vibe.

WHO'S IN Tents, campervans, caravans, glamping, camping, pets – yes.

ON SITE This terraced site consists of 43 spacious pitches separated by hedges and various arborea species for added shade. Electrical hook-ups available on some plots. New for 2016 are fully-equipped bell tents sleeping up to 2, sitting atop decking on stilts. They come equipped with bedding (sheets not provided), 1 double bed, kitchenette, refrigerator, gas stove and grill – picnic table also included outside. Luxury wooden cabins are also available. Laundry facilities; onsite grocery shop; bar/bistro. Boules, tennis court; badminton and volleyball; children's library; board games; ping-pong. No campfires.

OFF SITE With the Pyrénées just beyond your tent flaps, there's a wealth of outdoor pursuits on hand – caving, rock climbing, paragliding, rafting, canyoning and kayaking, to name but a few. There's also plenty of walking/hiking/cycling routes and the beautiful ancient village of Comminges is just a short stroll from the site.

FOOD & DRINK Le Bistro offers quality wines and a fresh daily menu of homemade dishes. Cyril also organises BBQs, evening dinners and wine tasting events.

GETTING THERE From Paris, take the A10 and then the A62 and then the A64 (in the direction of Tarbes); exit at Junction 21 (Aurignac direction) and finally head for Cassagnaberes.

OPEN Start of April–mid October.

THE DAMAGE Pitch, 2 persons, 1 car: €14.60–€22.50; with electricity €18.80–€26.70. Extra adults €4.50–€6.70, extra children €3.50–€5.60. Pets €2.50–€3.

camping la vie en rose

Escanecrabe, 31350 Haute-Garonne 00 33 6 71 01 49 57 campinglavieenrose.com

Nestled on the undulating southern slopes of bucolic Gascony – a land famed for it's *douceur de vivre* – Camping La Vie en Rose exhibits the fabled 'sweetness of life', and then some. Stretching across seven breathtaking acres of tranquil, wildflower meadow, fringed by enchanting oak woodlands, the views from this beautiful Haute-Garrone glamping site are breathtaking, with the peaks of the Pyrénées towering tantalisingly on the horizon.

After being met with the warmest of welcomes from hosts Emma and Jamie Fulton, the lucky glampers are shown one of five spacious bell tents. Well, we call them tents but that doesn't really do justice to the scale and style of these canvas palaces. Sat atop timber decking with shaggy rugs throughout, each bell boasts a lounge plus two separate bedroom tents including a deluxe 'superking' room that's ideal for parents. Outside, a fully-equipped campsite kitchen has the answer to all your culinary needs, while the über-luxurious timber washing lodge is the very definition of hi-spec, with hot power showers, marble washbasins, organic soaps and fluffy towels.

With an assortment of outdoor entertainment (a swimming pool, pétanque, slides and swings), a well-stocked games room (books, pool table, ping pong), and lots of other thoughtful touches (cots, high chairs, breakfast delivered fresh to your tent), it's clear that Camping La Vie en Rose is a site run by people who know the ingredients you need for a fuss-free family holiday. With all the comforts of a boutique hotel at a snippet of the cost, this is the ideal break for families looking to really get away from it all.

And when it's time to venture forth, this pocket of south-western France has a wealth of scenic and historical eye candy to sample. Head to the beach at Lac de la Gimone for a refreshing summer swim, or take your little lords and ladies to the fortified city of Carcassonne – a UNESCO World Heritage Site that hosts jousting, troubadours and medieval fairs. And of course, there's the Pyrénées calling all weekend-Wigginses to test their cycling stamina on the Col du Tourmalet Col d'Aspin.

Named after the signature tune of France's national songstress, Edith Piaf, a stay at Camping La Vie en Rose really is a 'Life in Rosy Hues'. Swinging lazily in the hammock, admiring this secluded patch of Pyrenean paradise, we reckon France's iconic diva would approve.

COOL FACTOR Life is seen through rose-coloured spectacles at this breathtaking slice of Pyrenean paradise.

WHO'S IN Groups, families – yes. Dogs, caravans, campervans, motorhomes – no.

ON SITE Five spacious bell tents with wooden flooring, a separate lounge, decking and shaded canvas awnings. Each tent has its own fully-equipped outdoor kitchen with gas hob and fridge, plus private shower/toilet room facilities with organic soaps and towels included. Swimming pool, outdoor lounge/Morrocan area (candlelit in evenings, perfect for glass of wine or as a shady reading area during the day). Free Wi-Fi, BBQ (including charcoal, fire starters, etc) and a washing machine.

OFF SITE Head up the mountains for a spot of wild swimming. Day trips to Les Laquettes, Lac de Mondeley and Lacs de Bastan are a popular option. There's car parking available and the latter boasts a café and beach. France's fourth largest city Toulouse is around an hour away. There are plenty of museums and exhibitions to see, including the fine art collection at the Musée des Augustins (0033 561 222 182), while a visit to the Cité de l'Espace (0033 567 222 324) – the national space centre – is out of this world. A gentle river cruise along the city's Canal du Midi is a fantastically peaceful way to round off your day-trip. Or why not treat yourself to a day of pampering in the restorative Pyrenean baths at the Balnéa spa (0033 891 701 919) in Loudenvielle.

FOOD & DRINK A continental breakfast of fresh fruit, bread, pains au chocolat and croissants is delivered to your tent each morning, as well as complimentary welcome gifts upon arrival. The surrounding farms and markets boast a wealth of fantastic local produce and Emma will happily point you towards the finest regional charcuterie and cheeses – the goats' cheese, Cheverie in Escanecrabe, is a must. Restaurant-wise, Auberge Champêtre (0033 561 882 271) in the village of Escanecrabe is excellent. Ten minutes away in Aurignac, the brasserie and garden restaurant of the sumptuous Hôtel St. Laurans (0033 561 904 955) serves up refined dishes in sophisticated surroundings.

GETTING THERE From Escanecrabe, go past the church on the left, take the next left and follow the signs to Camping La Vie en Rose.

OPEN June–September.

THE DAMAGE From €230 per night for 4 people, including breakfast.

pyrénées emotions

Col des Ares 31510 Malvezie, Haute-Garonne 00 33 5 61 88 14 67 www.pyreneesemotions.com

If an arduous journey makes your destination all the more appreciated, then you'll be kissing the 'Bienvenue' sign upon arrival at Pyrénées Emotions. Well, that's if you're arriving by bike at least. High up on the Col des Ares, it's little wonder this snaking incline tests the world's best cyclists (not to mention a few brave amateurs) during the Tour de France. But the trade-off for all the huffing, puffing and thigh-chafing? Well, just look around you. The lush, herbaceous landscape, dotted with grazing Mérens horses is splendid, and also blissfully quiet – hard to believe you're only 30km or so from the vibrant Pyrenean spa town and ski resort of Luchon.

The campsite itself is well-appointed, secluded and fastidiously-run by Franco-Dutch couple Laetitia and Stefan van Lanen. Relaxation and tranquillity are the order of the day here and a blissed-out bonhomie pervades amongst the site's 15 privileged pitches. Your hosts are on hand with everything from fresh bread in the morning to the best route to the nearby swimming lake at Saint Pé d'Ardet. All round Action-Man Stefan is your leading authority on hiking, biking and everything in between; he lives and breathes the outdoor lifestyle and is happy to arrange excursions. He's also qualified to lead canyoning, rafting, kayaking and climbing groups – something he does on a regular basis and the main reason he moved to the area.

After a day of white-water rafting down the Garonne, tackling the mighty Pic du Gar, or simply *flâneuring* past the Belle Époque villas of Luchon, campers can rest with their feet up in the campsite's restaurant, housed in a beautiful mountain lodge that's over a century old. The food isn't bad either, with continental breakfasts, light lunches and three-course meals available. Those in the know, meanwhile, congregate round the communal campfire (marshmallows are compulsory) and contemplate what tomorrow will bring. As Laetitia and Stefan surmise, their site offers a 'harmony of culture, nature, and adventure'. We second that emotion.

COOL FACTOR The only emotions are good ones at this chilled-out, high-altitude campsite.

WHO'S IN Tents, campervans, caravans, groups, dogs – yes.

ON SITE 15 pitches, 5 showers, 5 toilets. Electrical hook-ups available. Laundry and dish-washing facilities. Free Wi-Fi. Various outdoor activities can be arranged including rafting, kayaking, abseiling, mountain biking and white-water rafting. There is also a luxurious wooden gîte and B&B. The onsite restaurant is excellent. Communal campfire.

OFF SITE Outdoor enthusiasts will be in heaven here, with hiking and canoeing arranged from the site and run by multi-lingual instructors. Some of Europe's most iconic walks are also easily accessible, including the Pic du Gar, GR78 and Camino Francés all the way to Galicia's Santiago de Compostela. Bagnères-de-Luchon is just 30km from the site and boasts the famous Roman thermal springs and vaporarium (the only one of its kind in Europe). The prehistoric Caves of Gargas (0033 562 988 150) are also nearby and the ancient Romanesque city of Saint-Bertrand-de-Comminges boasts a breathtaking cathedral.

FOOD & DRINK Look no further than the onsite bar and restaurant. Campers can enjoy light lunches, continental breakfasts (with freshly-baked croissants) inside or on the terrace. You can even have a 3-course meal for €19 (kids eat for €9). Luchon has no shortage of places to eat: La Baluchon (0033 561 889 128) serves refined, contemporary French cuisine, with 3 courses from €30.

GETTING THERE Take the A64 motorway and leave at Junction 17 (Bagneres-de-Luchon) and follow the signs for Col des Ares. You'll find the campsite at the top.

PUBLIC TRANSPORT The nearest train station is Montrejeau-Gourdan Polignan. From here it is a 25-minute drive by car. Laetitia or Stefan can pick you up for a small fee.

OPEN Everyday from July–August. No check-ins on Mondays and Tuesdays for the rest of the year.

THE DAMAGE Large tent pitch, plus 2 adults with car and electricity €21 (plus 2 children €27). Small pitches €4; large pitches €7. Adults €5.50; children €3. Electricity €3. Dogs €2.

la vie en vert

09800 Augirein, Ariege 00 33 5 61 96 82 66   www.lavieenvert.com

If ever there was a campsite destined to be on a postcard, it's this one. The abundance of flowers, the babbling brook running along the back of a lovely old stone house, and 15 immaculately crafted pitches (plus a tipi), some right next to the river, make the site a bit of a chocolate-box delight. It's easy to find yourself wandering around with your camera or phone before you've even pitched the tent. Admittedly it lacks slightly in facilities – there's no pool and no communal room or café – but it does have a small kids' playground, homemade apple juice on tap and you can have breakfast in the house if you like. There's also a small library, fresh fruit and veg from local farmers on sale and a BBQ shack that you can set up right next to the river.

Then there are Claudine and Charles themselves – an ultra-hospitable pair who know the area well and can give you the lowdown on the many local highlights: biking and hiking trails, water sports on the River Bouigane, chapels, caves and a string of picturesque rustic villages in both directions, in particular Castillon-en-Couserans, which is a 20-minute drive away and has regular cultural events in summer. That's if you can wrench yourself away from all the calmness of the campsite, of course.

COOL FACTOR This cute, calm site keeps it (arbo) real.

WHO'S IN Tents, campervans, caravans, dogs – yes. Groups – no.

ON SITE 15 decent-sized pitches, all shaded, and 1 tipi. Washing machine; old-fashioned toilets, hot showers and a covered washing-up area. Kids' playground. No campfires but there is a BBQ area.

OFF SITE Hiking and horseriding can be arranged from the site. The Pyrénées Ariégeoises Natural Park has an array of top hiking routes and was created in 2009 in order to protect many endemic species, including the bearded vulture, capercaillie and Pyrenean Lily. It's a pleasant walk (or easy drive) up the slopes to Galey, with fabulous views and an interesting chapel. Vallée de Bethmal is also nice to visit and has a serene lake – good for family picnics and lazy wild swimming sessions.

FOOD & DRINK Claudine is happy to cook emergency evening meals for the odd camper in distress, but you're expected to be self-sufficient. A bio-breakfast can be prepared for €7 per person. The restaurant in Galey (0033 561 967 152) serves local produce and has a simple, rustic setting. There are also local cheese and meat farms in the area – ask at reception for information.

GETTING THERE Get yourself to Castillon-en-Couserans and take the road to Augirein, following the signs for La Vie en Vert. The site is just past the nursery – cross over the bridge and make a left (there are signs).

OPEN July–August.

THE DAMAGE Tent plus 2 people €15 per night. Tipi €32 per night (2 people).

camping aux mêmes

32140, Bellegarde, Gers 00 33 5 62 66 91 45 www.camping-gascony.co.uk

Time seems to expand at Camping aux Mêmes. In days gone by the site was a traditional Gascony farm, set in the heart of the Gers countryside, with rolling hills and magnificent views of the Pyrénées. It was bought by Janet and Peter back in 2003, who then made a home from the farmhouse and opened up the land to campers and caravanners. The rolling hills and views are still there, of course, embellished by a lovely blue swimming pool, a kids' playground and a bar area, from where you can enjoy the site's tranquillity.

Far enough away from the mountains to enjoy the warmer, more settled climate of the south of France, but close enough for days out in the peaks, Camping Aux Mêmes is a simple, uncluttered site that's perfect for anyone searching for peace and quiet. Young trees that Janet and Peter planted on their first arrival have now grown and matured to provide spots of dappled shade, while a couple of pleasant pitches on a lower terrace are shielded by fruitful fig and plum trees. From both areas you get views of the local church and sunflower fields – classic features of the area. This is a campsite that capitalises on traditional France, in other words, where you can leave behind the stresses and strains of everyday life and focus on other, more life-enhancing pursuits.

COOL FACTOR Friendly, family-run campsite in the peaceful Gascony countryside.

WHO'S IN Tents, campervans, caravans, dogs (on leads) – yes. Groups – by arrangement only.

ON SITE 20 large pitches (17 with water and electricity), some with partial shade and all with views over the Gascony countryside and of the Pyrénées. Hot showers, disabled facilities; children's play area, table tennis, swimming pool, shop, Wi-Fi, terrace café/bar open for lunchtime and evening meals in July and August. Campfires not allowed, but BBQs okay. Live music most weekends in July/August.

OFF SITE Head to nearby Masseube (3.5km), where there are tennis courts, a nine-hole golf course (0033 562 660 310) and a cinema. Sailing Lac de Thoux St-Cricq (0033 562 657 545) is also nearby. At the right times in summer, you can catch live music at the Marciac Jazz Festival (0033 562 093 198).

FOOD & DRINK The onsite restaurant serves lunchtime and evening meals in July and August. L'Auberge d'Astarac (0033 562 654 881) at Moncorneil-Grazan does great local food. O Mon Plaisir (0033 562 660 214) at Masseube has good local set menus, while, for something a little special, Les Quatre Saisons at Ornezan (0033 562 592 793) has slightly more pricey but excellent food.

GETTING THERE Take the D27 from Masseube towards Bellegarde, past the sports stadiums and on up the hill through the trees. Take the first road on the left and Aux Mêmes is the first farm on the right.

OPEN April–September.

THE DAMAGE Pitch and 2 people €25, extra adults €10, children (up to 11yrs) €5. Electricity €4; extra vehicle €6. Discounts: low season (April–June) €7 per night reduction; all season discount for 1 person €4 per night reduction.

domaine les angeles

Les Angeles, 32410 Cézan, Gers 00 33 5 62 65 29 80 www.domainelesangeles.com

Though affable Franco-Dutch couple Guido and Clara have only been running Les Angeles since 2008, the campsite's history goes back to 1985, when it was first converted from an old Gasconian farmhouse, and this doubtless explains the comfortable vibe you get when you first set foot on the site. What Guido and Clara have brought to this site is an air of cosmopolitanism, and the option to let everyone enjoy its wonderful serenity and location in the middle of a Gascony valley, surrounded by glittering sunflower fields and bristling vineyards.

Pitches are arranged around the edge of the site – generous rectangles protected from the sun by lovely old trees, which help lend the site a cosy, leafy atmosphere. You'll find the reception at the top of a gentle slope, next to picnic tables and a sparkling blue swimming pool. There's a sunny terrace and a paddling pool for little ones plus a playground with swings and a slide. If the weather forces you indoors there's a games room, pool table, library and bar. And you'll find plenty of up-to-date brochures to help you plan your stay. A few times a week during high season they arrange a *table d'hôte* dinner, which helps guests to get to know each other. You can also sample the region's wonderful produce – everything from local wines to foie gras. As Guido and Clara point out, though, Les Angeles is one of the best places to just relax with a book. Like being at home, perhaps, but without all the pesky distractions.

COOL FACTOR A lovely spot to relax and read your book in the middle of the Gascony countryside.

WHO'S IN Tents, campervans, caravans – yes. Dogs – no.

ON SITE 34 grassy spaces, most of which have electricity and beautiful views over the surrounding countryside. 2 wash-blocks containing 6 showers, toilets and washbasins. Minimarket. Washing machine (€5) and a couple of fridges for rent (€2.50/€4.50 per day). Boules, volleyball, table-tennis. No campfires but BBQs allowed.

OFF SITE There are lots of cultural and religious spots around, like the Abbaye de Flaran in Valence-sur-Baïse (0033 562 285 019) and Château de Lavardens (0033 562 581 061) in Lavardens.

FOOD & DRINK Drinks, ice creams, snacks, bread and croissants are available from the shop/bar. For a sociable drink, try La Légende Irlandaise in Jegun (0033 562 645 513), while Chez Vous in St-Puy (0033 562 689 852) serves local dishes and has a relaxed atmosphere. Restaurant des Thermes (0033 562 681 307) or Le Florida (0033 562 681 322), both in Castéra-Verduzan, serve regional cuisine and are good value. Nearby farms selling foie gras and other local delicacies include the Ferme de la Gouardère (0033 562 655 651) and Terre Blanche (0033 562 289 254) in St-Puy.

GETTING THERE Following the A62, take exit 7 or exit 8, then the N21 Agen to Auch. In Fleurance, take the D103 towards Vic-Fezensac. In Préchac, take a right to Cézan, and follow the road for 4km, following the purple signs.

OPEN June–September.

THE DAMAGE Pitch and 2 people €15–€22, extra adults €6–€7, children (7yrs or younger) €4–€5.

la brouquère

32330 Gondrin, Gers 00 33 5 62 29 19 44   www.brouquere.com

'Arrive as a guest, leave as a friend.' And with only ten pitches going at any one time the owners of La Brouquère haven't set themselves too difficult a motto to aspire to. Here in Gers, midway between the Mediterranean and the Atlantic, La Brouquère sits in a deliciously untouristy region of France. So, unless you become firm friends with a local farmer or spend dawn until dusk exploring the countryside, you'll definitely leave having got to know Sonja and Wouter a whole lot better.

One thing sure to leave an impression is their passion. Relocating from Holland a few years ago, the couple restored an old winery using its original stone for the structure of their gorgeous home, with bright blue shutters, a view of rolling hills, and, from June, blossoming sunflowers. There's a pleasant drive past vineyards to get here and an intimate camping vibe that greets you on arrival. All of La Brouquère's USPs share equal pride of place: the little swimming pool (actually, it's not much bigger than a hot tub, but it'll cool you down on sunny days), the terraced patio, the views and the house are all vividly enchanting.

In medieval times, this part of France fell slap-bang in the middle of crossfire between English and French armies based west of here at Bordeaux and at Toulouse further east. Nowadays, Gers is an unspoiled, rural landscape peppered with green vineyards and yellow sunflower fields. Its remoteness enables workmen to travel freely about their daily business, which for many is the production of foie gras and Armagnac. Such low tourist traffic is a big plus for curious travellers,

for whom La Brouquère makes an appealing, peaceful holiday choice.

Campers have the choice of pitching in the garden or on wilder land further back, with lots of space to lie on blankets whilst you peruse Sonja's comprehensive bumper-packed folder of local activities. Where to go first? What to do? The shared facilities are excellent. Or, if you're a product junkie who always ends up leaving your favourite shampoo in the shower, think about hiring the campsite's private bathroom – but book well in advance, it's a popular feature.

La Brouquère's homecooked food is also noted as a highlight by many a well-fed camper, with Indonesian, Indian, Greek, Italian and Swiss food all featuring – vegetarians are well catered for too. Pre-order bread and croissants at reception the day before and in the morning you can chow down on your breakfast in full view of uninterrupted Armagnac landscape. Vineyards are visible from your tent in one direction and, in the other, rolling hills separate you from the charming provincial town of Condom, a 10-minute drive away.

Biased or not, Sonja and Wouter believe that the Gers is the best region in all of France, that the locally-produced wine is better than any Bordeaux, and that 'don't worry' is your password to a happy stay at La Brouquère. And if, after a few days exploring or relaxing, you begin to agree with those opinions, you'll have the perfect excuse to return – and visit your new-found friends.

COOL FACTOR Tiny, friendly camping in the wonderfully untouristy Gers. Oh yeah, and there's wine and Armagnac brandy virtually on tap!

WHO'S IN This is an adults-only campsite. Tents, campervans, caravans and dogs (on a leash) – yes. Children – no.

ON SITE 10 spacious grass pitches for tents and cars. The owners also rent a fully-equipped rental tent (sleeps 4) and a rustic gîte (sleeps 5), just 600m away from the campsite nestled amongst the vineyards. There are 3 bathrooms, each with a large shower, a toilet and a sink and 1 private shower room with a toilet. 2 sinks for dishwashing (warm and cold water) and a washing machine. No fires are allowed. There's a boules court, Wi-Fi is available and a communal freezer for re-freezing cool blocks.

OFF SITE The tiny museum in Lupiac commemorates the birthplace of d'Artagnan, who fought alongside the Three Musketeers and is worth a look. The Thursday market at Eauze is also a must-see, while if you want to make like Formula One's Lewis Hamilton, then the race circuit 30 minutes away at Nogaro might appeal (0033 562 090 249). One-day courses start at €340.

FOOD & DRINK Gondrin's La Ferme du Cassou (0033 562 291 522) hosts 4 duck-tasting sessions a week and tours of their pâté prodution. If you like brandy, the best place to try it is Château de Cassaigne (0033 562 280 402), which offers free tours and tastings; a decent bottle of Armagnac will set you back around €25.

GETTING THERE The village of Gondrin is located on the D931 between Condom and Eauze, 50km from Auch and Agen. As you enter the village the campsite is well signposted.

OPEN May–September.

THE DAMAGE Off-season prices start at €17 for 1 pitch and 2 adults, with electrical hook-up and parking. See their website for more rates.

esperbasque

Chemin de Lagisquet 64270 Salies-de-Béarn, Pyrénées-Atlantiques 00 33 5 59 38 21 04 esperbasque.com

It's not hard to see exactly what Marianne Hessels fell for back in 1980. Equidistant from both the epic Atlantic coastline and the foothills of the Pyrénées, this one-time stud farm just outside the charming town of Salies-de-Béarn had her hooked at first sight. Today, thanks to the enterprising endeavours of this affable Dutch ex-pat, a sprawling slice of rural Aquitaine has been transformed into a campers' paradise – the wonderful Domaine d'Esperbasque.

Campers really are spoiled for choice here. The five different fields (The Park, The Hill, The Vineyard, The Oak, The Sheep Meadow) all have a unique charm and character. Take the Hill, with its beautifully terraced grass pitches set aside exclusively for tents, which boasts panoramic views over the valley into Salies-de-Béarn. Or the more family-friendly Park field, shaded by mature trees

and just a gentle canter from the nearby riding school – a vestige of the former farm's equestrian heritage. They also offer bright and airy safari tents, complete with complimentary deckchairs that are perfect for reclining with a glass of wine from the neighbouring vineyard and soaking up the view. Indeed, wherever you pitch up in this spacious site, the views are unbeatable.

There's a relaxed, hippified air to Domaine d'Esperbasque. With plenty for the kids to do (from trampolining and boules to swimming and darts), mums and dads are free to soak up the pleasingly lazy pace of life from the scenic terrace. As the sun descends over the surrounding Pyrénées, painting the tranquil night sky in warming hues of purple and sunburst, you'll know exactly what so enraptured Marianne on that momentous day over thirty years ago.

COOL FACTOR Gorgeous views and characterful, individual camping areas.

WHO'S IN Tents, caravans, campervans, dogs, families, groups (by pre-arrangement) – yes.

ON SITE 94 pitches (all with electricity) and 5 safari tents. 6 apartments also available. 3 sanitary blocks (2 disabled-friendly), 2 washing machines and a tumble dryer. A small bar with pool table, darts and with free Wi-Fi. A nice terrace with great views. Swimming pool and a shaded paddling pool for kids. A boulodrome field for playing petanque. Trampolines, swimming pool, go-karts, horseriding, organised activities and competitions including archery, football tournaments, talent shows. Indoor winter caravan storage available.

OFF-SITE Domaine d'Esperbasque is equidistant from both the Pyrénées and the Atlantic Ocean (both around 45mins drive away). The Bearn and Basque countryside boasts some stunning scenery and makes for a great hiking/biking trip. The lovely spa town of Salies-de-Béarn boasts several great restaurants and a golf course and the colonial Spanish border city of Pamplona is just under 2 hour's drive away. For the slightly unhinged, the San Fermin Festival's world-famous 'running of the bulls' takes place every July 6th–14th. For those who don't manage to escape unscathed, the healing shrine of Lourdes is just over an hour away.

FOOD & DRINK In high season, the local baker comes with freshly-baked baguettes and croissants every day. During low season, Marianne makes her own bread. There's also pizza night once a week and nightly dinners varying from Indian to local cuisine. You can buy plenty of local produce on site too. The pick of the local restaurants is La Belle Auberge (0033 559 381 528), a charming rural hotel in the surrounding village of Castagnède. You can get 2 courses plus plenty of delicious sides for only €26. For refined regional cuisine, head for the chic restaurant Les Voisins (0033 559 380 179) in Salies-de-Béarn. It's a little pricier than some of the other local eateries, but worth every penny. Marianne's neighbour, Lapeyre Guilhemas, also makes wonderful wine – pop next door for a visit and a glass or two. The region is also famous for its *foie gras* and *pâté*, with around 90% of France's artisan duck farms here in the south-west of the country.

GETTING THERE The site is located on the D933 about 10km from the A64. Take exit 7 and follow the signs to Salies-de-Bearn; at the roundabout with the fountain, don't go to the *centre ville* but follow the signs to 'Sauveterre de Béarn'. The campsite is about 3km from the roundabout.

OPEN March–end of October. Gîtes and apartments all year.

THE DAMAGE €17.94–€24.94 per night for 2 people, including tent or caravan, car, electricity and tourist tax.

glisten camping

Col d'Ibardin Campsite, 220 Route d'Olhette, 64122 Urrugne, Pyrénées-Atlantiques 0844 344 0196 glistencamping.com

Some otherwordly structures have landed in the Labourd countryside. With their geodesic shape and strikingly white outer shell, visitors to these parts could be forgiven for thinking they've stumbled upon south-west France's very own Roswell. Well, the little green men could do a lot worse than hole up at the dome village at Glisten Camping.

An innovative holiday experience, Glisten Camping brings some truly unique glamping accommodation to sunny south-west France. Like the domes themselves, the concept is simple. The brainchild of Cornish-based camping nut Simon Thomason, Glisten selects the best locations in south-west France then sets up the distinctively stylish geodesic domes which sleep a family of up to six. As Simon succinctly puts it, 'the great outdoors deserve a beautiful indoors'.

Inside, the domes are a triumph of ergonomic design that would have even Kevin McCloud struggling for superlatives. These stylish pods come complete with partitioned bedrooms, king-size beds and proper mattresses, hanging beds for the kids, and ultra-comfy Fatboy bean-bags. There's also a cool yet functional 'plancha' gas cooker and a spacious, covered al fresco dining area for those long, lazy, holiday meals. So chic are these dextrous dome-iciles, it wouldn't surprise us if the St Tropez set migrated westward along the coast for a spot of glamping.

As all cool campers know, location is everything, and Glisten scores top marks for that too. Col d'Ibardin, the first campsite on which the Glisten domes have been located, is a relaxed,

family-friendly retreat that boasts all the bells and whistles we've come to expect from campsites in this part of the world: clean, modern facilities, a swimming pool and a decent bar-restaurant. This bucolic Basque bolthole also lies at the foothills of La Rhune and is ideally located to explore the other natural delights the region has to offer. With its sweeping golden sands, enchanting pine forests and traditional mountain villages, it isn't hard to see what makes *Le Pays Basques* – where France's Atlantic Coast meets the Spanish border – such a magnet for camping fans. And while it also boasts some of Europe's warmest temperatures, the cooling sea breeze of this breathtaking Atlantic coastline means the only thing you need sweat over is what enchanting corner of this region to explore next.

COOL FACTOR Space-age domes that offer serious comfort.

WHO'S IN Glampers, familes, couples, kids – yes. Caravans, dogs – no.

ON SITE 10 geodesic domes sleeping up to 6, with a choice of standard or en suite. Swimming pools (2 for kids and 1 for adults), a children's play area, onsite bar restaurant, kid's club (summer only), small farm, and plenty of games, including petanque, table tennis and basketball.

OFF SITE Explore the surrounding hills and forests or take to two wheels – Glisten can organise bike hire for the whole family, as well as surf hire and lessons. For something less labour-intensive, take the vintage Train de la Rhune (0033 559 542 026) to the first summit of the Pyrénées – the views from over 900m high are spectacular. There's plenty of beaches to choose from too, with St Jean-de-Luz, Socoa and Hendaye among the nicest and nearest (15 minute drive). The Basque region straddles some of the most spectacular towns and resorts in both south-west France and northern Spain. Take in the glamour of Biarritz or chic San Sebastián (that's Donostia to the Basque).

FOOD & DRINK With a wealth of delicious local produce and treats to be sampled (including Bayonne ham and Gateau Basque), most dome-dwellers opt to cook their own food on the plancha grill provided. But 'La Kantina' – the onsite bar restaurant – also serves up decent, good-value meals and regional specialties such as *axoa*. Eat al fresco on the terrace or enjoy some private fuss-free dining with the takeaway service. Basic provisions can also be purchased from the onsite shop, open 7 days a week (summer holidays only). For something extra special, make the short pilgrimage to San Sebastián, the city with the most Michelin stars per square metre in the world. If your budget won't stretch to the haute cuisine heights of Arzak (0034 943 278 465), check out the harbourside taverns for some traditional *pintxos* and Rioja.

GETTING THERE From the north, take the N10 and the A63. Take exit 2 – 'St Jean de Luz south–Urrugne–Col Ibardin,' and at the roundabout take the exit for Urrugne. Turn left and continue on the D4 to Ibardin for 4km. At the intersection, continue straight towards Ascain. The site is located 200m down the road on the right.

OPEN April–October.

THE DAMAGE Prices per night start from £75 in low and mid season, minimum stay 2 nights. Weekly rentals range from £499 in low season to £1095 during peak season.

useful info

Got the tent, sleeping bag, stove, and corkscrew packed? Don't forget our top tips to keep your cool on those balmy French nights.

THE RIGHT SITE

Know the difference between an *aire naturelle* (campsite with a few pitches on a farm) and a *camping naturiste* (nudist campsite). For campers keen to dip into local life, nothing beats *camping à la ferme*. Limited to six *emplacements* (pitches) for 20 campers, you can hang out with the farmer, taste produce, admire animals and congratulate *Cool Camping* on yet another fabulous find.

THE RIGHT TIME

Skip French school holidays: spring holidays in April and October/November are reasonably quiet, but sites burst in July and August. Go for early July and bag your slot in advance. Sites generally open March to September or October. France is always one hour ahead of the UK.

RAIN, HAIL, OR SHINE

Watch the weather, particularly in mountainous areas and the south. To check, call 3250; visit www.meteo.fr/meteonet_en; or type your site's postcode into a text message and send it to 73250.

ON THE ROAD

Motorists drive on the right, and vehicles coming from the right have priority. Speed limits are 50 km/h (30 mph) in built-up areas, 90 km/h (55 mph) on the open road, 110 km/h (70 mph) on dual carriageways and 130 km/h (80 mph) on motorways – which cost. To calculate *péages* (tolls) pump your itinerary into www.autoroutes.fr. Children under 10 must not sit in front and must be in an appropriate seat in the back. Chatting on your mobile while driving lands a fine and the drink-drive limit is equivalent to two glasses of wine. Avoid buying pricey autoroute petrol; try a supermarket on a town's outskirts. Leaving the autoroute for lunch likewise leaves a sweeter taste. Motoring on traffic-jammed 'black' days in July and August is grim. Check traffic in advance with Bison Futé (00 33 8 92 68 78 88, France 08 26 02 20 22, www.bison-fute.equipement.gouv.fr) and avoid peak times, particularly Saturday. Tune into Radio 107.7 FM for the latest traffic news.

MAKING THAT CALL

If you're calling from the UK or from your mobile in France, dial the number *Cool Camping* lists, including the international access code '00' and France country code '33'. Calling from a payphone in France, drop the '00 33' and add a '0' before the remaining nine-digit number. French telephone numbers have 10 digits and no area code.

CULINARY NUGGETS

Every village has a market heaped with fresh fruit, veg, herbs, fish, and meat gagging to be cooked on a campfire. Check what the local farmer sells. Few shops open on Sunday and most break for a long lunch on other days. Bread accompanies every meal, though a baguette bought at sunrise is rock-hard by sunset. Every *boulangerie* bakes several times a day. Some campsites serve dinner.

DOWN THE HATCH

Tap water and water in fountains is drinkable unless marked '*non potable*'. In restaurants, ordering a jug of tap water is fine. The French seldom drink beer or tea (bring your own tea bags). The day is kick-started with *un café* (a short, sharp espresso) or tamer *café au lait* (milky coffee), and wine accompanies everything else. Look for *dégustation* (tasting) signs in wine-making areas.

DOWN THE PAN

Women's is *Dames*, men's is *Hommes*. French toilets are not always what they seem so, gals, you might find yourself parading past a man at a urinal. Once in, devices range from bog-standard toilets to a pair of elephant feet. Stand well clear before flushing.

WHAT TO DO IN AN EMERGENCY

(besides yelling 'AU SECOURS! (HELP)'

Fire call 18 from a landline or 112 from a mobile

Police (Gendarmerie) – call 17

Ambulance (SAMU) – call 15

Mountain rescue call 112; better still note the number of the local mountain-rescue squad before setting out

Lost/stolen passport report at the local police station and contact the British Embassy (01 44 51 31 00) in Paris to find the nearest British consulate to get a replacement

Lost/stolen credit card call 08 92 70 57 05, or MasterCard 08 00 90 13 87, or Visa 08 00 90 11 79

---

useful phrases

Campsite un camping
Pitch une emplacement
Large/small tent une grande/petite tente
Campervan un mobil-home/un camping-car
Caravan une caravane
Facility block le bloc sanitaire
Toilets/urinals les WCs/urinoirs
Showers les douches
Washing-up/laundry sink un bac lave vaiselle/lave linge
Drinking water l'eau potable
Recycling bins les bacs de recyclage
Sleeping bag un sac de couchage
Air mattress un matelas d'air
Campfire un feu de camp
Pink/white marshmallows les guimauves roses/blanches
Camping Gaz canister une bouteille de Camping Gaz

Corkscrew un tire bouchon
Tin opener une ouvre-boîte
Mallet un maillet

Where is the nearest campsite? Où est le camping le plus proche?
How much does it cost to pitch a tent here? Combien coûte une nuit en camping avec tente?
It costs a fixed €15 a day for two adults, tent and car. Nous avons un forfait journalier de €15 pour deux adultes avec tente et voiture.
Where are the recycling bins? Où sont les bacs de recyclage?
Do you have a spare tent peg/tin opener/lighter or matches? Avez-vous un piquet de tente/une ouvre-boîte/un briquet de poche ou des allumettes?
Could someone please clean the

toilets? Pourriez vous faire nettoyer les toilettes, s'il vous plaît?
There's no hot water. Il n'y a pas d'eau chaude.
Help! Someone has stolen my wallet! Au secours! Quelqu'un a volé mon porte-monnaie!
Where should I park? Où est-ce que je peux me garer?
Is it OK to build a campfire here? Est-ce qu'on peut faire un feu de camp ici?
What a beautiful view! Quelle vue magnifique!
Where's a good place to eat around here? Où est-ce qu'il y a un bon endroit pour manger près d'ici?
Do you speak English? Est-ce que vous parlez anglais?
Sorry, I don't speak French. Désolé, je ne parle pas français.

index